# How to Preach
# without Notes

# How to Preach without Notes

Charles W. Koller

Baker Books

A Division of Baker Book House Co.
Grand Rapids, Michigan 49516

Combined paperback edition published 1997 by Baker Books
a division of Baker Book House Company
P.O. Box 6287, Grand Rapids, MI 49516-6287

Combined hardcover edition first published 1969.
Previously published as separate volumes under the titles *Expository Preaching without Notes* (LC 62-21703) and *Sermons Preached without Notes* (LC 64-15866).

Third printing, March 1998

Printed in the United States of America

ISBN 0-8010-5761-2

For information about academic books, resources for Christian leaders, and all new releases available from Baker Book House, visit our web site:

http://www.bakerbooks.com

# Part 1

# Expository Preaching without Notes

# Contents

# Introduction

The last word has not been spoken or written in the field of homiletics. The need for fresh studies continues, and the interest never wanes. When Phillips Brooks had attained to fame as one of the world's greatest preachers, he continued to take lessons in homiletics.[1] Many others, after years of successful pulpit experience, have added to their effectiveness by the discovery of structural principles which had previously eluded them.

In the area of preaching without notes there has been a long felt need, to which the course, "Expository Preaching Without Notes," has aimed to provide some answers. For more than twenty years its distinctive principles have been taught to seminary seniors, all of whom had at least one year of previous training in homiletics, and many of whom had been preaching for years. Not only have these principles been taught at Northern Baptist Theological Seminary, but at a steadily growing number of other institutions as well. The response to the syllabus, which was published some years ago, has been sufficiently gratifying to warrant the hope that the course might be made helpful to many others if published in book form. It is hoped that certain chapters will be found particularly helpful: The Homiletical Devices (especially the "Key Word" and "The Multiple Approach"); The Heart of the Sermon; The Way to Note Free Preaching; and The Systematic Filing of Materials.

Preaching without notes does not mean preaching without *preparation,* as might be suggested by the familiar terms impromptu, extempore, extempory, and extemporaneous.

---

[1]Ezra Rhoades, *Case Work in Preaching* (New York: Fleming H. Revell Co., 1942), p. 13.

Preaching without notes does not mean *preparation* without notes. Indeed, carefully constructed notes are the basis of freedom from notes in preaching.

Preaching without notes does not mean that there should be no notes on the pulpit. As a matter of fact, the preacher is well advised to have these notes with him whenever he preaches; if at any time he should *need* them, he would need them *badly*.

Preaching without notes does not mean to stand free from the pulpit and thus *draw attention* to the fact that the speaker is preaching without notes; such diverting of the attention from the message might be as costly as improper attire, or bad grammar, or distracting mannerisms.

The material here presented has been developed through years of searching, gleaning, sifting, and testing in the laboratory of the class room. Every effort has been made to find the surest, simplest, most helpful procedures for effective expository preaching without notes. Gradually there have emerged certain proven principles, practical procedures, a basic homiletical pattern, and a streamlined system of notes for the easiest possible memorization, retention, and recall.

The preacher may be safely assured that when he has mastered the suggested techniques for getting an expository sermon out of the Bible, and setting it up for effective delivery without notes, he will have the techniques for preparing and delivering all other types of sermons as well. Occasionally a preacher, with or without training, will hit upon an excellent outline; but unless he understands just what he did, and how he did it, he will not be able to make such outlines come again two or three times every week. The principles are few and relatively simple, but are not commonly spelled out in the text books. To meet this need, is the specific aim of these pages.

The procedures here recommended include the same general and particular preparation that is urged for preaching from manuscript. Beyond this, it demands the utmost accuracy in the use of words, and the utmost precision in integrating the parts of the outline. The demand for conciseness, in a one page outline, presents a further life-long discipline, attended with life-long rewards.

These studies reflect help received over the years from innumerable sources. So far as possible, these sources are identified and gratefully acknowledged in these chapters and in the footnotes. In addition, the writer is indebted to many others, including that long succession of students in "Senior Preaching," whom he will always hold in grateful and affectionate remembrance.

Charles W. Koller

# 1

# The Scriptural Conception of Preaching

Preaching is that unique procedure by which God, through His chosen messenger, reaches down into the human family and brings persons face to face with Himself. Without such confrontation it is not true preaching. Since preaching originated in the mind of God, and is His own distinctive medium for reaching the hearts of men with a message that is calculated to save the soul, it is obviously His prerogative to set the standards. It follows that the only valid conception of preaching is the conception which God Himself has revealed in the holy Scriptures. It is unfortunate for the Christian cause when secular standards are substituted for the sacred pattern, and preaching becomes a mere instrument of culture or a means of teaching ethics and morals apart from the holy and authoritative demands of the living God.

The Scriptural conception of preaching is clearly reflected, as it relates to the messenger, and to the message.

## AS TO THE MESSENGER

1. *His Call.* In the Old Testament the preacher was a "prophet." This title is derived from the Greek *prophetes,* which in turn is a free rendering of the Hebrew *nabhi,* meaning "one who is called (by God), one who has a vocation (from God)." Thus, "the prophet was a man who felt himself called by God for a special mission, in which his will was subordinated to the will of God, which was communicated to him by direct inspiration."[1] It was this call which differentiated him from other men.

---

[1]William F. Albright, *From the Stone Age to Christianity* (Garden City, New York: Doubleday & Co., Inc., 1957), p. 303.

In the New Testament the preacher was an "apostle," "one sent from God" (Greek: *apestalmenos*), like John the Baptist (John 1:6), literally a "godsend." The apostle Paul, in nine of his Epistles, identifies himself as one "called to be an apostle." While the preacher at best is but an "earthen vessel" (II Cor. 4:7), through whom God reveals Himself to others, he is nevertheless the living point of contact between God and those whom He seeks to save through "the foolishness of preaching" (I Cor. 1:21).

2. *His Character.* In the ministry, as in no other calling, character is decisive. The Holy Spirit simply will not identify Himself with the unclean or unconsecrated. "Be ye clean that bear the vessels of the Lord" (Isa. 52:11). How completely God identifies Himself with the labors of His faithful spokesmen is shown in the ministry of Samuel. "The Lord was with him, and did let none of his words fall to the ground. And all Israel from Dan to Beersheba knew that Samuel was established to be a prophet of the Lord" (I Sam. 3:19-20).

It must be remembered that the fruitfulness or sterility of a man's ministry depends not nearly so much upon his native ability, his training, his skill, and his labor, as upon that which the Lord adds or withholds. "After preachers have preached ever so eloquently and long, when sinners are bowed, as great a wonder is wrought, and by God alone, as when Jericho fell."[2] The walls of Jericho did not fall by the shouts of Israel, but by the breath of God.

3. *His Function.* Nowhere is the function of the minister brought to a clearer focus than in the familiar words of the apostle Paul, which constitute what is perhaps the most important of all the 31,102 verses in the Bible for the minister, as a minister: "Now then we are ambassadors for Christ; as though God did beseech you by us, we pray you in Christ's stead, be ye reconciled to God" (II Cor. 5:20).

The man whose ministry is steeped in the atmosphere of this

---

2Edward D. Griffin, *The Art of Preaching* (Boston: Printed by T. R. Martin, 1825), p. 15.

text can never go far wrong, in doctrine or in spirit. He can not be objective or emotionally detached; he is an advocate for a cause, with eternities hanging in the balance. Under the burden of his message he will not think of himself as a pipe through which the truth flows out to others, but as a living embodiment of the truth to which he seeks to win others. He may not have the eloquence of a ready tongue, but will have that eloquence which is of the heart. His concern in the study will be not merely to prepare sermons, but, even more, to prepare his own heart. And when he preaches it will not be in feeble whispers, but with the spiritual vitality of the prophets and apostles, of whom he is a lineal descendant.

## AS TO THE MESSAGE

1. *Its Content.* All true preaching rests upon the basic affirmation, "Thus saith the Lord!" This affirmation occurs approximately two thousand times in the Scriptures. When the preacher faithfully communicates the Word of God, he speaks with authority. He is supplying something for which there is no substitute. Man does not need the Word of God to tell him what will become of his body, but he does need the Word of God to tell him what will become of his soul. Human ingenuity can not probe the future or solve the problems of eternity. For the answers to his questions of life and destiny, he must in utter helplessness look beyond himself. He can not by his own wisdom and effort find God. "No man cometh unto the Father but by me" (John 14:6); and "no man can come to me, except the Father which hath sent me draw him" (John 6:44). The Bible must light the way.

The Bible is not a record of man's religious discoveries. "It is the record of God's unfolding revelation of Himself, by the spoken word, by His intervention in nature and in history, and finally by His own entrance into the world as the God-man, Christ Jesus."[3] Not even the apostle Paul could claim that he had *discovered* God. He does say that "it pleased God ... to

[3]Lloyd M. Perry and Walden Howard, *How to Study Your Bible* (Westwood, New Jersey: Fleming H. Revell Co., 1957), p. 14.

reveal His Son" (Gal. 1:15-16), and that God has "made known unto us the mystery of His will, according to His good pleasure..." (Eph. 1:19). "It was not Paul who was clever enough to find out the secret; it was God who was good enough to make it known."[4]

Preaching in the New Testament was essentially the simple proclamation of the facts of the gospel. These facts fell into a sort of pattern which has been aptly termed "the apostolic pattern," and which is reflected in the sermon of Peter at Pentecost. This included the messianic identity of Christ, His sinless life, His atoning death, His bodily resurrection, and His eternal sovereignty. "The apostolic church saw the gospel, the good news, the *euaggelion,* as a fulfillment of prophecy, and saw its preaching as a continuation of the prophets' work."[5]

2. *Its Power.* "The Word of God is quick and powerful..." (Heb. 4:12). The gospel of Christ is "the power of God unto salvation..." (Rom. 1:16). It carries the thrust of a lancet, and along with it the balm that heals the soul. But everything depends upon the fidelity of the preacher and the purity and completeness of the gospel which is communicated, and upon which the promise of power is conditioned. Without this divine supplement, the sound of the sermon might be like the rushing of a mighty wind, but its spiritual power will be nil. The word of man does not become the Word of God by being loudly proclaimed or piously intoned.

"Lo, I am with you," says the Lord Jesus, following His instructions: "Go ye ... teaching them to observe *all things whatsoever* I have commanded you." Thus ends the Great Commission, and thus ends the Gospel of Matthew (Matt. 28:20). Mark goes one verse further, and records the fulfillment of this promise: "They went forth, and preached everywhere, *the Lord working with them, and confirming the word ...*" (Mark 16:20). The first large scale fulfillment came at Pentecost. The Great Com-

---

[4]George Barclay, *The Bible Speaks to Our Day* (Philadelphia: Westminster Press, 1945), p. 84.

[5]H. Grady Davis, *Design for Preaching* (Philadelphia: Muhlenberg Press, 1958), p. 109.

mission tells the preacher what to do; Acts 2 tells him how to do it. Everything is spelled out: the message, the "invitation," baptism, instruction, fellowship, service, victory! But when the preacher of a lesser gospel lays his poor offering on the altar, there is no answering fire from heaven. And the preacher stands piteously alone in the pulpit — a sight to make the angels weep!

For power in the pulpit, the preacher must speak from experience. Eloquence reaches its greatest heights when it is "the eloquence of Christian experience."[6] The preacher can not change lives by means of "eloquent hearsay." He can not share what he does not possess, or reveal what he has not seen. He can not win others to a faith to which he himself is not fully committed. Like the apostles, he must be able to testify, "We believe, and therefore speak" (II Cor. 4:13). As he "opens the Scriptures" (Luke 24:32) to his people, he must be in full attunement with the purpose and spirit of the Bible. He must reverence it, love it, and live it, if he is to share it helpfully with others.

"My word ... shall not return unto me void ..." (Isa. 55:11). There will always be a hearing for the faithful minister who declares humbly, intelligently, and with evident sincerity and good will, "Thus saith the Lord!" God honors His Word. Preachers may tend to become discouraged as they see how much of their preaching goes unheeded; but many a preacher would be mightily reinforced if he could know all that is going on in the hearts of an apparently unmoved audience as he faithfully and earnestly expounds the Word of God. Even that wicked King Zedekiah was not unaffected by the preaching of Jeremiah. Although he had consented to the persecution of the prophet, when he came to the dark hour of his extremity he anxiously inquired of Jeremiah, "Is there any word from the Lord?" (Jer. 37:17).

**3** *Its Aim.* In general, all Biblical preaching aims at persuasion to godliness. "Preaching is personal witnessing with the aim of

---

[6]Raymond Calkins, *The Eloquence of Christian Experience* (New York: The Macmillan Co., 1927).

communicating faith and conviction."[7] The sermon is "the meeting place of the soul with God,"[8] and seeks to channel the grace of God to believers and unbelievers. Andrew W. Blackwood makes the observation that Phillips Brooks, in about half of his 200 published sermons, addressed the seeker after God; and in the other half, the person who had already found Him. Spurgeon, in his sixty-three volumes of sermons, followed much the same course, maintaining about the same ratio.[9]

The sermon which aims at salvation "must be invested with edifying features; and the sermon which is preached primarily for the edification of the hearers must possess saving features."[10] To emphasize either conversion or Christian nurture without the other would be like seeking to produce roots without fruits, or fruits without roots. Faith and action, truth and duty, must go hand in hand.

In all Biblical preaching God seeks primarily, through His messenger, to bring man into fellowship with Himself. The aim, therefore, is not merely to impart knowledge, or provoke thought, or arouse the emotions, but to move the will to an affirmative response. And the response that saves the soul is always, of necessity, the response of a person to a Person. A valid, saving faith is not merely the acceptance of a "way of life," a philosophy, a principle, or a set of principles. It is the response of the creature to his Creator, the subject to his rightful Sovereign, the soul to the Savior. The only saving response is that of Saul of Tarsus, "Lord, what wilt thou have me to do?" (Acts 9:6; 22:10). This response to the risen Christ is the very password into the Kingdom of God. "By *me*, if any man enter in, he shall be saved . . ." (John 10:9). There is no other way (Acts 4:12). When Jesus was testing the faith of Peter, He did not say, "Peter, lovest thou

---

[7]James Wright, *A Preacher's Questionnaire* (Edinburgh: The Saint Andrews Press, 1958), p. 62.

[8]Halford E. Luccock, *In the Minister's Workshop* (New York: Abingdon-Cokesbury, 1944), p. 200.

[9]Andrew W. Blackwood, *The Preparation of Sermons* (New York: Abingdon Press, 1948), p. 27.

[10]David R. Breed, *Preparing to Preach* (New York: George H. Doran Co., 1911), p. 112.

my principles, my policies, my program"; but "lovest thou *me?*" (John 21:17).

After salvation, the emphasis is upon the *"things that accompany salvation"* (Heb. 6:9). The needed nurture and motivation of the Christian life involve the following specific objectives:

(1) Consecration, looking toward an ever deepening devotion and commitment to Christ and the "separated life." "Present your bodies a living sacrifice ... " (Rom. 12:1).

(2) Indoctrination, to be "no more children, tossed to and fro, and carried about with every wind of doctrine ... " (Eph. 4:14).

(3) Inspiration, to warm the heart with "the joy of the Lord" (Neh. 8:10): to put a doxology or hallelujah in the soul; to promote the spirit of praise and thanksgiving.

(4) Comfort. "Comfort one another with these words" (I Thess. 4:18). "Comfort ye my people" (Isa. 40:1), is no less an imperative than to call them to repentance or rouse them to heroic or sacrificial action.

(5) Strengthening. Believers need to be confirmed and fortified in the faith, "strengthened ... unto all patience and long-suffering ... " (Col. 1:11).

(6) Conviction. Mild surmises and lightly held opinions must ripen into convictions before they can be helpfully shared. The apostles spoke out of deep conviction when they said, "We can not but speak the things which we have seen and heard" (Acts 4:20).

(7) Action. "Be ye doers of the word, and not hearers only" (James 1:22).

Preaching should aim to communicate "the whole counsel of God" (Acts 20:27), on all levels of maturity and understanding. The young, the robust, the ambitious, have their needs as well as the old, the frail, the sorrowing. All alike need to be directed to Him who is the Source of all help. The supreme test of all preaching is: What happens to the man in the pew? To John the Baptist there was accorded the highest tribute that could ever come to a minister of the gospel: When they had heard John, "they followed Jesus" (John 1:37)!

# 2

# The Patterns of Scripture Presentation

In homiletical literature there is a bewildering profusion of classifications for sermons and other forms of presentation. There are classifications from the standpoint of content, from the standpoint of aim, and from the standpoint of structure. Terms are not uniformly defined, and there is much overlapping; but definitions there must be, to make any discussion intelligible. There is indeed a basic structural pattern, and patterns which are adaptations of the basic pattern, besides patterns which are quite unrelated. The distinctive feature of the "Basic" pattern is that the "Introduction" leads naturally to a thesis or proposition, and the body of the sermon is the elaboration of this thesis.

The following patterns and procedures are distinguishable.

## THE BASIC PATTERN

1. *Analysis.* This is the indispensable first step to an expository sermon outline in the Basic Pattern. It is a "work sheet" in the fullest sense. It should lift out the skeleton of the passage, revealing clearly the structure and progression of thought. It is strictly limited to the contents of the passage, and to the Biblical order of the material contained. It must not be too detailed; that would defeat its purpose. (This step is more fully discussed in a later chapter.)

2. *Exposition.* When an "Analysis" is expanded by interpretation and illustration it becomes an "Exposition," a Bible lecture. This includes exegesis of the passage based on close study of words and phrases used, and takes into account the immediate and remote context and the historical and geo-

graphical background. But an "Exposition" makes no application to the hearer, and carries no sermonic thrust calling for a response.

### 3. *Expository Sermon.*

(1) An "Expository Sermon" consists of "Exposition" plus application and persuasion (argumentation and exhortation). An "Exposition" becomes a sermon, and the teacher becomes a preacher, at the point where application is made to the hearer, looking toward some form of response, in terms of belief or commitment.

(2) An "Expository Sermon" derives its main points or the leading subhead under each main point from the particular paragraph or chapter or book of the Bible with which it deals.

In dealing with didactic passages or chapters, such as I Corinthians 13, the main points would obviously be generalizations or timeless truths expressed in the chapter, and identified by verse. In dealing with narrative passages, such as the story of the Prodigal Son, each main point might be a generalization, or it might be a particularization. The preacher might choose to draw out the lessons of the story and use these as his main points, establishing each piont by some detail from the story; or he might use as main points certain phases or details of the story, and proceed from these to the lessons which they teach. If the main point is a generalization, the leading subhead would be a particularization; and vice versa.

(3) An "Expository Sermon" in the "Basic" pattern makes use of a thesis (proposition, central idea, basic affirmation), in which the sermon has its unity and around which it is organized. An adequate thesis is a safeguard against wandering and irrelevance. Without it, a sermon might be like the wind which "bloweth where it listeth, and thou hearest the sound thereof, but canst not tell whence it cometh and whither it goeth" (John 3:8). "Expressed or latent, the proposition must exist; else a preacher can not speak to the point."[1] And for intelligent listening like-

---

[1] Austin Phelps, *The Theory of Preaching*, revised by F. D. Whitesell (Grand Rapids: Eerdmans, 1947), p. 57.

wise, an indication of the contemplated progression of thought is essential.

(4) An "Expository Sermon," as distinguished from an "Exposition," requires a sermonic introduction and conclusion.

4. *Textual Sermon.* A "Textual Sermon" is essentially the same as an "Expository Sermon," but employing a shorter Scripture passage, usually only a verse or a sentence or two. As generally conceived, it involves more intensive scrutiny of a less extensive passage. But many passages which should be treated as a unit are of such length as to make it practically impossible to classify the message as between textual and expository.

In a "Textual Sermon," the text may be analyzed and resolved into its parts, and the sermon structure based on its natural divisions; or the sermon may be built upon the implications of the text as a whole. A sermon based upon valid inferences from a text is no less a "textual" sermon than it would be if based on *analysis* of the text. But there must be no *unwarranted* inferences. "Take particular care not to lay down any proposition, or any question, which is not formally contained in your text, or which does not follow by a near and easy consequence."[2]

There are many texts which are so rich in meaning, with so much of concentrated truth and light, as to demand individual handling. But the text must be treated as more than a mere springboard or point of departure. The preacher must lead his people *into* the text, not *away* from it. For instance, that line in John 8:57 ("Thou art not yet fifty years old . . . . ") was not fairly treated when it was developed into a sermon on the peculiar advantages of vigor and opportunity of the young, those "not yet fifty years old." And what a rich context was overlooked, dealing with the pre-existence of Christ (v. 58), His incarnation (v. 42), His relation of Sonship to God (v. 54)!

---

2John Claude, *Essay on the Composition of a Sermon,* translated from the French, published in 1778, by Robert Robinson, Cambridge, England; included in *The Young Preacher's Manual,* by Ebenezer Porter (New York: Jonathan Leavitt, 1829), p. 162.

F. B. Meyer[3] suggests: "When the pivot-text is chosen, it is desirable, so far as possible to weave into the structure of the sermon all the main points of the surrounding paragraph." The method of D. W. Cleverley Ford[4] is to select a passage of Scripture; then to select from this passage a verse which to some extent summarizes the whole; then to find a theme suggested by this verse, and to expand it into a number of points, with application. The result generally is a combination of expository and textual preaching, with the main points based on implications of the text, rather than analysis of it.

5. *Topical Sermon.* A "Topical Sermon" has all the essential characteristics of a "Textual" or an "Expository" sermon; but bears no analytical relation to any one particular passage of Scripture. While the "Textual' sermon is the elaboration of a text, and the "Expository" sermon is the elaboration of a longer passage, the "Topical" sermon is the elaboration of a topic. Whether the topic is derived from Biblical or non-Biblical sources, the "Topical" sermon is not necessarily less Biblical in content and development than a "Textual" or an "Expository" sermon.

## PATTERNS RELATED TO THE BASIC PATTERN

In addition to the "Basic Pattern," by which the sermon is developed *deductively* from the thesis or proposition, there are other structural patterns, by which the sermon is developed *inductively*. Here the thesis, without which it would not be a true sermon, is withheld until the conclusion, which is indeed the thesis in reverse. The many structural patterns found in homiletical literature, under many classifications, seem to fall into the following familiar categories:

1. *The "Problem Solution" Pattern.* This pattern differs from the "Basic" pattern mainly in that the proportions of certain

---

[3]*Expository Preaching Plans and Methods* (London: Hodder & Stoughton 1912), p. 33.
[4]*An Expository Preacher's Notebook* (New York: Harper & Brothers, 1960). p. 19.

structural parts are changed. The "Basic" pattern might present the problem briefly in the introduction, along with suggested or attempted solutions; and would then, on the basis of an announced thesis or proposition, expound in the body of the sermon the one acceptable solution. The "Problem Solution" pattern expands the statement of the problem into a main division, and the statement of inadequate solutions likewise. These two main divisions are given the same rank and proportion as the third division, which deals with the acceptable solution. This approach can be very effective as the preacher secures the participation of his audience in exploring a problem and its possible solutions, instead of announcing the conclusion in advance and proceeding to establish its validity.

What is true of the "Problem Solution" pattern, as to emphasis and proportion, is similarly true of several closely related patterns: (1) The "Need and Satisfaction" pattern, which deals with a recognized need; possible ways of meeting the need; and the recommended solution. (2) The "Hegelian" pattern (named for the philosopher George William Friedrich Hegel, 1770-1831).[5] This pattern emphasizes "thesis-antithesis-synthesis"; the ideal, the actual, the reconciliation; action, reaction, struggle, suspense, climax; the familiar plot upon which most novels are said to be constructed: "boy meets girl, boy wants girl, boy wins girl." (3) The familiar "Nature-Cause-Results-Remedy" pattern is structurally comparable to the foregoing. It is a useful pattern if not used too often. Preachers are known to have "natured, caused, resulted, and remedied" their regular audiences to the point of exasperation.

2. *The "Narrative" Pattern.* This type of sermon is like an exploration in which the preacher conducts his people along a path of cumulative impressions leading to an inevitable conclusion. This was the prevailing pattern of the apostles. The sermon of Peter at Pentecost is a case in point. The apostles told the gospel story; the Lord "confirmed the word" (Mark 16:20) ; and the response at times amazed even the apostles. With an audience

---

[5]Blackwood, *The Preparation of Sermons*, p. 148.

that is hostile to the thesis, this may be the most helpful approach. The thesis is not divulged until the case is made, although the preacher himself keeps the thesis constantly in mind as the sermon progresses.

The material of the "Narrative" pattern may be either historical or biographical. If historical, the preacher relates a chain of circumstances (facts, cases, incidents, experiences, developments) leading to the central truth which he is seeking to drive home. This pattern is especially adapted to the biographical sermon, which is built around a person and not around a central truth. There are two approaches: (1) Under the first main point, tell the story of that life, preferably in chronological order; and under the second main point, draw out the lessons; or (2) Tell the life story, and indicate each phase by a main point, followed by the lessons derived; or reverse the order by first stating the lessons, as main points, and then developing these points with material from the related portions of the story.[6]

## PATTERNS NOT RELATED TO THE BASIC PATTERN

Two patterns which could hardly be classed as sermons are sufficiently useful to deserve consideration, and sufficiently different from each other to require separate treatment:

1. *The "Homily."* This pattern dates back to the early Christian churches, where it followed the prevailing Jewish practice of explaining in popular form the lessons of Scripture read in the synagogues.[7] This practice appears to have had its origin in the days of Ezra the scribe, who stood with others and "read in the book in the law of God distinctly, and gave the sense, and caused them to understand the reading" (Neh. 8:8). It is not developed around a topic or proposition, and differs from the sermon mainly in its "predominance of explanation over system." It follows the order of the Scriptural text, and aims merely to lift out for elaboration and application the successive parts of the

6Ilion T. Jones, *Principles and Practice of Preaching* (New York and Nashville: Abingdon Press, 1956), p. 111.

7*International Encyclopaedia* (New York: Dodd, Mead & Co., 1928), Vol. XI, p. 419.

passage as it stands. There is no effort at homiletical structure. It is necessary only that the limits of the text for the homily be determined by some internal unity of thought, and that the thread of unity be not buried and lost in the discussion.[8]

2. *The "Bible Reading."* Closely related to the "Homily" is the so-called "Bible Reading," which usually involves audience participation, and is likewise without homiletical structure. The Scripture lesson may consist of a single extended passage, or of unrelated verses gathered around a selected topic. F. D. Whitesell, in *The Art of Biblical Preaching*,[9] discusses "Bible Readings" as a possible procedure for beginners, or for certain types of Bible discussion groups. The usual procedure is to prepare a list of selected Scripture references, arranged in some progressive order, on some topic such as "The Power of Prayer"; then to "speak on the topic, going from one passage to another, making comments, giving explanations and illustrations."

Andrew W. Blackwood, in *Preaching from the Bible*,[10] devotes a chapter to "The Bible Reading" as a method for midweek services. Much of the reading is done in concert, and the leader aims to draw the group into active participation in the discussion.

Merrill F. Unger, in *Principles of Expository Preaching*,[11] associates the "Bible Reading" method with topical studies only. "The Bible Reading method rivets attention on the topic itself."

In churches where the "Bible Reading" method is virtually unknown, the use of this method on rare occasions can be quite effective. One pastor demonstrated this in his effort to enlist his members in tithing. On a given Sunday morning his deacons distributed to every person present a copy of the New Testament, in which the passages bearing on the Christian's obligation to give had been marked. Then the pastor, instead of preaching a regular sermon, led the congregation through the marked Scripture passages with comments and applications. The novelty of

---

[8] A. Vinet, *Homiletics*, translated by Thomas H. Skinner (New York): Newman & Ivison, 1853), p. 148.

[9] (Grand Rapids: Zondervan Publishing House, 1950), pp. 39-44.

[10] (New York: Abingdon-Cokesbury Press, 1941), pp. 153-168.

[11] (Grand Rapids: Zondervan Publishing House, 1955), p. 41.

the method appealed to the people, and the result was amazingly good.

\*      \*      \*

While there is merit in the various methods of presenting Biblical truth, and freshness in changing from one to another from time to time, the preacher will probably do well to *major* on the "Basic" pattern throughout his ministry.

# 3

# The Primacy of Expository Preaching

Expository preaching is only one of several types of preaching which have been mightily used and mightily blessed of God. A study of the great sermons in sacred literature reveals so much overlapping between these types as to make strict classification impossible. Nor is it essential for any given sermon to be purely topical or purely textual or purely expository.

Expository preaching, though always Biblical in content, is not always in the "Basic" structural pattern. "A sermon is often expository in its nature even though it may not be technically so in its homilectical structure."[1] But in order to be well received, the sermon must have unity, structure, aim, and progression; it must be sustained by Biblical authority, and must be intelligently presented. There is no doubt that expository preaching would be far more popular than it is, if it were more generally well done.

Textual preaching has much to commend it; likewise, topical preaching. No one method should be employed exclusively. But as a prevailing method, for year round ministering, expository preaching has the greater potential for the blessing and enrichment of both pastor and people. "Take heed ... unto yourselves, and to all the flock, over which the Holy Ghost hath made you overseers, to *feed the church of God ...* " (Acts 20:28) . This text, so largely used in ordinations, implies a generous use of the Bible, a copy of which is usually presented to the young minister. And what could be more appropriate in view of the prevailing spiritual undernourishment of our times!

---

[1]Jeff D. Ray, *Expository Preaching* (Grand Rapids: Zondervan Publishing House, 1940), p. 46.

Expository preaching feeds the soul. By acquainting the hearers with Biblical truth, the preacher is building up spiritual resources far beyond the immediate objectives of the sermon. Nutritionists are using the term "nutritional time bomb," with reference to particular nutritional deficiencies which may remain undiscovered for years and then suddenly manifest themselves in serious illness. Such is the experience of the spiritually undernourished who, under the stress of bereavement or catastrophe, suddenly discover that the soul is too weak to weather the storm.[2]

Expository preaching makes use of more Scriptural material than is generally true of textual or topical preaching. Through the knowledge of Biblical truth, God gives prompting, direction, and enablement for Christian living. And expository preaching as a prevailing method is likely to prove more helpful than other methods in developing a people rooted and grounded in the Word of God. Only when the believer has been thoroughly indoctrinated in the Holy Scriptures is he adequately fortified in the hour of temptation, and able to say, like Jesus in the wilderness, "It is written" (Matt. 4:4, 7, 10) ! Too many well meaning believers are coming to grief in our generation of widespread moral ambiguity because they do not know what is "written." Too many are like the woman of whom it was said that she had only one moral defect: She could not distinguish between right and wrong! A perennial emphasis on expository preaching may well be our best answer to the challenge of widespread Biblical illiteracy.

"Unhappily, even among theological students and ministers there is widespread ignorance of the content of the Bible. This is crippling to the would-be preacher."[3] But as he works at taking up the slack in the Biblical training of his people and seeks to declare "the whole counsel of God" (Acts 20:27) , he himself is the first to profit from the riches he discovers. Thus living within the Bible, he is constantly bringing himself and his people under the judgment of the Word of God; and as he

---

[2]Kenneth J. Nettles, in *The Watchman-Examiner* (Jan. 8, 1959), p. 32.

[3]Henry Sloane Coffin, *Communion through Preaching* (New York: Charles Scribner's Sons, 1952), p. 13.

extends his range of Scriptural truth, this wider coverage makes for a wholesome balance, and helps to prevent the disproportionate stressing of certain truths to the neglect of others. "A part of the rays of the sun separated from the rest will stain your page red or orange or violet, but if the full light of heaven falls upon it, it will leave it a pure white."[4]

"Problem Preaching" and "Life Situation Preaching" are definitely useful, and should not be disparaged. But expository preaching, with reasonably broad coverage of the Bible, made alive and relevant to the present age, may help more people by dealing with a much wider variety of problems and life situations. Problems which are too delicate to be handled topically may often be handled quite naturally in the course of expository preaching; and problems of which the preacher may not be at all aware may thus be brought under the light of Scripture. Willard Brewing, after a reference to preaching aimed at some particular problem, adds that there is another kind of preaching which may be "more effective still, that is, just turning on the Light which falls on every problem." He refers to Hebrews 4:12, where the "Word of God" is declared to be "a discerner of the thoughts and intents of the heart." And he couples with this passage of Scripture the apt comment of John Hutton: "The New Testament holds up a strong light by which a man can read even the small print of his soul."[5]

While there may be a problem in every pew, too much "Problem Preaching" or "Life Situation Preaching" does not provide the best kind of steady diet. "It tends to make people problem-conscious instead of Bible-conscious and God-conscious."[6] Preaching might become too horizontal, "savoring more of psychology than of religion, more of self-help than of the Bible."[7] The preacher might run out of "problems" or "situations"; or he might become so much of a problem preacher as to think of

---

[4]Griffin, *The Art of Preaching*, p. 20.

[5]Donald Macleod, *Here Is My Method* (Westwood, New Jersey: Fleming H. Revell Co., 1952), pp. 39, 46.

[6]Whitesell, *The Art of Biblical Preaching*, p. 22.

[7]W. E. Sangster, *The Craft of Sermon Construction* (Philadelphia: Westminster Press, 1951), p. 132.

people primarily in terms of problems, to the neglect of many areas of truth not so related. The timeliness which so often is the strength of this type of preaching seems to become a limitation upon its length of life. The expository sermon, on the other hand, may have the advantage of timelessness, while lacking nothing from the standpoint of relevance to an immediate situation. Along with contemporary application, it carries authority which is often lacking in sermons on contemporary themes with only occasional and perhaps vague references to Scripture.

The resources for expository preaching are inexhaustible. This type demands — and develops — a greater knowledge of Scripture than is necessary for other types. In the same progression, the preacher is challenged by an ever widening range of possibilities, with "endless variety at his disposal."[8] Not only will he be developing sermons dealing with paragraphs, but with chapters and with entire books of the Bible. Book sermons have been found particularly helpful in introducing some of the shorter, less well known books of the Bible, or in preparing a congregation for a series of sermons on a given book. An excellent discussion of this type of sermon is that of Ilion T. Jones.[9] He shows how a sermon outline on a book of the Bible may be constructed, by grouping the contents of the book under headings as the verses of a paragraph or chapter would be grouped, and developing each division in the same way. First, the point is stated; then elaborated with material from the book; then applied. A more dramatic handling of the book might be to discuss it under the three headings: the historical setting; the contents; the message. This would allow more time for the historical setting and the material from which the message is drawn, and would gather up the message in a series of brief and powerful thrusts at the end.

The preaching of an occasional sermon on the Bible as a whole is recommended by Corwin C. Roach,[10] as a salutary exercise

    8James S. Stewart, *Heralds of God* (New York: Charles Scribner's Sons, 1956), p. 109.

    9*Principles and Practice of Preaching*, pp. 109 ff.

    10*Preaching Values in the Bible* (Louisville: The Cloister Press, 1946), p. 296.

for every preacher. Next to sermons on the Bible as a whole, he would rank sermons on the books of the Bible, as a means of counteracting the tendency toward fragmentary preaching of the Bible. Similarly, Robert J. McCracken, in stressing expository preaching as a means of making the Bible more than a mere "compendium of handy quotations," favors occasionally devoting a sermon to the exposition of an entire book of the Bible.[11] Whether dealing with a paragraph of Scripture or a chapter or an entire book, there is need for practicing "the fine art of omission"; else the sermon might bog down in the abundance of material available.

Another effective type of expository preaching is that of preaching on Bible characters. Faris D. Whitesell, in his excellent book on this subject,[12] gives many reasons for placing this type of preaching in high priority. He points out that this is perhaps the easiest way to preach the Bible, the most likely to appeal to people and to hold their attention, and particularly to sustain the interest of young people, and the most likely to be remembered. And, for freshness and variety, there are approximately four hundred Bible characters from which to choose!

In the choice of subjects for biographical preaching, Andrew W. Blackwood suggests that "usually it is better to put the emphasis where the Bible puts it, upon the man who is doing the will of God. This is one reason why Genesis devotes more attention to Joseph than to all of its bad men put together."[13] With this emphasis the hearer may be helped to see himself in the person of another, and to find for himself the same blessing. All the while, it must be remembered that the Bible was not given to reveal the lives of Abraham, Isaac, and Jacob, but to reveal *the hand of God* in the lives of Abraham, Isaac, and Jacob; not as a revelation of Mary and Martha and Lazarus, but as a revelation of *the Savior* of Mary and Martha and Lazarus. It must be remembered also that the Bible generally provides only

11*The Making of the Sermon* (New York: Harper & Brothers, 1956), p. 35.
12*Preaching on Bible Characters* (Grand Rapids: Baker Book House, 1955).
13*Preaching from the Bible*, p. 57.

brief, incomplete sketches, and any use of the historical imagination must be strictly compatible with the recorded facts.

In dealing with characters who are not to be emulated, two dangers are to be avoided:[14] First, in depicting their flaws, there is danger of making a merely negative impact. A second danger is the temptation to present a distorted and unfair picture by making one or more faults loom disproportionately large. A biographical sermon that is completely fair will tend to correct any previous distortions.

"People both need and want the Word of God."[15] And the preacher who gives it to them will find his resources growing more abundant with every sermon he prepares. He shall be "like a tree planted by the rivers of water, that bringeth forth his fruit in his season" (Ps. 1:3). "Why go to the broken cisterns of this world's knowledge, when this ever-flowing fountain of divine truth yields rivers of the water of life?"[16]

---

[14]Frank H. Caldwell, *Preaching Angles* (New York: Abingdon Press, 1954), p. 61.

[15]Sangster, *The Craft of Sermon Construction*, p. 27.

[16]Faris D. Whitesell, *Evangelistic Preaching and the Old Testament* (Chicago: Moody Press, 1947), p. 184.

# 4

# The Advantages of
# Preaching without Notes

A survey of homiletical literature reveals, along with an endless variety of views and methods, that there is fairly general agreement on two points: First, it is recognized that most congregations prefer note free preaching. Secondly, it is agreed that each minister must find for himself the particular method that will best enable him to achieve such freedom from notes in the pulpit. For each minister to develop a method for himself might involve years of wasteful experimentation, and a high percentage *never* arrive at a successful method.

The reading of sermons in the pulpit does have its advocates.[1] One exponent says that "a reasonable amount of practice will enable anybody to read a sermon as freely as he preaches extemporaneously."[2] But sermons effectively read are so extremely rare that this procedure may be practically ruled out except for the most extraordinary circumstances. And while reading has been more or less acceptable in certain quarters, it has never been popular with the average audience.

There are, as there always have been, ministers who preach effectively from manuscript or copious notes in the pulpit, as well as some who read their sermons in full; but the same preachers would be even more effective if they could stand note free in the pulpit. This seems clearly to be the verdict of history.

---

[1]Charles L. Slattery, *Present Day Preaching* (New York: Longmans, Green & Co., 1909), p. 21.

[2]Bernard I. Bell, in *The Minister, The Method, and The Message*, by Harold A. Prichard (New York: Charles Scribner's Sons, 1932), p. 151.

## EXAMPLES FROM ANTIQUITY

The eloquent Cicero (106-43 B.C.,), who "enthralled Rome with his eloquence of speech,"[3] had strong convictions about facing an audience without the impediment of a manuscript. He was thoroughly trained in law and oratory; and his rank as the greatest orator of ancient Rome, and one of her most illustrious statesmen and scholars, qualifies him as an authority. He declared, "In delivery, next to the voice in effectiveness is the countenance; and this is ruled over by the eyes. The expressive power of the human eye is so great that it determines, in a manner, the expression of the whole countenance."[4]

Some of the ancient orators are said to have been of such disciplined memories that they sometimes dispensed with notes even in the *preparation* of their messages. Thus Quintilian, the Roman rhetorician, who had a distinguished professional career as a teacher of eloquence (c. A.D. 35-c. A.D. 97), gave instructions for *thinking out* a speech for delivery; and Cicero said that orations are written, not that they *may be* delivered, but as *having been* delivered.[5] The practice of preparing messages "by a process of mental composition is not unknown in the twentieth century. Its reliance is largely upon the general preparation that comes through extensive reading and wide experience. Thus a chosen text or theme will gather to itself a wealth of accumulated material which needs only to be placed in orderly arrangement.[6]

Andrew W. Blackwood reminds us that note free preaching was the method of Jesus and the prophets and apostles who, when they preached, spoke "from heart to heart and from eye to eye."[7] In the synagogue at Nazareth, when Jesus had "opened

---

[3]William A. Quayle, *The Pastor-Preacher* (Cincinnati: Jennings & Graham, 1910), p. 289.

[4]John A. Broadus, *On the Preparation and Delivery of Sermons* (New York: Harper & Brothers, 1944), p. 350.

[5]Henry J. Ripley, *Sacred Rhetoric* (Boston: Gould, Kendall & Lincoln, 1849), p. 170.

[6]Joseph Fort Newton, in *The Minister, The Method, and The Message,* by Harold A. Prichard, p. 179.

[7]*Expository Preaching for Today* (New York and Nashville: Abingdon-Cokesbury Press, 1953), p. 159.

the book" and began to speak, all eyes were fixed on Him (Luke 4:17-21). How incongruous it would have been for Jesus to have His eyes fastened on notes! "The fact that the mightiest of God's heralds in olden times preached without notes ought to create a presupposition in favor of this method now."[8]

## CONCENSUS OF MODERN OBSERVERS

Preaching without notes has been powerfully advocated by writers of our generation, as well as writers of the previous century.

"With the masses of the people, it is the popular method. No doubt some congregations have been educated into a toleration of reading, but it is almost always an unwilling acquiescence . . . ."[9]

"Without doubt the people at large are more taken with even a tolerable measure of success in extempore speaking than with the ablest addresses from a manuscript."[10]

"Hearers, of this I am sure, prefer what is called extempore preaching, better and more accurately described as unscripted preaching. . . . The less paper and the less reading from a paper, the less barrier to communication. . . ."[11]

Preaching without notes "will sometimes give a man of slender ideas and poor attainments . . . a superiority to another man with whom, in regard to sterling qualities, he could not sustain a moment's comparison, but who has not the power of freely addressing an audience."[12]

"Every time laymen are given a chance to express themselves they vote against the reading of sermons." "Practically all professors of public speech recommend free delivery without qualification."[13]

---

[8]Blackwood, *The Preparation of Sermons*, p. 194.

[9]Broadus, *On the Preparation and Delivery of Sermons*, pp. 329, 330.

[10]Wilder Smith, *Extempore Preaching* (Hartford: Brown & Gross, 1884), p. 12.

[11]Wright, *A Preacher's Questionnaire*, p. 68.

[12]Ripley, *Sacred Rhetoric*, p. 173.

[13]Jones, *Principles and Practice of Preaching*, pp. 194, 202.

Gilman, Aly, and Reid, in their excellent course book, *Fundamentals of Speaking,* declare, "The only speakers who should be allowed to use notes are those who do not need them."[14]

When Governor Alfred E. Smith was campaigning for the presidency he began reading his speeches. But he abruptly stopped, believing that the people lose interest when they see the speaker bending over a paper, and that they may think he is afraid to say what he really has on his mind.[15]

G. Campbell Morgan (1863-1942), "perhaps the greatest Biblical expositor of modern times . . . always spoke extemporaneously."[16]

Charles H. Spurgeon (1834-1892), generally recognized as one of the great preachers of all time, "preached extemporaneously, except for about a half page of notes which he used very little."[17]

George W. Truett (1867-1944), unexcelled as pastor-evangelist in his generation, preached with tremendous power, always without notes. For approximately forty-five years he served as pastor of the First Baptist Church of Dallas, Texas, which he built from a small, struggling congregation to a membership of approximately 9000 members, making it the largest congregation of white Baptists in the world. During the latter half of his ministry he was away from his own pulpit about half the time; he "belonged to the world"; but the spiritual impact of his ministry kept the church life in high momentum to the very end. Those who heard him could scarcely imagine his preaching otherwise than without notes.

## TESTIMONY FROM EXPERIENCE

Clarence E. Macartney, famous author of many popular books of sermons, preached without notes since his junior year in the seminary, and since that time "never preached either with a manuscript or with any notes whatsoever in the pulpit." In

---

14Gilman, Aly, and Reid, *The Fundamentals of Speaking* (New York: The Macmillan Co., 1951), p. 127.

15*Ibid.,* p. 126.

16Whitesell, *The Art of Biblical Preaching,* pp. 150-151.

17*Ibid.,* pp. 156-158.

his book, *Preaching without Notes*,[18] he declares, after forty years of preaching, that "in season and out of season, year after year, and to the average congregation, there can be no question that the sermon that does the most good is the sermon which is preached without notes."

Dean Charles R. Brown, in the Lyman Beecher Lectures for 1922-23,[19] declares, "The man who preaches without manuscript reaches levels of joy in his preaching which I am sure the preacher from manuscript knows not of." But, "In my own practice," says Dr. Brown, "while I never use a manuscript in preaching, there are five sentences in my sermon which I always write out in advance and know by heart — the first one and the last four."

Fred Townley Lord,[20] former President of the Baptist World Alliance, had this to say: "I have always felt happier looking at a congregation than looking at a manuscript. I learned that directness of speech and direct contact with an audience were worth more than a labored literary style."

Faris D. Whitesell,[21] outstanding preacher and teacher of evangelism, says, "If a man ever needs liberty and freedom in preaching, it is when delivering an evangelistic message. Look the people directly in the eyes all the time, speak sincerely, and preach with a mighty sense of mission and urgency."

John Wesley[22] said, "Look your audience decently in the face, one after another, as we do in familiar conversation."

Harold J. Ockenga,[23] renowned pastor of the historic Park Street church in Boston, Massachusetts, has preached without notes for over thirty years, and strongly recommends this method, based on comprehensive preparation and careful outlining of sermons.

---

18 (New York: Abingdon-Cokesbury Press, 1946), pp. 145, 160.

19*The Art of Preaching* (New York: The Macmillan Co., 1944), pp. 87, 113.

20*My Way of Preaching*, edited by Robert J. Smithson (London: Pickering & Inglis, Ltd.), p. 92.

21*Evangelistic Preaching and the Old Testament*, p. 50.

22*John Wesley on Pulpit Oratory*, revised and abridged by Ross E. Price (Kansas City, Mo.: Beacon Hill Press, 1955), p. 19.

23"How to Prepare a Sermon," *Christianity Today* (Oct. 13, 1958), pp. 10-12.

## CONFIRMATION FROM THE LABORATORY

"Psychologists, conducting tests under laboratory conditions, have found that people remember that which is read to them, with forty-nine per cent efficiency. Retention increases to sixty-seven per cent when the thought is expressed, not by reading, but by direct address. We want our message to be remembered."[24]

The eye is itself "an organ of speech," and is needed in every communication. Along with spiritual communication, it radiates also a physical energy, as does the "electric eye" which opens the door into the modern railroad station or supermarket. Halford E. Luccock tells of the display of an invention called a "look-at-meter," which dramatically demonstrated this fact. In this delicate contrivance even a casual glance was enough to deflect the sensitive plate.[25] The Ancient Mariner of Samuel T. Coleridge "holds him with his glittering eye." Orators have been doing this from the beginning of time. When Candidates Nixon and Kennedy, in those crucial television appearances, made their supreme appeals to the country, with the presidency of the United States at stake, they spoke without notes. Why? How much more should the appeals of the minister of Jesus Christ, with eternities at stake, be delivered without the impediment of notes!

"There is power in the eye, no less than in the voice, to convey all varieties of emotion — indignation, surprise, determination, appeal."[26]

"It is the eye, the tone, the living thought of the speaker that moves and persuades the hearer."[27]

"Eye contact between preacher and listener should be as intimate and continuous as possible. This does not merely help

---

[24] John N. Booth, *The Quest for Preaching Power* (New York: Macmillan Co., 1943), p. 222.

[25] Luccock, *In the Minister's Workshop*, p. 198.

[26] Wilder Smith, *Extempore Preaching* (Hartford: Brown & Gross, 1884), p. 128.

[27] F. Barham Zincke, *The Duty and Discipline of Extemporary Preaching* (New York: Charles Scribner & Co., 1867), p. 15.

direct the listener's attention; shades of meaning are conveyed that would otherwise be lost."[28]

David R. Breed[29] speaks of "the emancipated eye" of the note free preacher, and of the added power which this gives him in delivering his message.

Robert E. Speer insisted that the speaker keep his eyes on the audience. "There is more power in your eye, sometimes, than you may imagine."[30] A speaker may attract the attention of a restless member of his audience by merely looking at him, and thus bring him to quietness and attentiveness.

In stressing the importance of the conclusion of the sermon, Ilion T. Jones lists a number of emphatic "don'ts." One of these is: "Don't once break eye contact with the people ... be completely free from manuscript or notes."[31] Obviously, what makes for power in the closing moments of the sermon will make for power throughout the body of the sermon.

28Webb B. Garrison, *The Preacher and His Audience* (Westwood, N. J.: Fleming H. Revell Co., 1954), p. 236.

29*Preparing to Preach*, p. 322.

30*How to Speak Effectively without Notes* (New York: Fleming H. Revell Co., 1928), p. 17.

31*Principles and Practice of Preaching*, p. 167.

# 5

# The Importance of Structure

The structural specifications for a good sermon are comparable to the specifications by which the primitive Indian fashioned his arrows. He realized that his very survival might depend upon the excellence of his arrow. The shaft must therefore be absolutely straight, lest it wobble in flight; the point must be sharp enough to penetrate; the feathers must be in just the right amount to steady the arrow in flight, yet not to retard its flight or dull its thrust. Similarly, the sermon must have a clear thought running straight through the length of it, a sharp point at the end, and just enough "feathers" to cope with the atmosphere through which it must pass on its way to the target.

Preaching without notes is largely a matter of structure. So is pulpit power. While some of our great preachers have succeeded without adequate structure in their sermons, their success has been due to extraordinary compensating factors. A keen mind, a vivid imagination, breadth of learning, experience and observation, and intensity of feeling, coupled with native oratorical talent, may make a powerful impact. But even greater effectiveness might be achieved if there were structural excellence also. Without sound structure, a real message may prove obscure and impotent. "It is possible, of course, to fill twenty minutes or longer with sermonic matter that is without form and yet not entirely void."[1] But sound structure will add immeasurably to the power of a sermon, and good homiletical habits are a priceless resource to the pulpiteer.

An outline that stands out clear and sharp is the first long step to freedom in the pulpit. And it does not need to be offen-

[1]Sangster, *The Craft of Sermon Construction*, p. 62.

sively angular. Properly elaborated or clothed, it can be a thing of beauty as well as strength. As one authority aptly points out, "A good outline is never the cause of failure in a sermon."[2] While technique alone does not insure a good sermon, the *want* of technique makes a good sermon highly improbable. Sound structure can make the difference between futility and effectiveness in a sermon, and can, over the years, lift a preacher from mediocrity to excellence.

A sound structure is helpful not only to the preacher, giving him a sense of timing, progress, and proportion, but to his audience as well. Intelligent listening requires that the course of thinking be made clear to the hearer. Donald G. Miller, in *The Way to Biblical Preaching*,[3] protests against that "cult of sermonic tricksters in our time whose aim seems to be to hide from the hearer the points at which an advance in thought is made." Clear, smooth transitions are a mark of excellence in a sermon, and an evidence of clear thinking on the part of the preacher. Clarity of expression is not incompatible with profundity; as a matter of fact, the two may be said even to have an affinity for each other; and to achieve simplicity is a triumph indeed.

The kind of outline that is structurally adapted to memorization, retention, and recall is not achieved without labor, but is worth all that it costs. It has been truly said that much poor preaching is due to "suppressed perspiration."[4] An excellent outline, however, is not enough, though it be constructed with the accuracy of a Swiss watch, and though it be a literary achievement of the highest order. "The major sources of preaching power are spiritual. Hence they lie far beyond the reach of homiletics."[5]

Excellence of structure can not compensate for the absence of the Holy Spirit. Without the guidance and empowerment of

---

[2]H. E. Knott, *How to Prepare a Sermon* (Cincinnati: The Standard Press, 1927), p. 23.

[3](New York: Abingdon Press, 1957), p. 94.

[4]G. Campbell Morgan, *Preaching* (New York: Fleming H. Revell Co., 1937), p. 14.

[5]Blackwood, *Preaching from the Bible*, p. 182.

the Holy Spirit, the preacher, however skillful in homiletical techniques, would be only "a homiletical carpenter" producing and delivering "wooden" sermons.

Structural soundness can not supply that life of holiness which is basic to pulpit power. There is an eloquence of the lips, and there is an eloquence of the heart. Of Aaron, it was recorded, "He can speak well" (Exod. 4:14); but there is no message of Aaron to be found in the Scriptures. Moses, on the other hand, regarded himself as "not eloquent ... slow of speech, and of a slow tongue" (Exod. 4:10). But from Moses we have a legacy of messages mighty in power, reflecting that eloquence which is of the heart.

Technique can not make up for want of content. With all that is being said in our generation about *"communicating"* and about *"relevancy* in preaching," there must first be something to *communicate,* something to *make relevant.* "It is more important clumsily to have something to say than cleverly to say nothing."[6]

A flawlessly prepared sermon remains lifeless and powerless until the preacher throws himself heart and soul into the message. In such delivery the sermon becomes much more than the sum of its parts, and the preacher becomes more than the sum of his talents, his training, his experience, and the labor expended. His love for his people, his devotion to his Lord, his high sense of calling, plus the accompaniment of the Holy Spirit make the preacher invincible, as God fulfills the ancient promise: "Them that honor me, I will honor," saith the Lord (I Sam. 2:30).

---

[6]Webb B. Garrison, *Creative Imagination in Preaching* (New York: Abingdon Press, 1960), pp. 79-80.

# 6

# The Sources of Preaching Material

A preacher will not long hold the interest of his people if he preaches only "out of the fullness of his heart and the emptiness of his head." The pastor must reckon with the probability of having to prepare about one hundred and fifty messages a year, including Sundays, Wednesdays, funeral services and special occasions. This adds up to an enormous output. The only safeguard against poverty of thought is by way of constant exposure to the sources of preaching material, and constant replenishment from these sources. Laying up resources is a matter of years of sustained effort and meditation. Sermons are developed more or less unconsciously, and there is no substitute for the prolonged general preparation behind the immediate specific preparation.

Perennial freshness in the pulpit calls for an adequate background of indirect as well as direct preparation, and this calls for adequate materials. Lester Harnish makes the excellent suggestion that the minister should have a library costing at least as much as the car he drives, and should spend four hours a day, five days a week, in concentrated reading and study.[1] J. H. Jowett gave picturesque expression to the same need: "We must cultivate big farms, and we shall have well-stocked barns, and we shall not be moody gleaners searching for thin ears over a small and ill-cultivated field."[2]

A common criticism of topical preaching is that it is too remote from Scripture, too remote from authority. A common criticism

---

[1]*We Prepare and Preach*, edited by Clarence S. Roddy (Chicago: Moody Press, 1959), p. 65.

[2]*The Preacher: His Life and Work* (New York: Richard R. Smith, Inc., 1930), p. 121.

of expository preaching is that it is too remote from the people, too remote from modern life. Expository preaching may tend to dwell too much on the other side of the Isle of Patmos, and topical preaching may tend to dwell too much on this side of Pearl Harbor. A proper balance must be found, and can be found, in drawing upon the sources available.

1. *Scripture.* The Bible is the great inexhaustible reservoir of Christian truth. The daily reading of it will insure the preacher an unfailing supply of pulpit themes for the edification of his people, and an abundant source of illustrative material. One authority[3] recommends only one *book of illustrations,* namely, the Bible. A preacher of the Bible will often be amazed at what he discovers in searching the Scriptures, and how often his people will exclaim, "Is that in the Bible?" Particularly in the Old Testament, there are many incidents which would lend freshness to current preaching because they are so little known.

But how can a preacher draw upon sources with which he is not familiar? To some, the Bible is a largely unexplored gold mine. Men have been known to go through a full seminary training without having studied the entire Bible or even having read it through so much as once. "A seminary professor advised the members of an entering class to be sure to read the Bible through once during the three years of their training. . . . When the class graduated, not one member had read the Bible through while in the Seminary."[4]

The preacher will do well to utilize materials in the Scriptures before going outside the Bible. Explain Scripture with Scripture. The best commentary on the Bible is the Bible itself. The apostles were powerful partly because of their familiar use of the Old Testament. Roger Nicole points out that "More than ten per cent of the New Testament text is made up of citations

---

[3]Rhoades, *Case Work in Preaching,* p. 89.
[4]Simon Blocker, *The Secret of Pulpit Power* (Grand Rapids: Wm. B. Eerdmans Publishing Co., 1951), p. 23.

or direct allusions to the Old Testament. The recorded words of Jesus disclose a similar percentage."[5]

Declaring "the whole counsel of God" includes the Old Testament and the New Testament, history and prophecy, the Psalms of praise and the Book of Lamentations, theology, ethics, etc. It will involve careful exegetical study of passages, not from intellectual curiosity, but to discern the mind of God; not as a work of mere literary craftsmen, but as saving truth transmitted through human channels. Marginal references and cognate passages should be consulted; a good concordance is indispensable; and there should be a generous use of a Bible dictionary, a Bible atlas, and some good commentary, and complete dependence upon the Holy Spirit, the Supreme Teacher, who "will guide you into all truth" (John 16:13).

2. *History.* Familiarity with the history of the kingdoms and empires with which the people of God interacted in Biblical times will add immeasurably to an understanding of the Scriptures. And later history will reveal the relevance of Biblical truth to later generations. "History is the great interpreter of Providence and of the Scriptures also."[6] And since history has a way of repeating itself, it sheds light on the present and on the future as well. In a gathering where one of the speakers had repeatedly urged that the facts be looked in the face, an elder member replied, "Yes, we must look the facts in the face; but we shall not fully *understand* the facts until we have viewed them also from the rear." Some of the mighty messages of Moses and Joshua and Samuel were reinforced with references to history, revealing a point of strength which might well be emulated today.

3. *Literature Other Than Scripture and History.* A balanced program of reading would include, in addition to devotional readings, some biography, poetry, fiction, archaeology, studies in the arts and sciences, and other general reading. Not to be

---

[5]*Revelation and the Bible,* edited by Carl F. H. Henry (Grand Rapids: Baker Book House, 1958), p. 138.

[6]Breed, *Preparing to Preach,* p. 134.

overlooked, is the hymnal, where much of the world's finest and most helpful poetry may be found. In addition to books, there would be magazines and newspapers. Some weekly digest of current events, national and world-wide, would be helpful. But in all his reading the minister must be extremely selective, remembering that time is precious, and the reading of any given book or magazine or article rules out the reading of something else that might be more valuable.

4. *Experience.* Preaching at its best is the sharing of profound personal experience. The apostles told freely of their own personal experience, and their testimony was mightily blessed. "We can not but speak the things which we have seen and heard" (Acts 4:20). But "no doctrine can live in the intellect which does not renew itself in experience."[7] Effective testimony in the pulpit requires a background of experience in constant process of renewal. But let the preacher make sure that the experience he relates is true, that it is indeed his own, and that he is not the hero of his own story. Occasionally a preacher may be tempted to make use of that ill-advised pulpit expression: "Pardon a personal reference." Such apology is never warranted. If the preacher is sharing an experience with the humble and sincere intent of clarifying or enforcing a truth to make it more helpful to his hearers, he does not need to be pardoned. And if the personal reference aims in some way to glorify the preacher, it *should not* and *will not* be pardoned.

Some of the most enriching experiences come through observation of the world around us, and through conversation, by which we enter into the experiences of others. The parables of Jesus reflect alert observation of the processes of nature and the ways of humanity, as well as the needs of the human heart revealed through conversation.

5. *Imagination.* Dullness is the bane of much preaching. Imagination can make an otherwise dull sermon come alive, by bringing hidden realities into view, by setting familiar facts in

---

[7]Halford E. Luccock, *Communicating the Gospel* (New York: Harper & Brothers, 1954), p. 72.

fresh relationships, by seeing resemblances and implications which escape the casual observer. Thus the ancient Scriptures are made to live. A vivid historical imagination is a real gift of God. But in the exercise of this gift, the preacher must make sure that any speculation, conjectural details, and plays upon fancy are identified as such, to his hearers. And let the preacher beware of cleverness! "It is impossible at one and the same time to create the impression that you are clever and that Jesus is wonderful."[8]

The imagination may express itself in several ways:

(1) *Visualization.* This is the portrayal of incidents with dramatic insertion of interesting and significant details which are commonly overlooked. This type of appeal has probably never been more important than in our day of television and magazines for all ages.

(2) *Supposition.* A hypothetical illustration may be no less effective and helpful than a true incident, so long as the preacher makes clear what he is doing.

(3) *Parable.* This was a favorite teaching device of Jesus the Master Teacher. Forty of his parables are recorded in the Gospels. The parable is still a useful device, provided that there is no confusion between facts and fiction.

(4) *Figures of Speech.* More than twenty figures of speech were recognized by the older rhetorics. But only a few are in common use. One is the *simile.* To say that the Hudson River is like the Rhine would be a literal comparison, not a figure of speech. But when the speaker says, "The Hudson River flows like the march of time," that is a simile. Here an imaginative element is supplied, lifting the river into comparison with something entirely out of its realm. An *analogy* is an *extended* simile, built not upon the resemblance of two things, but the resemblance of their relationships. A *metaphor,* on the other hand, is an *abbreviated* simile. The simile declares, "God is like a rock"; the metaphor says, "God *is* a rock" (Ps. 71:3). The teachings of Jesus abound in metaphors, such as, "Ye are the salt of the

[8]Quoted from Principal Denny, by James Wright of Scotland, in *A Preacher's Questionnaire,* p. 12.

earth . . . the light of the world" (Matt. 5:13-14) ; the "mote" in the eye; "pearls before swine" (Matt. 7:4, 6) .

A further figure of speech effectively used by Jesus and by many others is *personification,* attributing personality to impersonal objects or abstractions: "The trees shall clap their hands" (Isa. 55:12) ; "The stones would cry out" (Luke 19:40) . Closely related is one other figure of speech, the *apostrophe,* in which the speaker turns from his audience and addresses an imaginary object or an abstract idea or a person not present: "Woe unto thee, Bethsaida! . . . " (Matt. 11:21) .

A judicious use of the imagination can add freshness, beauty, and effectiveness to the sermon. If excessive, the exercise of the imagination may draw attention to itself and become an actual hindrance to the effectiveness of the message. And the supreme concern of the man of God is the *message!*

# 7
# The Homiletical Devices

The homiletical devices here presented are used consciously or unconsciously by most preachers much of the time. They become immeasurably more helpful if recognized and understood. They are equally serviceable in developing the thesis of the sermon, or in developing its main points; and they help to answer the familiar question, "How do I put flesh on the bones of my outline?"

1. *The Six "Rhetorical Processes."*

(1) *Narration.* The introduction of a sermon consists primarily of the narration (or affirmation) of Scriptural facts or historical background, or of current circumstances relating the speaker, the audience, the occasion, the subject, the Scripture, and the thesis to one another.

(2) *Interpretation.* This may proceed by way of paraphrase, definition, amplification, or description (comparison, contrast, association). A further procedure might be through "the seven interrogatives" (discussed later). Or, the development might be by analysis of the proposition or any of the main points, in logical progression (cause to effect, concrete to abstract, general to specific, familiar to unfamiliar — or vice versa). Still another development might be by chronological progression, or according to places or persons.

(3) *Illustration.* Here all the "sources of preaching material," previously discussed, come into play. At this point the preacher will be grateful for the accumulated materials which he has gathered in folders for instant use. (For a filing system so simple and practical as to encourage its perpetual use, see the chapter on "The Systematic Filing of Materials.")

(4) *Application.* The truth may often be more effectively applied to the hearer by implication than by direct statement. A well chosen illustration is often the most effective means. Application may involve the hearer as the sermon progresses, or it may be withheld until the conclusion.

(5) *Argumentation.* To use argumentation does not mean to become controversial or to display a contentious spirit. In general, audiences are reasonable and more or less inclined to follow a logical presentation. Thus there is a place for reasoning, in a gracious spirit, and for rebuttal, and the introduction of proofs, and corroboration by testimony from all sources.

(6) *Exhortation.* Whatever exhortation there may have been during the course of a sermon, the conclusion must bring the message to a focus and call upon the hearer for some sort of response. The formulation and delivery of the conclusion challenge the preacher to his very utmost in grace, tact, and good taste. He is speaking for a verdict, and the test of his sermon is the response that he elicits from the person in the pew. (See chapter on "The Seven Basic Appeals in Scriptural Preaching.")

2. *The Seven Interrogatives* (Pronouns and Adverbs). Next to the thesis or proposition itself, probably the most critical point in a sermon outline is the point where the thesis is resolved into the parts which become the main divisions of the sermon. At this point, the "interrogative" can be exceedingly helpful. It becomes the connecting link by which to get over from the thesis to the main points of the sermon. The procedure is simply "to raise the most relevant question that the thesis leaves unanswered, and let the points which follow answer this question."[1]

(1) *Who?* (Introducing a sequence of persons to be enumerated, identified, classified, or included in the application of some principle)

or *whom,* coupled with one of the prepositions: to, from, for, against, by, with, through, in, on, over, under, behind, of, before, after.

---

[1]John Malcus Ellison, *They Who Preach* (Nashville: Broadman Press, 1956), p. 69.

(2) *Which?* (Introducing a sequence of things, choices, or alternatives)

or *which,* coupled with one of the prepositions above.

(3) *What?* (Introducing a sequence of meanings, implications, definitions, particulars, characteristics, inclusions, or exclusions)

or *what,* coupled with one of the prepositions above.

(4) *Why?* (Introducing a sequence of reasons or objectives)

(5) *When?* (Introducing a sequence of times, phases, or conditions)

(6) *Where?* (Introducing a sequence of places)

    or *Whence?* (Place, origin, source, cause?)

    or *Whither?* (Place, goal, result, extent, conclusion?)

    or *Wherein?*

(7) *How?* (Introducing a sequence of ways)

In developing a thesis, an "interrogative" may be applied either to the subject of the thesis, or to the predicate, or to the object of the verb, or the object of a preposition in a modifying phrase. While the "interrogative" is generally not expressed in the sermon, it is always there, in as much as every affirmation is, in effect, an answer to an interrogative.

3. *The Key Word.* One of the most helpful of all homiletical devices is the "Key Word." If there is structural unity in a sermon, there is a "Key Word," not necessarily expressed or even recognized, that characterizes each of the main points and holds the structure together. The need for such a "Key Word" may be illustrated by an extreme example. A preacher of pioneer days is said to have introduced one of his sermons as follows: "My text is, 'Adam, where art thou?' My sermon has three points: First, Where was Adam? Secondly, Why was Adam where he was? And thirdly, A few remarks about baptism." Obviously, he had not tested his structure by means of a "Key Word."

The value of a clear cut thesis and a "Key Word" that exactly fits each of the main divisions can scarcely be overstated. The "Key Word" opens a corridor down the length of the sermon structure, with direct access from the front entrance to every room, instead of leaving the preacher and his hearers wandering uncertainly from room to room. It is basic to that kind of sound homiletical structure which best lends itself to preaching without notes.

A "Key Word" is always a noun or a noun form of a verb or an adjective. Examples:

(1) Noun: attributes, barriers, causes, devices

(2) Noun form of verb: begin*nings,* refus*als,* infer*ences,* commit*ments,* expect*ations,* disclos*ures*

(3) Noun form of adjective: actual*ities,* weak*nesses*

A "Key Word" is always plural.

A "Key Word" must be used with absolute accuracy; otherwise it has no value.

A "Key Word" should be specfic. For instance, "things" is too general. To use such a broad term as "Key Word" for the points of an outline is like using a bushel basket or a wheelbarrow to carry three apples.

The range of possible key words is practically unlimited. The following brief list is only suggestive, and could be expanded enormously by the use of a dictionary of synonyms.

| | | | |
|---|---|---|---|
| abuses | attainments | compulsions | destinies |
| accusations | attitudes | conceptions | details |
| acts | attributes | concessions | devices |
| actualities | | conclusions | differences |
| admonitions | barriers | conditions | directions |
| advantages | beginnings | consequences | directives |
| affairs | beliefs | contrasts | disciplines |
| affirmations | benefits | corrections | disclosures |
| agreements | blessings | credentials | discoveries |
| aims | | criteria | distinctions |
| alternatives | calls | criticisms | doctrines |
| angles | causes | customs | duties |
| answers | certainties | | |
| applications | challenges | dangers | elements |
| approaches | changes | decisions | encouragements |
| areas | charges | declarations | essentials |
| arguments | claims | defenses | estimates |
| aspects | clues | deficiencies | events |
| aspirations | commitments | definitions | evidences |
| assertions | comparisons | degrees | evils |
| assumptions | compensations | demands | examples |
| assurances | compromises | denials | exchanges |

exclamations
exhortations
expectations
experiences
expressions

facets
factors
facts
failures
faults
favors
fears
features
finalities
forces
functions
fundamentals

gains
generalizations
gifts
graces
groups

habits
handicaps
hopes
hungers

ideas
imperatives
implications
impressions
improvements
impulses
incentives
incidents
indictments
inferences
injunctions
insights

inspirations
instances
instructions
instruments
intimations
invitations
items

joys
judgments
justifications

kinds

lessons
levels
liabilities
losses
loyalties

manifestations
marks
methods
mistakes
moments
motives
movements
mysteries

needs
notions

objections
observations
obstacles
offers
omissions
opinions
opportunities

particulars
peculiarities

penalties
perils
phases
phrases
pledges
points
possibilities
practices
premises
prerogatives
principles
priorities
probabilities
problems
processes
promises
promptings
pronouncements
proofs
prophecies
propositions
provisions

qualifications
qualities
questions

realities
realizations
reasons
reflections
refusals
remarks
remedies
reminders
requirements
reservations
resources
responses
restraints
results
revelations

rewards
risks
rules

safeguards
satisfactions
secrets
sins
sources
specifications
statements
steps
stipulations
successes
suggestions
superlatives
suppositions
surprises
symptoms

tendencies
testimonies
tests
thoughts
threats
topics
totalities
truths

urges
uses

values
views
violations
virtues
voices

warnings
ways
weaknesses
words

The "Key Word" generally involves the use of a "Transitional Verb," which is always a "transitive" verb requiring an object, or a verb coupled with a preposition that requires an object. In either case the object is the "Key Word." The following "Transitional Verbs" are set in natural combinations with "Key Words," to demonstrate their normal use.

"This text *raises . . . questions.*"
"The Lord *makes . . . promises.*"
"The Apostle *delivers . . . charges.*"
"The Prophet *points out . . . reasons.*"
"The situation *calls for . . . responses.*"
"Faithfulness *leads to . . . satisfactions.*"

Further suggestions of possible "Transitional Verbs":

| | | | |
|---|---|---|---|
| announces | emphasizes | names | stipulates |
| answers | enumerates | notes | suggests |
| anticipates | exemplifies | | supplies |
| | explains | offers | |
| concedes | expounds | | teaches |
| | expresses | presents | |
| declares | | proclaims | draws attention to |
| demands | identifies | produces | |
| describes | implies | pronounces | results in |
| deserves | indicates | | sets forth |
| desires | introduces | reveals | |
| | | | touches upon |

4. *The Multiple Approach.* This simple device has been an eye opener and a turning point in the homiletical experience of many young ministers and older ministers as well.

Approach the passage first from the standpoint of the reader, to note the message or lessons which are obvious. Then approach the passage from the standpoint of each person or group of persons involved, including God and Christ and the Holy Spirit. What does the passage reveal to each or about each? What does each one say, or do, or think, or purpose, or learn, or discover, or experience?

Preachers who have felt, after preparing one sermon on a given passage, that they had just about exhausted its homiletical possibilities, have been able, with relative ease, to find several more outlines in the same passage, by means of the "multiple approach." A seminary class in senior homiletics were having difficulty getting a sermon outline on an assigned chapter which happened to be Acts 7. Introduced to the "multiple approach," the same students were able in class, in a few minutes, to produce three or four acceptable outlines. Thereafter, the assignment of several outlines on a given passage became commonplace. The following approaches to the chapter were suggested, with possible developments indicated, and with an abundance of Scriptural material in the chapter to undergird each division.

From the standpoint of Stephen: He bore the *marks* of a good witness of Jesus Christ: I. He knew his Lord; II. He testified for his Lord; III. He emulated his Lord (particularly in his dying hour).

From the standpoint of those who stoned Stephen: Persons with a form of godliness may be guilty of grievous *sins,* continuous with the sins of their fathers: I. Breaking God's Law, v. 53; II. Resisting God's Spirit, v. 51; III. Rejecting God's Son, v. 52.

From the standpoint of Israel, including the forefathers: Neglect of spiritual opportunities may lead to departure from God, in three *stages*: I. Indifference to His Goodness (deliverances through Joseph, Moses, and Joshua did not result in faith); II. Defiance of His Leaders (Moses and the Prophets); III. Rejection of His Son.

From the standpoint of God: *Obstacles* which the grace of God had to overcome in bringing salvation to His people: I. Famine in the Land of Promise; II. Enslavement in the Land of Refuge; III. Death of God's Leaders; IV. Derelictions of God's People.

# 8

# The Steps in Preparing
# an Expository Sermon

1. Gather the *Preliminary Data* (preparatory, factual data) which are essential to an understanding of the passage. The primary source is the Bible, preferably a Bible with cross references and marginal notes, and with probable dates indicated at the beginning of the chapters. Next in importance is the Bible Concordance, then the Bible Dictionary, the Bible Atlas, and Bible Commentaries. Take note of any preaching significance which may appear in the facts thus gathered.

2. Make a brief *Analysis* of the Scripture passage, to discover the structural pattern. In didactic passages (as distinguished from narrative passages) the Analysis may often be developed into a sermon outline by supplying a title, an introduction, and a conclusion, and elaboration by means of the "Rhetorical Processes."

A careful analysis will usually reflect the main thrust, the primary emphasis, of the passage. But the same passage may carry secondary implications which are no less worthy of development in a sermon. In many passages it would be difficult to determine which emphasis is primary and which is secondary. Thus a given passage of Scripture may be many-sided and may lend itself to a variety of legitimate uses.

3. If no sermon outline is suggested by the Analysis, take the following steps to a *Sermon Outline*:

(1) Ask, What lessons or timeless truths are expressed or implied or suggested in the passage?

(Take the "multiple approach" and explore the passage by

tracing through it the course of every person in it, noting what the passage reveals to each or about each.)

In some narrative passages, the didactic element is prominent (Deut. 6:6-9), with clear expressions of timeless truth. Where no timeless truths are *expressed*, look for timeless truths *implied*. In many narrative passages, there may be more truths implied than expressed. Or, there may be truths which are neither expressed nor implied, but only *suggested*. Beyond valid *inferences* which may be drawn, appropriate *observations* may be made; or, there may be an occasional possibility of deriving a helpful thought by *"rhetorical suggestion,"* as in the passage, "take also a little honey" (Gen. 43:11), which might become the caption for a topical sermon. But where a thought is derived by "rhetorical suggestion," it is necessary for the preacher to make this clear to his audience, lest he be charged with ignorance or dishonesty. Obviously that which is derived by "rhetorical suggestion" is not *exposition*. Carelessly handled, it could become *imposition*.

If a truth is not clearly expressed or unmistakably implied, there is need for special care. As Stuart Chase points out, in "Tips on Straight Thinking," an example or two may not be enough to establish a sound generalization. "Reasoning by example," even in the days of Aristotle, was put "high on his list of fallacies that led unwary minds to false conclusions."[1] When faced with a single example, ask, How typical is this? Does it prove the point, or merely illustrate it? Is there enough material to warrant a reasonable inference? The train always starts after the whistle blows, but that does not prove that the whistle started the engine.

(2) Characterize with a "Key Word" the first such lesson or timeless truth which suggests itself.

(The Key Word supplies the thought for the transition from the Thesis to each of the main points in a given outline.)

(3) Find parallel points or lessons answering to the same Key Word.

---

[1] *Reader's Digest*, June, 1954, p. 121.

(These are your main points, your "Romans.")

(4) Find the common principle which these parallel points establish, and by which these points are held together.

(This is your Thesis, Proposition, Basic Affirmation, Statement, or Central Idea.)

(5) Identify your Subject; and formulate a Title or Topic to suit the message.

(The subject of the sermon is not necessarily the title or topic of the sermon. Thus, the title or topic might be "The Supreme Beatitude"; the subject might be "Giving"; and the thesis might be, "It is more blessed to give than to receive." The subject is what the preacher is going to talk about; the thesis indicates what he is going to say about it.)

(6) Prepare an Introduction and a Conclusion.

(7) Develop the outline with the aid of the "Homiletical Devices."

A close exegetical study of every verse is essential, in the light of its context, both immediate and remote, and with careful discrimination between literal and figurative language. The minister must know what it means and preach what it says.

The following examples from the New Testament and the Old Testament will illustrate the "multiple approach" and the use of the "key word."

*Example — Acts 8:26-40*

From the standpoint of Philip.
> *Conditions* to effective witnessing:
> > I. He must respond to the Spirit's leading (vss. 26, 27; 29, 30).
> > II. He must proceed tactfully (vs. 30).
> > III. He must use the Scriptures (vss. 32-35).
> > IV. He must present Jesus (vs. 35).
> > V. He must follow through to completion (vss. 37, 38).

From the standpoint of the Ethiopian.
> *Steps* to salvation:
> > I. He must be open to the truth (vss. 28, 31).
> > II. He must understand (vs. 30).
> > III. He must believe (vs. 37).
> > IV. He must obey (vs. 38).

From the standpoint of the Holy Spirit.
>  *Leadings* of the Holy Spirit:
>  > I. He led Philip to the place (vss. 26, 29).
>  > II. He led Philip to the man (vss. 29, 30).
>  > III. He led Philip to an appropriate Scripture (vs. 35).
>  > IV. He led Philip to a happy result (vs. 39).

From the standpoint of any seeker after salvation.
>  *Aids* along the way to salvation:
>  > I. The Holy Spirit (vs. 29).
>  > II. The Holy Scriptures (vss. 28-33).
>  > III. The soul-winner (vss. 30, 35, 37, 38).

*Example — I Samuel 12*

From the standpoint of Samuel (Inspirational Sermon).
>  Thesis: The eloquence of Samuel was the result of spiritual *qualities* which make for spiritual power:
>  > I. His integrity of character (vs. 4).
>  > II. His faithfulness to his calling (reasoning with them — vs. 7; rebuking — vs. 17; exhorting — vs. 20; warning — vs. 25; comforting — vs. 22).
>  > III. His devotion to his people (vs. 23).

From the standpoint of Saul (Ordination Sermon).
>  Thesis: Saul was shown three *factors* for a leader of God's people to take thoughtfully and prayerfully into account:
>  > I. The man he follows (godly — vs. 5; powerful in prayer — vs. 18).
>  > II. The people he leads (forgetful — vs. 9; self-willed — vs. 12; chastened — vs. 19).
>  > III. The God he serves (righteous — vs. 7; gracious — vs. 8; faithful — vs. 22).

From the standpoint of God (Devotional Sermon).
>  Thesis: God gives four *manifestations* of grace which claim our devotion:
>  > I. He permits what he does not desire (vs. 13).
>  > II. He delivers us from danger (vs. 11).
>  > III. He warns when we go astray (vs. 18).
>  > IV. He encourages when we are under discipline (vs. 22).

From the standpoint of Samuel's people (Evangelistic Sermon).
>  Thesis: God extends four *helps* to those whom he would save:
>  > I. The example of every godly life (vs. 3).
>  > II. The instruction of every faithful teacher (vs. 7).
>  > III. The warning of every divine visitation (vs. 18).
>  > IV. The intercession of every burdened believer (vs. 23).

# 9

# The Preliminary (Factual) Data

To preach intelligently on a passage of Scripture, the preacher must be familiar with certain relevant facts which lie largely outside the passage. It does not follow that he is to spell out his findings in the sermon. They do provide background, and will flash through the sermon at times; but the principal value is to give the minister himself an assured grasp of the passage. The hostess who sets a delicious meal before her guests could not do so without an intelligent understanding of the ingredients and processes involved, but the guests would hardly be pleased with a recital of all the facts behind the meal.

An adequate background for dealing with a Scripture passage would include at least the following preliminary (preparatory, factual) data:

1. *The Speaker or Writer.*

(1) Who spoke the words of the text? Was it God, a prophet, an apostle, a saint, a fool, or the devil? "We must make a distinction between what the Bible records and what it approves. ... The Bible no more morally approves of all that it records than an editor approves of all that he prints in his newspaper."[1]

(2) What kind of a person? What was his character, his age, his condition? The mighty eloquence of Moses, in Deuteronomy, becomes ever more remarkable when it is realized that the speaker was an aged veteran, 120 years old, who had borne one of the world's heaviest responsibilities for forty years, and who had regarded himself as a man "slow of speech, and of a slow

---

[1]Bernard Ramm, *Protestant Biblical Interpretation* (Boston: W. A. Wilde Co., 1956), p. 171.

tongue" (Exod. 4:10). Similarly, Joshua's farewell address was delivered at the age of 110. And Daniel, when thrown into the lion's den, was not the young stripling visualized by some, but a man of ninety, still taking risks for his Lord. Neither was the Apostle Paul, in Romans 7, a young convert meeting the first counter-attacks of Satan, but an experienced veteran of the Cross, still having to struggle with his old nature.

(3) What was the speaker's background; his ancestry; his training; his experience?

(4) What was his relation to the persons addressed?

2. *The Persons Addressed.*

(1) Who? (Identity and Status)

(2) What kind of persons spiritually — believers; unbelievers; backsliders?

(3) Anything noteworthy about their situation — socially, economically, or politically?

3. *The Time.*

(1) When? (Exact or approximate time, definite or tentative)

(2) What significance in the time, as related to other events? (Contemporaneous or otherwise suggested)

Many Bible incidents come alive when seen in their historic setting. The timing often looms large. It means something to discover that during the Babylonian captivity, while Daniel was standing in pagan Babylon as a living monument to the living God, Ezekiel was ministering comfort to the wretched exiles "by the River Chebar," and Jeremiah was ministering to the disconsolate survivors among the ruins of Jerusalem. And the final soul-stirring appeal of Hosea means more when it is remembered that it was followed in three years by the tragic fulfillment of the judgments of which he was warning his people.

A Bible with probable dates indicated at the chapter headings can be exceedingly helpful. While none of the chronologies would claim to be completely accurate, the probable dates do have a value in arranging and relating the facts of sacred history.

4. *The Place.*

(1) Where? (Exact or approximate place, definite or tentative)

(2) Any significance attaching to the place? (Anything unique or noteworthy, perhaps growing out of other events connected with the same place or vicinity, before or after?)

It is significant that Moses halted his people at Beth-peor, "House of the Opening," so named because located before a break between the mountains, and here poured out his heart in those farewell appeals recorded in Deuteronomy. Here, before what was virtually a literal gateway into the Promised Land, he led his people in a series of "revival meetings" to prepare them spiritually for survival and well-being after entering in.

Joshua, like Moses, exercised great wisdom in setting up his final rally of the people of Israel. The place, Schechem, was alive with sacred memories. Nearby was the place where Abraham's altar had stood; nearby was the well of Jacob, and later also the tomb of Joseph. Most important of all, here Joshua had gathered his people once before, for that unforgettable dedication service which followed the conquest of Canaan. Now twenty-five years have passed; Joshua is 110 years old and at the end of his days; and Israel is in a sadly backslidden state. When Joshua had poured out his heart in that farewell appeal, the response was overwhelming! High among the contributing factors must have been Joshua's choice of place.

Where was the Apostle Paul when he wrote joyfully of being blessed "with all spiritual blessings in heavenly places"? He was sitting in prison, not knowing whether he would ever be free again! An exposition of Ephesians would lack much if it failed to take into account the question of place.

5. *The Occasion.* What were the circumstances which prompted or called forth the message?

6. *The Aim.* All Scriptural messages aim at godly living in general; but what was the particular immediate response at which the speaker or writer was aiming?

7. *The Subject.* The subject of the passage is obviously the subject of the "analysis" of the passage, but not necessarily the subject of a sermon, because the latter may deal primarily with only one aspect of the passage.

In expounding the Word of God, there is a grave responsibility upon the preacher to convey the truth without distortion. The need for accuracy is greater than with any other type of information or knowledge which may be communicated. The discipline of strict accuracy should be carried into every detail of the preparation until such accuracy becomes a fixed habit. With eternities at stake, the hearer can not afford to be in error, nor can the spiritual teacher whom he trusts.

As one famous American has wisely said, "Every man has a right to his opinion, but no man has a right to be wrong in his facts."[2] It is a gratifying and rewarding experience, when referring to materials gathered long ago, to know that one's own handwriting on a memorandum is a dependable guarantee of its accuracy.

Thoroughness, in the gathering of factual data, is scarcely less important than accuracy. One of the surest, quickest ways to a mastery of the Bible is for the preacher to master the content of every passage as he deals with it, and also the research materials related to it. Let the research be done with such thoroughness that it need not be repeated; and let the materials be carefully preserved. If not used immediately, such materials are valuable for later use; and if used, they can be used again. When a book of the Bible has been mastered, as to factual data, it seems an unfortunate waste of time and energy to pass on and not preach a series of related messages. "A connected series on any subject by a man of quite moderate ability will make far more permanent impression than an equal number of isolated sermons by a brilliant speaker. The congregation recall what was said last time, they look forward expectantly to what will be said next time. . . ."[3]

Honesty in the pulpit is taken for granted — and should be. But carelessness in dealing with facts may bring the preacher

---

2Bernard Baruch, as quoted from *Pathfinder*, in *Reader's Digest* (March, 1948), p. 61.

3Quoted by Blackwood, in *The Preparation of Sermons*, p. 261, from B. H. Streeter, *Concerning Prayer* (New York: The Macmillan Co., 1916), pp. 275, 276.

under suspicion. One writer of a few years ago, Herbert H. Farmer, quotes a reference of Samuel Butler to the "irritating habit of theologians and preachers of telling little lies in the interest of a great truth."[4]

There are pitfalls of misinterpretation into which devout believers may fall, resulting in distortions of the truth. A preacher may borrow an interpretation from a devout Bible scholar, who had previously borrowed it from another equally devout but perhaps misguided Bible scholar. And so the inventions of devout men may unwittingly be passed around as "the Word of God." Let the Bible speak for itself! What does it actually say? And what does it mean?

Scriptural truth has suffered much through the wresting of text from context. Tender sermons have been preached from the text, "A little child shall lead them" (Isa. 11:6), in utter disregard of the context: "the wolf, the lamb, the leopard, the kid, the calf, the young lion, and the fatling"! Similarly inappropriate is the use, as a benediction, of that expression of mutual distrust between Jacob and Laban, "The Lord watch between me and thee, when we are absent one from another" (Gen. 31:49). And what church-goer has not been challenged to go and "turn the world upside down" for the Lord! Of Paul and Silas, it was said that they "have turned the world upside down" (Acts 17:6). But who said it? That was not the approving testimony of an inspired writer, but the slander of an unbelieving mob! The integrity of the pulpit demands accuracy, thoroughness, and a scrupulous regard for text and context.

The following sketch of "Preliminary Data," on Deuteronomy 6, will suggest in minimal terms the background necessary to an accurate interpretation of the chapter. This sketch is the preacher's work sheet, a concise notation of facts and references which he has gathered and which might be helpful in the preparation of the sermon. Several of these items are of such significance as to be almost certainly reflected in the sermon. And material not specifically used is nevertheless helpful as background preparation.

---

[4] *The Servant of the Word* (New York: Charles Scribner's Sons, 1942), p. 73.

### Deut. 6
#### *Preliminary Data* (Work Sheet)

1. *Speaker or Writer*

    Moses — 5:1

    "Prophet" — 34:10

    "learned . . . mighty in words and deeds" — Acts 7:22

    Age 120, mirac. preserved — 34:7

    "slow of speech and of a slow tongue" — Exod. 4:10

    40 yrs. leader of Isr. — Exod. 4:29 to Deut. 34:6

2. *Persons Addressed*

    "All Isr." — 5:1; 6:3, 4

    Only such as were less than 20 yrs. old at Kadesh — Num. 14:29

3. *Time*

    1451 B.C. (Moses born 1571 B.C.; called in 1491 B.C., Exod. 3)

    End of 40 yrs. in wildern., just before death of M.

4. *Place*

    "Valley, over against Beth-peor" — 3:29; 4:46; 34:6

       — In "plains of Moab" — 34:1

    Beth-p. is a city of Moab, near Mt. Peor, E. of Jordan, opp. Jericho

       — 4 or 5 mi. no. of Mt. Nebo in ridge of Pisgah

    Beth-p., literally: "House of the opening"

5. *Occasion*

    His approachg. death and their anticip. entr. to Canaan — 4:22

6. *Aim*

    Establ. in Isr. the knowl., fear, and love of God, and obed. to Him

7. *Subject*

    Instructions for securing Israel's well-being in Canaan

\*     \*     \*

*Note:* In recording the Preliminary Data —

    (1) Use terse statements, usually one line, not paragraphs.

    (2) If a statement exceeds one line, indent the part that is carried over.

    (3) Abbreviate wherever possible without obscuring the meaning.

    (4) Show Scriptural authority for each point, where possible.

# 10
# The Analysis of the Scripture Passage

An "analysis" is not a "sermon outline." An *analysis* resolves a Scripture passage into its parts; a sermon outline is a *synthesis,* in which the component parts, from many sources, are put together to form a whole.

In preparing an analysis, the purpose of it should be kept clearly in view. As indicated earlier, it is a "work sheet," which aims to present a true skeleton of the passage, revealing clearly the structure and progression of thought. It must be kept concise, generally within a range of about twelve to eighteen lines.

Before actually resolving the passage into its parts, the context should be examined, to confirm the proposed limits of the passage and to aid in the understanding of the passage. "If we know the flow of thought leading to a passage, and the flow of thought away from it, we can predict with some certainty the flow of thought within the passage."[1] Attention should be given not only to the immediate context, but also to the larger connections, which are often decisive in arriving at a correct interpretation.

The analyzing of a Scripture passage is done in three steps:

1. Read the passage the first time to discover the subject and the story, if dealing with a narrative passage; or the subject and the main thrust, if dealing with a didactic passage.

It is important that the major emphasis be established, and that the relation of the subsidiary themes be likewise determined. "Then if one of the secondary themes becomes the theme of the sermon it should be developed in such a fashion that its relation to the major theme will be clearly seen."[2] Thus, what-

---

[1] Ramm, *Protestant Biblical Interpretation,* p. 137.
[2] Miller, *The Way to Biblical Preaching,* p. 70.

ever the theme of the sermon, the atmosphere of the Scripture passage will be truly reflected.

2. Divide the passage into paragraphs; then draw out the topic sentence of each paragraph, or state otherwise its principal idea. This step brings out the main points of the analysis.

3. Read each paragraph again, as many times as necessary to discover the subordinate or contributing ideas which sustain, explain, or elaborate upon the principal idea. This step brings out the sub-points.

Be particularly on the lookout for the following helps or clues:

    (1)   Any change of persons speaking, or addressed, or otherwise involved (Hos. 14).

    (2)   Any progression or successive stages as to time, place, action, or incidents (Luke 15:11-32).

    (3)   Any enumeration of examples or instances (such as instances of divine providence in Acts 7:2-53).

    (4)   Any cumulative enunciation of ideas, principles, or teachings (as in I Cor. 13).

    (5)   Any pairing, grouping, or parallelism of ideas, on the basis of similarity (Ps. 19).

    (6)   Any contrast, opposition or interchange of ideas (I John 4:1-5).

    (7)   Any indication of cause and effect (Matt. 25:34-43).

    (8)   Any division of the whole into its parts (as of the body, in I Cor. 12).

    (9)   Any repetition of certain clauses, phrases, or words (as "By faith," in Heb. 11).

    (10)   Any transitional clauses or phrases; or connective words such as: "therefore, moreover, nevertheless, finally, else, thus, but, and, or."

In formulating the analysis —

1. Limit the analysis to actual contents of passage.

2. Retain the sequence of material as given in passage.

3. Indicate with each main point all verses included in its sub-points.

4. Indicate with each sub-point the exact verse or verses covered.

5. Be concise, not "losing sight of the forest because of the trees."

6. Omit parenthetical material, if incidental; otherwise indicate that it is parenthetical.

In passing from the analysis to a sermon outline, the way may be clear and obvious, or quite the contrary. In the latter case, the mental paths to a sermon outline are not too difficult, as outlined in the previous chapter on "The Steps in Preparing an Expository Sermon." Even if the analysis does not provide a structural basis for a sermon outline, the preparation of it has been valuable. Like the preparation of the "preliminary" or "factual data," it has helped toward that "saturation" which is so necessary to effective exposition, and which so often provides the springboard for the message to follow. The introduction may begin with some general observation emerging from the passage or the factual data or the analysis; or with some striking expression encountered, some question arising, or some thought or incident suggested.

It is in the *didactic* passages of Scripture that the preparation of an analysis is most rewarding. Here the structural pattern of the Scripture passage may often be developed directly into a sermon outline, of course with suitable adaptations. The inspired writers did not always follow clear rhetorical patterns, and evidently were not concerned about the homiletical convenience of a later day. Fragmentary and elliptical passages are not infrequent. Parenthetical material may make a logical analysis difficult. Translations are often imperfect. And passages which were doubtless understandable when written are often obscure to us.

Let the preacher be grateful for those obscurities which call for deep pondering and painstaking study. For such effort, there is no substitute. What is often mistaken for genius is but an uprush of that which has been deposited over a long period of conscious effort. Even a genius has to learn all that he knows.

After intensive study, time should be left for the subconscious mind to function. First comes the labor of investigation; then incubation; then illumination. One is often amazed at the resources which have been stored up in the subconscious, and the way that unrelated fragments, long forgotten, combine in the development of new ideas. But recovery from these hidden resources may come slowly. Sermon topics and related Scripture passages should therefore be selected not later than Tuesday before the Sunday when the sermon is due. Illustrations will come to mind as the week progresses, as well as new ideas and fresh ways of expressing familiar truths. To begin the sermon a week earlier may be better still, to avoid nervous strain and to give more time for the sermon to mature.

The following "analysis" covers a full chapter of twenty-five verses. Its main points might well become the main points for a sermon outline. An introduction would have to be supplied, including a sermonic thesis or proposition; also a conclusion. The discussion, besides making use of all the "rhetorical processes" (previously discussed), should illumine the entire chapter, making use of such material as is relevant to the thesis chosen, and judiciously omitting the rest.

### Deut. 6
#### Analysis (Work Sheet)
#### Instructions for Israel's well-being in Canaan

vss.   1-3  *Importance of these instr.*
        vs. 1    They are God-given
        vss. 2-3  They are designed to insure favor of G. in prom. land
                vs. 2    That thy days may be prolonged
                vs. 3a   That it may be well with thee
                vs. 3b   That ye may increase mightily

vss.   4-5  *Love Him*
        vs. 4    As the one and only supreme Lord
        vs. 5    With all powers of body, mind and spirit

vss.   6-9  *Declare Him*
        vs. 6    Keep His words in thine heart
        vss. 7-9  Fill household with knowl. of God

vss. 10-12  *Remember Him*
        vss. 10   When thou comest into possession
        vss. 11-12  When thou hast eaten thy fill

vss. 13-25  *Serve Him*
           vss. 13-16  **Exclusively**
           vss. 17-19  **Diligently**
           vss. 20-25  **Perpetually**

# 11

## The Heart of the Sermon

Sound structure and effective delivery depend upon a clear cut thesis or proposition. This is the heart of the sermon. To this, every part of the sermon must be relevant and structurally adjusted. The thesis may or may not embody the key word and transition to the main points in the body of the sermon. If the key word and transition are not expressed in the proposition, a separate transitional sentence must be provided as an addendum. A smooth and effective transition is one of the decisive marks of excellence in a sermon. And an awkward transition may weaken the entire structure and delivery.

Occasionally the thesis may be so clearly implied in the introduction of the sermon as to make its formal statement unnecessary; but the preacher must have it definitely in mind, and it must be clear to the listeners as well. A sermon without recognizable purpose and progression may lead to bewilderment rather than conviction and decision. In those rare instances when it seems best to withhold the thesis till the end, it is no less essential for the preacher to have the thesis clearly in mind, and for the audience at least to see progression in the discourse.

A thesis or proposition may be tested by the following criteria:

1. It should indicate the course of the discussion which is to follow. It is a promise which the discourse must faithfully redeem; it must therefore be formulated with scrupulous accuracy. If it is too broad, the development will fall short of its promise; if too narrow, the expectations of the audience will be set too low for appreciative listening.

2. It should be, in effect, a generalization conveying a timeless,

universal truth, modestly and temperately stated, without embellishment or exaggeration.

3. It should normally be a simple sentence, although it might be incorporated as the main clause in a sentence including also a purely transitional clause.

4. It should be perfectly clear. Structurally, this is the most important sentence in the entire sermon, and must be free from even the slightest touch of ambiguity. Nowhere are brevity and simplicity at a greater premium than here. J. H. Jowett expressed the conviction that "no sermon is ready for preaching, nor ready for writing out, until we can express its theme in a short, pregnant sentence as clear as crystal." He found the getting of that sentence "the hardest, the most exacting, and the most fruitful labor" in his study.[1]

5. It should comprehend the whole thought of the sermon. It is "the gist of the sermon in one sentence."[2] "The rest of the sermon, called the body of the sermon, is the development according to specific principles of that one Christian truth or idea."[3] "The discourse is the proposition developed; the proposition is the discourse abridged."[4]

To confine the proposition within proper limits is no less important than to make it cover the full scope of the sermon. If it is to stimulate expectation, it should not disclose too much, since attention and interest depend largely upon the element of suspense.

6. It should be important enough to warrant the elaboration to follow in the body of the sermon. "No pulpit has room for diminutive propositions."[5]

7. It should generally be sermonic in character, expressing or implying some response, on the part of the audience, toward

---

[1]*The Preacher, His Life and Work* (New York: George H. Doran Co., 1912), p. 133.

[2]Jones, *Principles and Practice of Preaching*, p. 84.

[3]Blocker, *The Secret of Pulpit Power*, p. 18.

[4]Vinet, *Homiletics*, translated and edited by Thomas H. Skinner, p. 67.

[5]Austin Phelps, *The Theory of Preaching* (New York: Charles Scribner's Sons, 1911), pp. 321, 322.

which the preacher is moving. "A discourse which makes no spiritual or moral appeal or demand is not a sermon."[6]

The thesis of the sermon is, in a true sense, *the conclusion in reverse*. The thesis looks ahead to the conclusion; and the conclusion looks back to the thesis. Each finds its complement in the other.

A distinction needs to be made between a *sermonic thesis* and a *didactic thesis*. A didactic thesis aims to teach or inform; a sermonic thesis aims to persuade, and therefore, carries a personal thrust. A didactic thesis might affirm, "All authority rests in the hand of God." But there is no sermonic thrust, as there would be in the following formulation: "Man should submit to the authority of God." A better formulation, psychologically, might be: "We fare best when we submit to the authority of God." A didactic thesis might read: "Children of God manifest certain characteristics." A sermonic thesis would read: *"True* children of God...." or "Children of God *should* manifest...."

However expressed, the sermonic proposition must convey the idea of necessity, duty, or desirability. Occasionally a thesis might be didactic in structure and yet sermonic in character, as in the following formulations: "It is more blessed to give than to receive." "Temptation can be successfully resisted."

### THESIS AND TRANSITION ILLUSTRATED

*Example I*

TITLE:     *"How to Deal with Temptation"*

SCRIPTURE: Matthew 4:1-11

    *Intr.:*

       1. Temptation to sin is our common lot.
       2. Temptation successfully withstood, can be a means to spiritual blessing.

THESIS:    3. Temptation can be successfully resisted.
           (Interrogative: "How?")

TRANSITION:  — Like Christ, we must meet certain conditions:
              (Key Word: "Conditions")
       I. *We must know the Word of God.*    ("It is written.")
      II. *We must believe the Word of God.*  ("It is written.")
   III. *We must obey the Word of God.*    ("It is written.")

---

[6]G. Campbell Morgan, *Preaching*, p. 88.

*Concl.:* If we, like Christ in the wilderness, know ... believe ... obey ... we too shall rise in triumph. ...

(Here the Transition is indicated as an addendum to the Thesis. Therefore, it is treated as a sub-point, without being numbered. Here the Thesis is a "simple" sentence; and the Transition likewise. The same Thesis *might* be stated as part of a "complex" sentence, as in the following example.)

*Example II*

THESIS: *Temptation can be successfully resisted,* upon three conditions which Christ met:

(Here the underscored main clause is the Thesis. Ordinarily, the clearer construction is to cast the Thesis in the form of a "simple" sentence, and to add a Transition that is likewise "simple.")

*Example III*

THESIS: Christ here met three conditions for successfully resisting temptation:

(This is the simplest form of Thesis, in that it supplies its own Transition and Key Word, "Conditions," and the answer to its own implied Interrogative, "How?")

# 12

# The Structural Components
# of the Sermon

Strong sermons are made up of strong parts. A sermon that is strong in one part and weak in another will be correspondingly lacking in effectiveness. If the structure is strong throughout, the introduction really introduces, the illustrations really illustrate, the conclusion really concludes, and the message is a message indeed.

1. *The Title or Topic.*
(1) Should be brief. Brevity tends to bring attention to a focus, whereas long titles tend to scatter thought. Andrew W. Blackwood draws attention to a rule of thumb in the newspaper world, to the effect that "a line of newspaper publicity should contain no more than four strong words."[1] Including such brief words as "the," "and," "to," etc., a good general rule seems to be to hold the total to about seven words.

(2) Should be attractive. It has been observed that the success or failure of a book is often determined by its title, and that sermons which have lived have generally had attractive titles. The sermon title on the bulletin board or in the newpaper is the minister's first approach to his potential audience, of whom only eight per cent attend Sunday morning worship and only two per cent attend church on Sunday evenings. Industry spends huge sums developing apt slogans to sell its products, and the minister needs to exercise a similar concern in phrasing his sermon topics.

[1] *The Preparation of Sermons*, p. 94.

(3) Should be indicative of the content of the sermon. A good title suggests more than it expresses. But while it may convey only a hint as to the substance of the sermon, what it does reveal must accord strictly with the material to be presented.

(4) Should be suited to the sacredness of the preaching task. A title can be fresh, attractive, thought-provoking, without sacrificing reverence. It is not necessary for the title to be clever; but reverent, it must be.

(5) Should be related to the needs and interests of the hearers. They are not just so many individuals; each is the center of a universe, to which the minister must gain entrance with saving truth. They may not care what became of the Hittites and the Jebusites; they want to know, "What will become of us?" They come to church from three motives: For Christ's sake, for the sake of others, and for their own sake. The last is the lowest of the legitimate motives that bring people to church, but it is the one motive which brings the overwhelming majority of those who come.

Perhaps the ultimate in a successful title was achieved in a tract by Dwight L. Moody, which was distributed among the prisoners in a penitentiary. This tract, entitled "How the Jailor Got Caught" (the Philippian jailor, Acts 16:25-34), was read by one desperately wicked convict, and became the means of his conversion and complete transformation. W. B. Riley[2] suggests a similarly attractive title for women behind the counters in department stores: "The Conversion of a Saleslady," based on the conversion of "Lydia, a seller of purple ... whose heart the Lord opened ..." (Acts 16:14).

2. *The Introduction.*

(1) Should prepare the hearers for a favorable and intelligent reception of the Scriptural truth which is to be presented. This is necessary even when preceded by the most careful indirect preparation through hymns, prayers, and the reading of the Scriptures. To secure attention is not enough; it must be *favorable* attention. The man who left a tract for the waitress, but

---

[2]*The Preacher and His Preaching* (Wheaton, Ill.: Sword of the Lord Publishers, 1948), p. 99.

forgot to leave a "tip," secured attention, but not *favorable* attention. Persuasion, which is the ultimate aim of the sermon, generally begins with the introduction.

A strong opening statement is exceedingly important. Thereafter, the introduction would normally unfold after the manner of a chain reaction, with each successive point flowing out of the preceding point. As a rule, audiences prefer to be thus eased into the subject rather than plunged into it.

(2) Should state the thesis, revealing the proposed line of development. Broadus makes the observation that "to state one central idea as the heart of the sermon is not always easy ... but the achievement is worth the effort."[3] And the hearers are far more likely to follow with interest if given some indication of the direction to be taken.

(3) Should make clear to the audience the relevance of the topic to the occasion, the audience, the text, and the thesis.

(4) Should provide a natural transition from the thesis to the body of the sermon. This transition serves also as the bridge between the main divisions of the sermon. Normally this will involve the use of a *Key word* that exactly fits each of the main points of the sermon. If no key word can be found to fit all the main points, the structure needs to be revised. If the outline is logically sound, the transition will be natural and easy; otherwise the preacher fumbles. Homiletical achievement is probably nowhere more surely reflected than in the transition from the introduction to the body of the sermon. Dull, pedantic, labored transitions will discourage even the friendliest audience.

In the "Basic" sermonic pattern, the sermon proceeds *inductively* from the opening sentence down to the thesis; then *deductively* to the conclusion. In other homiletical patterns, such as the "Narrative" or the "Problem Solution" patterns, where the sermonic thrust is withheld till the conclusion, the audience should be given the benefit of a "didactic" thesis to make intelligent listening possible.

---

[3]Broadus, *On the Preparation and Delivery of Sermons*, revised by Jesse B. Witherspoon, p. 52.

3. *The Main points* (designated by Roman numerals).

(1) Should be stated as sentences or clauses, concise but complete, except where the transitional sentence or the context completes the thought. A "cue" or a "topic" may not be enough to recall the thought when the notes have grown cold. For an illustration, a cue or topic is usually adequate; likewise, for points in a Scripture "Analysis," with the open Bible supplying the details.

(2) Should be mutually exclusive. Overlapping can be disastrous to memorization and recall, for extemporaneous preaching. Points can be kept mutually exclusive "by following what is known as *a single principle of division,* which means that the topics are derived from the main idea or theme from the same point of view."[4] For instance, the Apostle Paul, in Philippians 3:13, 14, emphasizes three kinds of grace which the Christian needs: The grace to forget; the grace to concentrate; the grace to persevere.

(3) Should be mutually adapted as to proportion, unity and sequence. Co-ordinate points should be of approximately equal force and importance, and should be given comparable proportions of elaboration. Unity requires that the points be tested by referring back to the proposition which they are to support, to make sure that this support is real. Sequence of points may generally be determined by a natural order of thought which is instinctively felt.

There must be progression, discernible to the audience, and this should lead cumulatively to a strong finish. This does not mean that the climax should come invariably at the end. As one excellent authority points out, when people have come to expect the climax at the end they may brace themselves against the anticipated appeal, or they may begin to look for hat and gloves, knowing that the end is near. The better way, he suggests, is to have no settled order, but to change as much as possible the position of the climax.[5]

---

[4]Hunter and Johnson, *A Manual of Systematic Discourse* (Maryville, Tenn.: Edwin R. Hunter, 1947), p. 7.

[5]Smith, *Extempore Preaching,* p. 53.

Negative statements belong in the early part of the sermon. "It is frequently necessary to clear the ground before one can put up his own structure, but one should not still be clearing the ground in his concluding sentences."[6]

Humor, likewise, belongs in the early part of the sermon. If wisely and sparingly used, it may have real value. It relaxes people and may open the mind to some serious truth or appeal. Pathos may be useful either at the beginning or at the end of the sermon. At the beginning, it may prepare the hearers for the reception of the message; at the end, it may warm the hearts toward the exercise of duty, kindliness, or love. But pathos, like humor, is to be used sparingly and with great care, in the pulpit.

(4) Should be parallel in form, so far as possible. Parallelism of ideas, expressed in parallel form, is essential to logical and visual memory. If the first point is phrased as a question, the remaining points should be questions. The same uniformity of pattern should be sought with reference to phrases, or nouns, adjectives, or other parts of speech standing in the position of emphasis in co-ordinate points.

But parallelism must not be carried to the point of unnatural phrasing or labored efforts at uniformity. Parallelism in form cannot make unlike points equal; and fanciful expedients which bring about resemblance in form may bring, along with it, confusion of thought. Particular caution should be exercised in the use of alliteration and antithesis, which too often result in something as unhelpful and as distasteful as a forced rhyme. Parallelism of structure can not bring into unity such points as can not be brought under one common key word. And three or four unrelated sermonettes do not make one sermon, however parallel the statement of points.

Hardly less important than parallelism and *co-ordination* is the related principle of *subordination*. It is a homiletical expedient of the highest importance, which seems never to have received adequate attention. The salvation of many an outline may be achieved through the judicious subordination of points

---

[6]Carl S. Patton, *The Preparation and Delivery of Sermons* (Chicago: Willett, Clark & Co., 1938), pp. 63, 64.

which are too valuable to discard, yet impossible to co-ordinate with other points in a given series. Though overlapping or not of equal weight or significance with the other points, such a point might have real value as a sub-point undergirding one of the main points.

(5) Should be co-extensive with the thesis. At times it may be necessary to narrow the proposed thesis or broaden the scope of the main points, or vice versa.

(6) Should be Scripturally undergirded. It is desirable for all sermons, and essential for expository sermons, that each main point or the leading sub-point thereunder be supported with adequate Scriptural undergirding, usually in the exact words of Scripture. This undergirding should be visible, logical, and undebatable. It establishes authority, it prevents straying from the Scripture passage, and it helps to insure accuracy of utterance. It keeps both the preacher and the audience aware that he is communicating not his own views but the Word of God.

4. *The Sub-Points* (designated by Arabic numerals). The sub-points should be, in general, like the main points, (1) complete statements, (2) mutually exclusive, (3) mutually adapted, and (4) parallel in form.

In expository preaching, on a narrative passage of Scripture, a "Roman" may be a generalization, stating a lesson, a principle, or a timeless truth; or it may be a particularization, stating an instance of the application of a principle. If the Roman is a generalization, the leading "Arabic" thereunder would normally supply from the given Scripture passage a specific application of that principle. If the Roman is a particularization, the leading Arabic thereunder would normally be the statement of a principle implied or suggested by the particular instance given in the Roman.

Beyond the leading Arabic under a given Roman, there is wide latitude in drawing upon the "sources of preaching material." Here any or all of the "homiletical devices" may come into play (the "rhetorical processes," the "interrogatives," the "key word"). Quite often the Arabics under a given Roman will unfold like the points of the introduction, after the manner of a chain reaction, each point flowing naturally into the next.

5. *The Illustrations.* Many a sermon has been saved by an effective illustration. And many a preacher has been saved from mediocrity by a special giftedness in the use of illustrations. In college chapels, it seems that the speaker is more often evaluated on the basis of his illustrations than on any other basis. The part of the sermon most likely to be remembered is the illustration. For this reason, one writer declares, "I am not very fond of illustrations, except from the Bible, largely because I often find that they are remembered when the points illustrated are forgotten."[7] The use of illustrations is not therefore to be discouraged; as a matter of fact, one good illustration to each main point would be about right. But the choice of illustrations calls for the greatest of care.

(1) Should be conducive to the purpose of the message. No matter how good the illustration, unless it contributes to the momentum, clarity, and force of the sermon, it must be left out. Some illustrations are like sham windows which admit no light, and some actually divert from the thought which the illustration should reinforce. Not only must the illustration be suited to the point; its relevance must be immediately recognizable to the audience.

(2) Should be true. Confidence in the integrity of the preacher is basic to the acceptance of his preaching. Loose statements in the pulpit will quickly destroy this confidence. Worse still, God will not bless the use of untruth. A legend, a parable, a fable, or a dream may make an excellent illustration if clearly identified as such. If there is the sightest doubt as to the authenticity of an illustration, let the speaker indicate the source; and let him never be tempted to relate as his own the experience of someone else.

(3) Should be plausible. There are times when truth is stranger than fiction. If a story is true, but implausible, it is worse than valueless as an illustration.

---

[7]Geoffrey W. Bromiley, in *My Way of Preaching*, edited by Robert J. Smithson (London: Pickering & Inglis, Ltd., 1956), p. 15.

(4) Should be in good taste. Nowhere else does a preacher display more clearly his refinement or want of refinement than in his choice of illustrations. The cultural standards of the pulpit tend to become, over the years, the cultural standards of the pew; and discerning congregations have been known to set pulpit candidates aside because of poor taste in the choice of illustrations. Cleverness can not compensate for the want of good taste, and a good laugh can not erase its effect.

An occasional bit of humor, if relevant and incidental to the serious purpose of the message, may be "a beautiful instrument in the service of truth";[8] but a comedian in the pulpit is not what the churches need or desire.

6. *The Conclusion.* When Peter, in that powerful sermon at Pentecost, had progressed to a certain point, his hearers were crying out for the conclusion: "What shall we do?" This is the question which a sermon should raise, and which the conclusion should answer. To withhold the conclusion would have been utterly heartless on the part of Peter. To the extent that any sermon succeeds, it builds up the reasonable expectation of an answer to questions, problems, and needs which have been set forth. An adequate conclusion is therefore essential. Not less futile than the diagnosis without a remedy, is the rambling discourse which leaves a puzzled congregation asking, "So what?"

(1) The conclusion should somehow reflect the proposition or the main points, or both. As indicated earlier, the conclusion is, in effect, the proposition in reverse. A concise recapitulation can be a powerful concluson, and the value of repetition is not to be lightly regarded. Webb B. Garrison[9] calls attention to some significant conclusions growing out of extensive studies under the guidance of Arthur Jersild: "Repetition is the most effective single method of securing emphasis ... (the) power of repetition (is) greatest when the various presentations are sep-

---

[8]Luccock, *In the Minister's Workshop,* p. 192.

[9]*The Preacher and His Audience,* pp. 163, 164.

arated by other items of discourse ... optimum emphasis comes from three repetitions."[10]

(2) The conclusion should bring the message to a burning focus. There is validity in the old axiom, "The object of the sermon is more important than the subject"; and to this "object" the whole sermon must lend itself, down to the last words of the conclusion. Moses closed one of his powerful appeals with the words, "Therefore choose life, that both thou and thy seed may live" (Deut. 30:19). Joshua concluded his great farewell address with the words, "Choose you this day whom ye will serve ..." (Josh. 24:15). Jesus concluded the Sermon on the Mount with an illustration about two foundations (Matt. 7:24-27); and another of His discourses, with that classical challenge, "Go and do thou likewise" (Luke 10:37).

(3) The conclusion should appeal to the individual for a response in some concrete form: either an action or a resolve, a pledge of dedication or rededication to Christ at some clear point, or a response of thanksgiving. Throughout the sermon, and particularly in the conclusion, the hearer must be made to feel that the message is a personal matter. "Thou art the man!" This is the impression which every sermon should make. The appeal may be expressed directly, or through implication — by means of a solemn question, a verse of Scripture, or a simple, earnest statement of Biblical truth.

(4) The conclusion should avoid the introduction of new material, except for some clinching illustration or poem or verse of Scripture, making sure of a strong closing sentence for the final impact.

---

10"Modes of Emphasis in Public Speaking," *Journal of Applied Psychology,* Vol. 12 (1928).

# 13
# The Way to Note Free Preaching

One of the greatest joys of the ministry is the spontaneity of note free preaching. Freedom from notes is worth all that it costs. It depends mainly on three factors in preparation: saturation, organization, and memorization.

## SATURATION

Whatever method of preparation the preacher may follow, he needs to be thoroughly familiar with his material. He must know the subject in all its ramifications. "No man can be eloquent on a subject that he does not understand," as Cicero, the greatest orator of ancient Rome, declared two thousand years ago.[1] Even inspiration can not work in a vacuum.

The preacher must not begrudge the time spent in gathering his factual data and preparing his Scripture analysis on the way to his sermon outline. "It is a general principle that anything which costs the producer little is of little value to others."[2] One of the penalties of plagiarism is that it so largely by-passes the processes of saturation. For the expenditure of time and thought and labor, there is no substitute. A good procedure is to select the sermon topic early; meditate upon it daily; let the sermon grow; then write the outline in one sitting.

The main business of a preacher is to prepare and deliver sermons. Strong churches are not gathered around weak pulpits. And if the discipline of thoroughness and accuracy in prepara-

---

[1]Gilman, Aly, and Reid, *Speech Preparation* (Columbia, Mo.: Artcraft Press, 1946), p. 29.

[2]Wilson T. Hogue, *Homiletics and Pastoral Theology* (Winona Lake, Ind.: Free Methodist Publishing House, 1940), p. 31.

tion seems rugged at first, nothing that the minister does is more rewarding; and in time such sermonizing becomes one of his greatest joys.

## ORGANIZATION

A professor of preaching who had been hearing student sermons for nearly forty years was asked if he had any particular impression that stood out. His answer, without a moment of hesitation, was, "Want of content!" If organization is to be significant, there must be something to organize. The art of preaching is more than "the art of expanding a two minute idea into a thirty minute sermon." Some sermons do recall the words of that member of the British Parliament who said of his opponent, "He has a genius for compressing a minimum of thought into a maximum of words." But for every sermon that fails for want of content, there is probably another that fails because of inadequate organization.

For retention and recall, in note free preaching, the structure "must be simple, obvious, natural, so that it fixes itself in the mind; and it must be clearly articulated in its parts."[3] With a good outline, the preacher commits to memory a progression of thought rather than words, and is never tied to a particular phraseology. A rambling discourse, on the other hand, practically defies memorization, and keeps the preacher bound to his notes.

In political campaigns, the importance of eye contact has been recognized by the use of the "teleprompter," a device by which the prepared speech is unrolled before the speaker, line by line, as the speech progresses. From the elevated position of the speaker, he appears to be looking directly at his audience, when in actuality he may be reading from the teleprompter. His hands are free, there is no turning of pages, and the illusion is complete.

For television performers and for moving picture actors and actresses, there is a device known as the "idiot sheet." It is a large screen carrying the script, to prompt the memory in case

---

[3]Richard S. Storrs, *Preaching without Notes* (New York: Hodder and Stoughton, 1875), p. 109.

the lines should be forgotten. It is so placed as to give the impression of eye contact with the audience, while serving its purpose as a safeguard to the memory.

For the preacher, without the help of such devices as the "teleprompter" or the "idiot sheet," there are other ways of achieving note free delivery. The methods vary widely as to merit and practicality, but among them there is one best method for every man of God.

One way of preaching without notes is to write out and memorize the full manuscript. This has been the method of some of our great preachers. But to memorize a ten page manuscript for every service calls for prodigious feats of memory; and few preachers could endure the staggering demands of such a procedure two or three times a week, or oftener. The time element alone would be generally prohibitive. There is danger also that a memorized manuscript might tend more toward the impression of a declamation than of a sermon.

If, in preparation for the pulpit, a full manuscript is written from a carefully prepared outline, the danger of memorizing words instead of thoughts is greatly reduced. For many preachers, however, visual memory and logical memory may become confused as they try to recall what has been written both in the outline and in many pages of manuscript. The same confusion is to be feared when the preacher writes out his manuscript first, and then makes an abstract or analysis of his manuscript for pulpit use.

Some have followed the practice of taking the full manuscript into the pulpit, with careful underscoring of the points in one, two, or three colors. This is somewhat like the preparation for reciting or passing a test on an assigned textbook. One does not attempt to memorize entire paragraphs or pages or chapters, but the structural skeleton in terms of underscored topic sentences. The points thus underscored constitute, in effect, an abstract or analysis of the manuscript which is to be orally reproduced in the pulpit. Such an analysis may differ widely from an independently constructed outline, and would be far less effective. And there would be the big problem of turning so many pages in the course of the sermon.

For the great majority of preachers, it seems fairly well established that a carefully prepared outline, the product of hours of labor, is the best preparation for the pulpit. This involves lifelong discipline to consciseness and accuracy of expression. While concise, the outline must carry enough of the sermon so that it can be recalled as needed, perhaps weeks or months or even years later.

The discipline of accurate expression in sermon outlines is more exacting than in sermon manuscripts, and is more likely to be maintained throughout life because it does not involve the extra hours per week for writing out the sermons in full. When this accuracy of expression becomes habitual, it carries over into all written and oral discourse.

Ideally, the outline should be so formulated that its main points and many of its sub-points may be imbedded practically verbatim in the body of the sermon. This will conserve any apt phrasing which has been achieved in the course of preparation. If there has been due concern for transitions and connectives, and the exact words of the outline should be used in oral delivery, the points should flow naturally and unobtrusively into the movement of the sermon. And there is not the impression of glibness which sometimes results from memorizing a manuscript. As one hearer remarked after a memorized sermon, " We *can* know our lines *too well.*"

Writing out the sermon in full does not necessarily insure accuracy of expression. There is much extemporaneous writing as well as extemporaneous speaking. And hasty, slipshod writing may be more harmful than beneficial to style. The full sermon may best be written out after its delivery, to avoid that confusion of logical and visual memory which may result from having both an outline and a full manuscript written out beforehand. Besides this, there may be still a better way. With modern facilities for tape recording, the practice of recording all sermons as preached, and typing them afterwards from the tape has much to commend it.

A few brave souls go into the pulpit regularly with no notes of any kind. For most preachers, with two or three new messages to deliver every week, this would be sheer recklessness, and an invitation to disaster. While the acknowledged ideal is to *preach without notes,* a carefully prepared outline is essential in preparation and *might* be needed in delivery.

The better the outline, the greater is the likelihood of its not being needed in the pulpit. But there may be times when the preacher, whatever his usual practice may be, will need his notes. This could happen if he is weary or physically below par, or if he has been prevented from getting adequate preparation, or if there is an emergency in the preaching service itself. It seems wise, therefore, to have notes that can be carried into the pulpit. A full manuscript will scarcely do. "Either the speaker will very early resort to a close reading of it, or he will go on without reference to it at all, until suddenly needing it, he will find himself wholly unable to find his place."[4]

One author suggests that "generally, the written notes will be ample if they embrace about $1/4$ of the words of a sermon." This would include the proposition and main divisions written in full, with illustrations and Scriptural quotations indicated by a mere word or two.[5]

Another author presents a plan of writing the sermon in full, then making an abstract consisting of paragraph headings, which would cover one side of half a sheet of note paper, and which would serve in the final phase of preparation. This might be carried into the pulpit for possible reference, although the author insists that the preacher strive to be completely note free in the pulpit.[6] The mental hazard of having labored with both a manuscript and an abstract has been previously indicated.

John Erskine, the author, gratefully recalls how one of his professors, George Rice Carpenter, taught him to write. First, a skeleton of the essay was required, with each paragraph represented by a single sentence. "By the time we had shaped this outline to his satisfaction and our own, nothing remained but to fill out the paragraphs and smooth away the angularities of the

---

[4]Hunter and Johnson, *A Manual of Systematic Discourse,* p. 77.

[5]Smith, *Extempore Preaching,* p. 18.

[6]Zincke, *The Duty and the Discipline of Extemporary Preaching,* p. 50.

frame."[7] This is excellent procedure for the preparation of a sermon, even if a full manuscript is to be written out afterwards.

For convenient handling, a loose leaf note book of 5 x 7¾ inches is often favored as first choice. Such a note book is about the size of the average Bible, and a leaf will fit easily between the pages of the Bible. By writing on both sides, it is possible to carry a full sermon outline on the two sides of one sheet; or it could be carried on one side of two opposite sheets in the note book. This presupposes conciseness, and abbreviations wherever possible.

Some highly successful pulpiteers prefer to use a sheet, 8½ x 11 inches, folded across the middle so as to make four pages, turned so as to fit conveniently into the Bible. The outline is written (by hand) down the two inside pages facing each other. Any excess material is carried over to the third page, leaving the first of the four pages blank.[8]

A still better plan, perhaps, for the preacher who is reasonably confident of not using his notes in the pulpit, is to place his outline on one side of one sheet of 8½ x 11 inches, thus providing longer lines and greater flexibility in notation. Folded once, this will fit easily into the Bible. It presents the advantage of keeping the whole outline in view throughout the phase of preparing, and leaving room on the back side of the sheet for detailed data with which the outline itself should not be encumbered. For brevity, every preacher must develop his own system of shorthand or abbreviations. About thirty-six lines, closely hand written, on one side of a sheet, should generally suffice. This is the plan which the author strongly prefers, and recommends above all others.

In certain cases it may be necessary, for strict accuracy, to read statistics or quotations too involved to trust to memory. But in public discourse it is generally better to cite statistics in round numbers that can be carried in memory by both the speaker

---

[7] Jones, *Principles and Practice of Preaching*, p. 89.
[8] Harnish, in *We Prepare and Preach*, edited by Clarence S. Roddy, p. 68. See also *The Public Worship of God*, by J. R. P. Sclater (New York: Richard R. Smith, Inc., 1930), p. 113.

and the audience, and to give in simple paraphrase a quotation too involved to remember verbatim. In the case of Scripture citations, the minister will steadily enrich his pulpit resources if he carefully selects the exact phrases, clauses, and verses which he will use, and quotes them from memory. The same would be true with reference to selected stanzas of hymns, and short poems.

## MEMORIZATION

In preparing for the pulpit, as in all areas of learning, there is no escape from a certain amount of pure memorization. Perhaps half of the total effort is expended in "saturation"; another forty per cent in "organization"; and a final ten per cent in "memorization." A good memory is largely the result of cultivation. And subject matter in which we are genuinely interested and with which we are thoroughly familiar is not difficult to retain. "The best way is, to attempt no memorizing of sentences or words whatever. Let the mind be entirely concentrated on the ideas to be developed, and the end to be accomplished by the sermon."[9] But the observance of a few simple rules, growing out of the experience of many, over long periods of time, will help enormously toward efficient memorization.

1. *The use of visual aids in outlining.* With most people, the visual memory is stronger than the oral memory, and perhaps stronger than the logical memory. This accounts for the familiar confession, "I remember your face, but not your name."

(1) Indentation. Subordination is instantly recognized by indentation. Let the sub-point be set to the right, about six spaces, beneath the point which it supports or elaborates. And let the illustration be similarly set in, as an addendum to the particular point that it illustrates.

(2) Underscoring. This is generally reserved for the title of the sermon, the "Intr.," the "Concl.," and the main points. Some have favored the use of different colored pencils for keeping the outline clearly in mind.[10] Others definitely prefer only one color. Too much underscoring will blur the visual image.

---

[9]Smith, *Extempore Preaching,* p. 99.
[10]Rhoades, *Case Work in Preaching,* p. 19.

(3) Numerals, not letters. Use a Roman numeral for a main point, an Arabic numeral for a sub-point, and an Arabic in parentheses for further subordination — I, 1, (1). In enumerating points, the mind does not function in terms of "Reason A," "Reason B," and "Reason C"; but in terms of "The first reason," "the second reason," and "the third reason." A point is not to be numbered unless it is one of two or more points in a series.

(4) Handwriting, not typewriting. For concise notation, handwriting affords greater flexibility, especially in getting a point on one line. Besides, the handwritten page, by the added effort involved and by its irregularities in penmanship, gives a stronger visual image. It has even been argued that the sermon outline should be written in pencil rather than ink, so that a whole line may be erased and a new line written in if necessary. Certainly, to substitute a fresh typewritten copy for an outline over which one has labored for several hours is to forfeit the benefit of the visual image which has already impressed itself on the memory.

(5) Points and cues, not paragraphs. A "cue" is a word or phrase which aims to bring a complete thought to mind; a "point" is the expression of the thought itself. A cue is often adequate for recalling an illustration, but for other uses a point is preferable. Robert E. Speer, in his well known booklet, *How to Speak Effectively without Notes*,[11] urged that each point in a speech be put in the form of a statement, and not a mere phrase or catch-word. Conciseness of statement is of course implied, and is of utmost importance to clarity and retention in memory.

2. *Brevity of statement.* Every line represents a paragraph; a paragraph normally runs to about one hundred words; and an outline for a thirty minute sermon would run to approximately thirty to thirty-six lines. Abbreviations may be freely used, provided the meaning is clear; and words like "and," "the," etc., may often be omitted without obscuring the sense.

Brevity is not only a convenience; it is also an element of force. "Whatever can be said in fifty words and is said in seventy-

---

[11]p. 15.

five is weakened by about fifty per cent." The preacher who disciplines himself to the use of one side of one sheet of paper (8½ x 11 inches) for a sermon outline is not only helping himself toward a note free pulpit delivery; he is at the same time developing two additional qualities which are highly desirable — accuracy and force.

Eloquence flows out of saturation and deep feeling; and where the preacher is saturated with his subject, the sermon outline does not need to be elaborately spelled out. The briefest reference will bring back the full thought, much as a "cue" of two or three words will bring to mind an illustration requiring two or three minutes to relate. Details which may need to be recalled months or years later, and which could not be retained in memory, may be carried on the back side of the outline.

3. *Statement of parallel points in parallel form, if possible.* This was discussed in the preceding chapter.

4. *Limitation of points to a maximum of five in a series.* The memory tends to bog down when there are more than five points in a series. Psychological tests in the field of education have revealed that when there are more than five items between which to choose, the discernment becomes more or less blurred and the choices are correspondingly less reliable. Perhaps there is some sort of connection between a man's mental capacity and processes and the fact that he has five digits on each hand and foot. The primitives count by fives, or by the score, with one gesture indicating the sum of all the fingers and toes.

There is no merit or sacredness attaching to any particular number of points. F. W. Robertson, of Brighton, England, cited by Andrew W. Blackwood[12] as "perhaps the most influential book preacher in the past hundred years," had particular inclinations toward outlines with two contrasting truths. T. W. Callaway, a Southern Baptist pastor, published a book of one thousand sermon outlines of three points each.[13]

---

[12]*Expository Preaching for Today*, p. 14.

[13]*One Thousand Threefold Scripture Outlines* (Grand Rapids: Zondervan Publishing House, 1943).

Harry Emerson Fosdick, who for thirty-eight years taught Practical Theology at Union Theological Seminary in New York City, said that the body of a sermon should usually have not more than four points; because too many points confuse the hearer. In exceptional cases, nevertheless, his sermons would run to five, six, or even seven points.[14]

John A. Broadus[15] points out that when there are as many as five or six heads, "they must follow each other in a very natural order, or the average hearer will not easily retain them in mind. Accordingly, judicious and skillful preachers seldom have more than four heads of discourse."

5. *Observance of the natural laws of memory.* The familiar formula calls for impression, association, and repetition. These have been stressed for years in many courses in memory training and methods of study.

(1) Impression. In establishing the memorial supper by which Jesus, the Master Teacher, designed to be remembered "till He come," He engaged nearly all the senses: seeing, hearing, tasting, smelling, feeling, touch, and motion. The more senses we engage, the more impressions we have, and the more likely we are to remember.

In the use of church drama as a means of ministering to the souls of men, the importance of pantomime is emphasized. This "expression of thoughts and motions through bodily action" is important because a drama is *seen* as well as *heard*.[16] The same is true of the minister, whose posture, gestures, facial expression, and changes of pitch, tempo, and intensity play such a vital part in the effective communication of the spoken word. Since these physical factors are so prominent in communicating the message, participants in drama are taught to do the work of

---

14Edmund H. Linn, "Fosdick as a Preacher," in *Andover Newton Quarterly* (Newton Centre, Mass.: Andover Newton Theological School, LIII, No. 4, 1961), p. 35.

15*On the Preparation and Delivery of Sermons,* revised by Jesse B. Weatherspoon, p. 113.

16Fred Eastman and Louis Wilson, *Drama in the Church* (New York: Samuel French, 1942), pp. 77, 81.

memorization on their feet, walking through the accompanying action and reading their speeches aloud. Thus the memory of thoughts and words is reinforced by the association of visual and oral impressions, and the further senses of touch and motion.

(2) Association. The processes of learning and remembering proceed from the familiar to the unfamiliar. Somehow a connection must be established. The associations need not be logical, but should be as vivid and as forceful as possible, to strengthen the likelihood of remembering.

(3) Repetition. Of superlative importance is the law of distributed effort or spaced learning. "The man who sits down and repeats a thing over and over until he finally fastens it in his memory is using twice as much time and energy as is necessary to achieve the same results when the repeating process is done at judicious intervals."[17]

"Material studied for fifteen minutes a day for four days ... will be remembered much better than material studied an hour one time and never reviewed."[18] "Practice of an hour a day for five days is more effective than five hours in a single day."[19]

It is possible to study too long at a time, and to study oneself stupid. We study best when we are rested, happy, healthy, and interested. A good night's sleep is an excellent preparation for mental effort of any kind. And a practice which could be decisive in the attainment of freedom from notes, at least for Sunday mornings, is that of preaching the sermon to oneself the very last thing before going to sleep on Saturday night. But it must be the *very last* thing before falling asleep. Then, upon awakening, the very first thing, even before rising from the bed, think the sermon through again. It is often amazing how clearly the whole sermon comes back after the night work that has been going on in the subconscious during sleep.

The procedure of actors and actresses, who have enormous

---

[17]Dale Carnegie, *Public Speaking and Influencing Men in Business* (New York: Association Press, 1937), p. 109.

[18]Thomas F. Staton, *How to Study* (Nashville, Tenn.: McQuiddy Printing Co., 1954), p. 23.

[19]Gilman, Aly and Reid, *The Fundamentals of Speaking*, p. 133.

chores of memorization, may be of suggestive value for the preacher. Four steps are commonly involved: (1) Read the script in full; (2) Copy the script *in longhand;* (3) Record the words on a tape, and have them played back almost continuously, in the living room, kitchen, etc., till they have been more or less fully absorbed; and finally (4) Write out the full script again, in longhand, from memory.

One further precaution is important: Just before the time of speaking, go over the notes once more to refresh the memory; trust God and go ahead!

\*      \*      \*

The following abbreviated outline reflects the proposed pattern of notation — as to underscoring, capitalization, indentation, numbering and statement of points, parallelism, and brevity. Illustrations are omitted. Many of the words in the outline could well be abbreviated, thus assisting the visual memory by providing more room on a line and more white space on the page.

Acts 2
THE WORLD'S MOST ATTRACTIVE CHURCH

*Intr.*:

1. The old "First Church" never equaled in spiritual attractiveness and spiritual effectiveness.
   (1) A happy church — "with gladness . . . praising God" (vs. 46, 47).
   (2) A popular church — "having favor with all the people" (v. 47).
   (3) A fruitful church — "The Lord added . . . daily" (v. 47).

2. The old "First Church" must have had something we do not have.
   (1) To thrive in old Jerusalem, not achievement of puny church.
   (2) To lift sagging standards, stem tide of dishonesty, corruption, immorality today, task too formidable for puny church.
   (3) To restore N. T. power, we must restore N. T. pattern.
       — Four elements of strength are revealed in this chapter:

I. THEY WERE A UNITED MEMBERSHIP.
   1. At Pentecost — "all with one accord in one place" (v. 1).
      (1) Togetherness, unvarying pattern of power — house in readiness for heavenly Guest.
      (2) Want of togetherness destructive of worship, evangelism — no light thru broken wires.
   2. After Pentecost — "they *continued* in . . . fellowship" (v. 42).

II. *THEY WERE AN INFORMED MEMBERSHIP* — "we all are witnesses (v. 32).

   1. They knew the gospel — greatest body of truth ever put together in sermon (Peter's sermon).

   2. They understood the mission of the church — Great Commission — evangelism and nurture.

   3. They continued learning — "in the apostles' doctrine" (v. 42).
      — cf.: "I would not have you ignorant," six times in N. T.

III. THEY WERE A SPIRITUAL MEMBERSHIP.

   I. The original 120 had been "filled with the Holy Spirit" (v. 4).
      — Not like cup, half full, pathetically trying to run over.

   2. The later 3000 received the Holy Spirit (v. 38).
      — Like 3000 clocks, all sizes, moved by same current, same time.

   3. The combined group were ministering in power of Holy Spirit.
      — Nothing so attractive as real spirituality — can't remain "small but spiritual."

IV. THEY WERE A WITNESSING MEMBERSHIP.

   1. The pattern of Pentecost: "all . . . began to speak" (v. 4).
      — Not necessary to be eloquent, but vocal.

   2. The divine imperative: two-fold testimony — lips and life.
      — "Exhort . . . showing thyself a pattern . . ." (Titus 2:7, 15).

   3. The supreme divine embarrassment: lack of consecrated witnesses.
      — Hope of world, not occasional giant or genius, but multitude of ordinary people with clean hands, pure hearts, ready testimony.

*Concl.*: Church has not lost its charter; Great Commission still stands; power of God is not diminished; restore N. T. pattern, restore N. T. power.

# 14

# The Way to Perennial Freshness

Good craftsmanship does not necessarily insure against monotony. Something more is needed. As Halford E. Luccock has so aptly pointed out, "We have a moral obligation to be interesting"[1] A drowsy church is not a church on the move, and a yawning member is not in process of heeding a call to higher ground. William A. Quayle[2] declares that it is a sin to be uninteresting in proclaiming the gospel, and devotes an entire chapter to a discussion of "The Sin of Being Uninteresting."

To be interesting, the speaker must know what interests his audience. "The difference between a bore and a good conversationalist is that the bore has not discovered the distinction between what interests him and what interests his hearers."[3]

The preacher must learn what farmers have long since learned, that "crop rotation is the rule of fertility." For the preacher this means constant change of materials, methods and emphases. He "must not always labor to carry the people beyond themselves, nor to ravish them into ecstasies; but he must always satisfy them, and maintain in them an esteem and an eagerness for practical piety."[4] This calls for certain safeguards to homiletical freshness which experience has developed:

1. Adapt the preaching to the changing times and seasons, and to the changing needs, moods, and circumstances of the congregation. On the Sunday following the attack on Pearl Harbor

---

[1]*Communicating the Gospel*, p. 138.

[2]*The Pastor-Preacher*, pp. 124-133.

[3]Wright, *A Preacher's Questionnaire*, p. 66.

[4]John Claude, in *The Young Preacher's Manual*, by Ebenezer Porter (New York: Jonathan Leavitt, 1829), p. 140.

someone made the observation, in one of our large cities, that most of the sermon topics announced for the day gave no intimation that the preacher had even heard of Pearl Harbor, or was aware that our country had been plunged into war. Surely God would have a message to fortify His people for the grim days ahead! Timeliness makes for freshness. And timeliness does not rule out timelessness, if the preacher draws sufficiently upon the Scriptures for his message.

2. Adapt the preaching, at different times, to the various age groups and to the various intellectual, social, and economic levels of interest within the congregation. This will be a broadening experience for both the preacher and his people, and will develop a symmetrical congregation. Jesus showed equal concern for the highly placed Pharisee Nicodemus and the fallen Samaritan woman. Paul ministered alike to Jews and Greeks, to King Agrippa and the slave Onesimus. "I am made all things to all men, that I might by all means save some" (I Cor. 11:22).

3. Use a variety of approaches among "The Seven Basic Appeals in Biblical Preaching," discussed in a later chapter.

4. Vary the homiletical types of sermons, between the "Basic Pattern" (Expository, Textual, Topical), the "Problem Solution Pattern," and the "Narrative Pattern," discussed in a previous chapter.

5. Vary the Scripture material and emphasis, avoiding ruts and hobbies. Of a certain scholarly, but monotonous, preacher it was said, "If he doesn't Greek-root you to death, he will Hebrew-stem you to death." The preacher should not fear a certain amount of repetition; it is both necessary and desirable. One sermon on a subject may not be enough. The preacher must, like Peter, stir up the pure minds by way of remembrance (II Peter 3:1); and he must maintain a certain pressure upon the unyielding till they are won. But it must be repetition with variety.

"*All* Scripture is given by inspiration of God, and is profitable..." (II Tim. 3:16). No part, therefore, is to be neglected either because of its obscurity or because of its being too well known. "Like some well advertised and badly exploited beauty spot of nature the real splendor of many passages has been obscured by the heavy traffic to which they have been subjected."[5] Sometimes the traffic is only seasonal, and the same text when treated out of season may prove delightfully fresh. Or, in the immediate context of a passage traditionally reserved for certain seasons there may be suggestions rich in possibilities for fresh sermonic treatment.

For perennial freshness, the principal resource is the Bible, but the preacher must make it live. Hardly less important than the diet itself is the manner in which it is served. Hospital dieticians recognize the need of making the food tray as attractive and tempting as possible to encourage the appetite of the patient. Frequently the appetite is helped by merely changing the dishes in which the food is served.

6. Approach the thesis or proposition from various angles. Five possibilities are suggested by Austin Phelps:[6]

(1) The speaker. "I wish to share with you. . . ."

(2) The audience. "The difficulties which some of you are facing. . . ."

(3) The occasion. "The observance of this day calls for. . . ."

(4) The text. "This text explains. . . ."

(5) The sermon. "This message will deal with. . . ."

7. Vary the number of points and sub-points, not using three points just because that is the number most often used, and not avoiding the use of three points just because the practice has been overdone. If the number of divisions is always appropriate to the text or thesis to be developed, there will be no monotony.

8. Dramatize incidents of Scripture, especially those which are obscure or little known. This can be done without becoming theatrical or sensational, or catering to the secular tastes of the multitude. Of Jesus, it is recorded that "the common people heard him gladly" (Mark 12:37). Plainly, they were fascinated both by what he said and the fresh, pictorial way he said it. "Without a parable spake he not unto them" (Matt. 13:34). Audiences appreciate the picturesque.

---

[5]Roach, *Preaching Values in the Bible,* p. 270.

[6]*The Theory of Preaching* (New York: Charles Scribner's Sons, 1911), pp. 362, 363.

An excellent example of visualizing a Scriptural scene is found in Alexander Whyte's message on "The Man Who Knocked at Midnight."[7] The night is dark ... lights out ... everybody in bed ... a knock at the door ... a friend asking for three loaves ... no answer ... he knocks again ... a weary voice from within ... a refusal ... more waiting ... he knocks again ... the door opens ... the friend gives him all he needs. "Ask, and it shall be given you; seek, and ye shall find; knock, and it shall be opened unto you" (Luke 11:5-10).

9. Draw preaching material from a wide range of sources: Scripture, history, literature other than Scripture and history, experience, and imagination (discussed in a previous chapter). "No amount of clever arrangement can conceal poverty of substance...."[8]

10. Quote occasionally from striking poems or hymns, especially little known stanzas of familiar hymns or stanzas from unfamiliar hymns. Truth often shines more brightly when clad in verse, and much of the world's most inspiring poetry is to be found in hymnals.

11. Enlarge the vocabulary, especially as to "key words" and "transitional verbs." Synonyms or near-synonyms are often a welcome relief from over-worked "key words." Instead of ways, use paths, methods, procedures, channels; or substitute a phrase: directions, instructions, suggestions, or intimations — as to how. And instead of reasons, use encouragements, incentives, promptings, motivations, etc. Occasional paraphrasing of the transitional sentence may give further relief.

12. Avoid the practice of indicating invariably the number of points to be given. The element of anticipation may often be better sustained by the use of such terms as "several," "some," "certain," or "the" than by indicating an exact number. There is a psychological penalty upon spelling out too fully in the introduction what is to be presented in the body of the sermon.

---

[7]*Lord, Teach Us to Pray* (New York: George H. Doran Co., Tenth Edition), p. 169.

[8]Bromiley, in *My Way of Preaching,* edited by Robert J. Smithson, p. 14.

*        *        *

Basic to all freshness in the pulpit is the demand that the preacher be himself, and not an imitator of others. Left to themselves, no two preachers will develop the same sermon on a given text, because no two preachers have exactly the same intellectual endowments or the same background of individual experience.

# 15

## The Essentials of an Effective Preaching Service

The effect of a preaching service is to be measured by its spiritual outcome. Clear aim is a prime qualification in the modern apostle, as with the Apostles in the New Testament. John bears witness "that ye might have life" (John 20:31); "that ye sin not" (I John 2:1); and "that your joy may be full" (I John 1:4). Peter's concern in his first sermon was that they might "repent and be baptized" (Acts 2:38); and in the closing words of his last Epistle it was that they might "grow in grace" (II Peter 3:18). Paul pled, "be ye reconciled to God" (II Cor. 5:20); and "walk worthy of the vocation wherewith ye are called" (Eph. 4:1).

How is the fruitful outcome of Christian preaching to be assured? What are the essentials?

### A GOOD CROWD

Beyond the best efforts of the preacher, whatever his preparation and his spiritual state, the outcome of his labors will depend largely upon his audience. It follows that every legitimate means should be employed to secure a good attendance. Webb B. Garrison tells, in this connection, of an alleged recipe for rabbit stew in an ancient Irish cookbook. Every step is carefully spelled out. The first step reads: "Catch your rabbit." "Public address systems make it possible to speak to more and more, yet the majority of speakers are addressing fewer and fewer."[1]

Attendance alone is not enough. There must be co-operative

---

[1] *The Preacher and His Audience*, pp. 17, 18.

listening. If the audience is favorably disposed and giving close attention the speaker is correspondingly inspired. "Preaching is emphatically not the exclusive responsibility of the preacher alone. To effective preaching, the hearer contributes, if not as much as the preacher, then certainly much more than he usually realizes."[2] According to Geoffrey W. Bromiley, "Sermons fail more often through bad hearing than through bad preaching."[3]

Even more decisive than the attitude of the hearers toward the preacher, is their spiritual state. As Earle V. Pierce points out, "The power of the preacher is multiplied or reduced according to the fullness or lack of fullness of the Holy Spirit on the part of the church.... at least one half of the spiritual power is in the pew."[4] In the average audience there are men and women of spiritual vision and understanding, and others who have very little of either. In any event there must be a willingness to receive the truth. "If any man willeth to do His will, he shall know..." (John 7:17). But God does not reveal Himself to unwilling eyes; He does not speak to unwilling ears; He does not come with blessing into unwilling hearts.

With all the diversities of the average audience, the preacher must secure favorable attention and seek to reach the hearts of all. The services must be made attractive and every impediment removed, to insure a favorable setting for the message.

## A GOOD SETTING

1. *Careful ushering* helps to get the service off to a good start. Good ushering may not be noticed, but poor ushering will scream its way into the consciousness of the visitor. His first and his last impression of the service may come through the usher. Good ushering involves much more than leading a worshiper to a pew and taking up the offering a bit later. The usher must not only extend a friendly welcome and make sure that the worshiper has an order of service and a hymnal; he must remain

---

2Herbert H. Farmer, *The Servant of the Word* (New York: Charles Scribner's Sons, 1942), Peface.

3*My Way of Preaching*, edited by R. J. Smithson, p. 16.

4*Ye Are My Witnesses* (Philadelphia: Judson Press, 1954), p. 102.

alert throughout the service to every circumstance that bears upon the physical comfort of the worshiper.

An Usher's Manual for the pastor and the head usher can be enormously helpful. There are a number of excellent Manuals available at nominal cost.[5] Let the head usher lead his group in the reading and discussion of the Manual, and let a group of reserve ushers be likewise prepared. The practice of asking every male member of the church to take his turn at ushering has much to commend it, provided he is adequately instructed for the task.

2. *Proper temperature.* A room that is too warm or poorly ventilated makes for drowsiness as well as discomfort. And a chilly temperature in a single Sunday service may decrease the attendance for weeks to come. Physical discomfort and good listening do not go together.

3. *Adequate lighting.* Dimly lighted churches are often depressing to the spirit, and the preacher will find it harder to keep his audience awake than in a well lighted sanctuary. As for those who sit in the pews, they expect enough light to read the hymnal and the order of service without straining.

4. *Proper acoustics.* It is estimated that about thirty-five per cent of those who attend church are in some degree deficient in hearing. And those with normal hearing are often frustrated by bad acoustics or the failure of the public address system. How distressing for the preacher to find, after doing his utmost in the pulpit, that some of his people could not hear him! Here again, trained and alert ushers can help save the service.

5. *Favorable atmosphere.* Reverence, refinement, and friendliness in the pulpit are generally reflected in the pews. Communion services, by their very nature, encourage reverence; and so

---

[5] Willis O. Garrett, *Church Usher's Manual* (Philadelphia: Judson Press, 1924).

*Principles of Church Ushering,* compiled by Church Ushers Association of New York, 1951.

Paul H. D. Lang, *Church Ushering* (St. Louis, Mo.: Concordia Publishing House, 1946).

does a well conducted baptismal service. Evangelistic pastors have noted that the services which open with the ordinance of baptism are the services most likely to close with visible responses to the evangelistic invitation.

6. *Suitable music and singing,* with every hymn and every special rendition contributing definitely to the spiritual momentum of the service. Music during prayer tends to scatter the thoughts of the audience. Either the prayer or the music, or both, will be largely lost to the congregation. Beautiful music should be provided a place of its own, and audible prayer likewise.

7. *Attention to minor details:* (1) Pulpit Bible opened beforehand; (2) Hymns indicated on the hymn board; (3) Order of service supplied to the organist well beforehand; (4) Ear-phones and amplifying system tested before each service; (5) Clock regulated, and so placed as to be plainly in sight for the preacher, but behind the audience where it will not distract from the service; (6) Punctual beginning. To start five minutes late means five minutes of irritation at the beginning; to close ten minutes late means ten minutes of irritation at the end. Together, this adds up to fifty hours wasted, for an audience of two hundred; and much of this waste will represent sheer irritation.

## A GOOD SERMON

There is absolutely no limit to the number of people who can stay away from poor preaching. The demands of the pulpit call for the very utmost efforts of the ablest preacher with the most abundant mental and spiritual preparation. When a preacher goes to the pulpit with less than his best, he begins to deteriorate. This may account for the loss of momentum occasionally to be seen in the ministry of a man who was outstanding at the age of thirty and mediocre at fifty. Even when the preacher has done his utmost in mental and spiritual preparation and in the delivery of his sermon, it might fall flat, through factors unseen and beyond his control. Fortunately, such experiences are of rare occurrence.

On a cold, rainy, gloomy Saturday a certain pastor sat working on his sermon from breakfast till noontime, with little to show for the morning's labor. Impatiently, he laid down his pen and sat looking disconsolately out the window, feeling sorry for himself because his sermons came so slowly. Then there flashed into his mind a thought that was to have a profound effect on his later ministry: "Your people will spend far more time on this sermon than you will. They will come from a hundred homes; they will travel a thousand miles, in the aggregate, to be in the service; they will spend three hundred hours participating in the worship and listening to your sermon. Don't complain about the hours you are spending in preparation; your people deserve all that you can give them!"

## A GOOD DELIVERY

Dignity and warmth are of course basic; either without the other would be futile. Beyond this, the speaker must project his voice with sufficient volume to be easily heard by the most distant person in his audience, and with such distinct enunciation as to be readily understood. Proper pitch and tempo are likewise important to a pleasing delivery. An audience that listens faster than the preacher speaks is bored. And an audience distracted by mannerisms or faults in speech, dress or decorum, is partly lost to the service. A good delivery may make a poor sermon reasonably effective; a bad delivery may make the best of sermons ineffective.

# 16

# The Basic Appeals in Biblical Preaching

The preacher, in every legitimate appeal from the pulpit, is addressing himself to the hearer's conscience. Conscience is the awareness of the voice of God speaking through the Holy Spirit to the soul — instructing, encouraging, approving; or correcting, warning, rebuking. To preach without reliance upon the co-operation of the Holy Spirit through the voice of conscience would be sheer presumption. But while every Biblical appeal is ultimately an appeal to conscience, there are many *roads* to the heart. A long list of appeals could be  enumerated; but, when overlapping has been eliminated so far as possible, there seem to be about seven basic appeals through which the preacher may approach his audience.

The preacher with only one appeal is like a musical instrument with only one tone. However sweet the tone, when it loses its freshness it loses its charm. Sometimes a preacher does not realize how monotonous he has become in his evangelistic appeal, and how trite and threadbare in his pulpit vocabulary. It has been said that each generation needs a fresh coinage of theological terminology. The old terms, through long wear, seem to slip through the mind without taking hold, like an old dime worn so smooth and thin that it slips almost imperceptibly between the fingers. Freshness of appeal, coupled with an ever broadening Scriptural base of preaching, makes for long pastorates and wins an ever widening constituency of men and women, children and adults, rich and poor, high and low.

The presentation of theological truth must be comprehensive

enough to illumine the mind, to stir the emotions, to move the will, to win the whole man — "heart, soul, mind, strength" (Mark 12:30). To every man and every mood there is an effective and an ineffective approach. And to every approach there are degrees of attractiveness and persuasiveness. A lecturer in medical school was encouraging his students, perhaps facetiously, with the assurance, "Eighty-five per cent of your patients will get well — with your help, without your help, in spite of your help." But the minister has no such comfort. He knows that unless his hearers are given the right prescription and persuaded to accept the remedy, a flat hundred per cent will be lost. Not one of the seven basic appeals can safely be neglected.

1. *The appeal to altruism,* a benevolent regard for the interests of others.

When Moses was appealing to Hobab to guide the people of Israel through the wilderness to the Promised Land, he said, "Come thou with us, and we will do thee good." Hobab refused. But when Moses pled for Hobab to come for the good that he could *do,* instead of the good that he would *receive,* Hobab responded (Num. 10:29-33). The appeal to altruism reaches many who will not respond to any appeal on the basis of self interest. The second commandment, which speaks of "visiting the sins of the fathers upon the children," lends itself to this appeal (Deut. 5:9). And many have been moved by the words of Jesus, "There is joy in the presence of the angels of God over one sinner that repenteth" (Luke 15:7, 10).

2. *The appeal to aspiration,* the universal hunger for spiritual happiness — the sense of completeness.

The noblest of mankind reflect this thirst for holiness, and the meanest soul that breathes has holy moments when the better self seeks expression. This longing was reflected by the thief on the cross: "Lord, remember me when thou comest into thy kingdom" (Luke 23:42). The rich young ruler spoke out of a similar longing: "what lack I yet?" (Matt. 19:20)

In other cases the longing is for spiritual qualities and satisfactions which have been lost. Through the memory of better days, many a heart can be reached with a message of hope, forgiveness, restoration. "By the rivers of Babylon, there we sat down, yea, we wept when we remembered Zion" (Ps. 137:1). When Ezekiel came and "sat where they sat" (Ezek. 3:15), he doubtless found many hearts receptive to the grace of God. To the backslidden church at Ephesus, with its rich traditions of spiritual power, it was most natural that the appeal should be as it was: "Remember from whence thou art fallen..." (Rev. 2:5).

In the remarkably fruitful ministry of George W. Truett, the appeal to aspiration and to altruism loomed large.

3. *The appeal to curiosity,* susceptibility to that which appears novel, unfamiliar, or mysterious.

This appeal might be regarded as an appeal to the imagination in that it promises to bring reality into view. By its intimations it sustains the element of suspense and anticipation, upon which the interest of the hearer so largely depends. Jesus made effective use of this appeal. To Nathanael, who had never met Him, Jesus said, "when thou wast under the fig tree, I saw thee" (John 1:47). To the Samaritan woman, He said, "If thou knewest..." (John 4:10). To Zacchaeus, who had never seen Jesus, He said, "today I must abide at thy house" (Luke 19:5).

The following sermon topics make legitimate use of this appeal: "The Curiosity of the Angels" (I Peter 1:12); "Fishing on the Wrong Side of the Boat" (John 21:6); "Praying on the Wrong Side of the Creek" (apparently based on some incident outside the Scriptures). The appeal to curiosity is peculiarly subject to abuse, in terms of irreverence, and even dishonesty, where truthfulness suffers at the hand of cleverness.

4. *The appeal to duty,* the divine urge to do a thing because it is right, or to refrain from a thing because it is wrong.

With the majority of people, this is probably the least popular of all appeals. It is nevertheless a familiar Biblical approach: "These ought ye to have done" (Matt. 23:23); "We ought to obey God" (Acts 5:29); "Ye ought to support the weak" (Acts 20:35); "Six days in which men ought to work" (Luke 13:14). With some people, who will do anything that they feel they *ought* to do, this may be the most powerful of all appeals. Charles G. Finney used it with great effectiveness.

5. *The appeal to fear.* This Biblical appeal has been much neglected, to the great loss of the church and those whom the church, through this omission, has failed to win. Punishment is not a popular theme with preachers or with congregations, partly because some things preached have been untrue, alien to the spirit of the New Testament, and dishonoring to God. God is not vengeful or vindictive. The wrath of God, synonymous with the judgment of God, is not like "the wrath of men," which "worketh not the righteousness of God." But, like the punitive laws of our country at their best, the punishment of God is remedial, deterrent, and protective of society.

God uses this approach when lesser appeals have failed. Saul of Tarsus, when God dealt with him, "fell to the earth . . . trembling and astonished" (Acts 9:4, 6). The Philippian jailer "came trembling" (Acts 16:29). Jesus used this appeal in the Sermon on the Mount — "If thy right eye offend thee, pluck it out . . ." (Matt. 5:29); in the parable of the rich fool (Luke 12:16-21); and in His reference to the family with one member in hell (Luke 16:19-31). The prophets used this appeal. Nathan, confronting King David, induced remorse and repentance — "Thou art the man" (II Sam. 12:7). Jonah stirred Nineveh — "Yet forty days and Nineveh shall be overthrown" (Jonah 3:4). In apostolic times, "fear came upon all the church" (Acts 5:11); and when Paul preached "judgment," "Felix trembled" (Acts 24:25).

Fear of punishment is not the highest incentive to right conduct, but it often succeeds when other appeals have failed. "Be sure your sin will find you out" (Num. 32:23). Fear of being caught keeps many persons honest, and restrains many others from crime. Fear dictates fantastic expenditures for armaments, and motivates much individual conduct. An amazing percentage of Christians have been turned to Christ by fear, coupled with loving, tactful guidance to the way of salvation.

6. *The appeal to love.* Every conceivable appeal is an appeal to one of three loves: love of self, love of others, or love of God.

All three are reflected in the "first and great commandment" and the second, which is "like unto it" (Matt. 22:37-40) . "Love the Lord thy God ... thy neighbor ... thyself" (Luke 10:27) . The calculated motivation in any appeal is the hope of favoring or the fear of grieving or injuring oneself or God or others. The supreme motivation is love toward Christ. "The love of Christ constraineth us" (II Cor. 5:14) . "We love Him because He first loved us" (I John 4:19). To know Him is to love Him, and to "preach Christ" (II Cor. 4:5) remains the supreme function and prerogative of the man in the pulpit.

7. *The appeal to reason.* The Prophet Samuel "reasoned" with his people (I Sam. 12:7). The Prophet Isaiah makes a similar appeal: "Come now, and let us reason together, saith the Lord" (Isa. 1:18) . And in the middle verse of the New Testament it is recorded that the Apostle Paul "reasoned" with the Jews and others daily in the synagogue and the market (Acts 17:17, A.R.V.) . Jonathan Edwards and Charles G. Finney were outstandingly successful with the appeal to reason, which is merely an appeal to intelligent self-interest. With many thinking people it is the most powerful of all appeals.

\*    \*    \*

Whatever the inclinations or special aptitudes of the preacher may be, he will strengthen his ministry, enlarge his fruitfulness, and advance his own mental and spiritual development by maintaining a variety of appeals with the many diversities of his people constantly in view.

# 17
## The Minister's Vocabulary

One of the most pronounced evidences of culture or the want of culture lies in one's use of words. One of the surest means of determining one's mental age or general intelligence is the vocabulary test. To be poor in words is usually to be poor in mind. The thought processes are largely confined within the limits of one's vocabulary. And to increase the range of one's thinking, it is necessary to increase the vocabulary by means of which one's thinking is articulated. "Tests of more than 350,000 persons from all walks of life show that, more often than any other measurable characteristic, knowledge of the exact meanings of a large number of words accompanies outstanding success."[1]

A rich vocabulary is a mighty asset in the pulpit, enabling the preacher to project an idea from his own mind into the minds of others without loss or blur. In developing such a vocabulary, three aims are to be kept constantly in mind.

1. *Accuracy.* A good rule of life for the minister is to keep three books invariably at his desk, where he can reach them without straining and without leaving his chair: The Bible, the Concordance, and the Dictionary. He can not afford to pass over an unfamiliar word without looking it up. How is it spelled? How is it pronounced? What does it mean? Thus a vocabulary is developed, and a sensitivity to the meaning of words, and to the various shades of meaning. Careful thinking and careful speaking go together. And as the preacher patiently disciplines himself to accuracy of expression he gains in freshness also, through the use of a steadily growing vocabulary.

---

[1]Blake Clark, "Words Can Work Wonders for You," *Reader's Digest* (May, 1961), p. 73.

Accuracy contributes to force. As Mark Twain aptly declared, "The difference between the right word and the almost right word is the difference between lightning and the lightning bug."[2] And further force is often gained by the use of specific rather than general terms. Many have paid tribute to "the power of the specific."[3] Thus a reference to a storm may be less effective than to speak of it as a windstorm, a rainstorm, a hailstorm, a snowstorm, or a sandstorm. Likewise there may be greater force in the terms, cheating, lying, stealing, than in the general term, dishonesty.

For accuracy in communicating the meaning of a Scripture passage it is necessary at times to refer to the original language. A common misreading of Scripture, at communion services, occurs through misplaced emphasis in the passage, "Drink ye all of it." Does it mean, "Drink ye *all-of-it*"? The Greek version, by its case endings, immediately dispels any doubt, and reads, "Drink *ye-all* of it" (Matt. 26:27).

2. *Clarity*. Use always the shortest, simplest, most familiar word that exactly fits. This does not limit the preacher to a small vocabulary. On the contrary, if there is richness and breadth of thinking, a large vocabulary is essential if every thought is to be expressed in words that *exactly fit*.

Ilion T. Jones quotes an apt expression of Fritz Kunkel, who characterized words as "ignition devices."[4] He points out that it is not enough for the gospel to be *proclaimed;* it must be *communicated.* To this end, the words used must be understandable to the hearers; else the "ignition" fails. This does not rule out the duty of the preacher to stretch the mental horizons of his people and, in disciplined thinking, to expand their vocabulary; but it does emphasize one of the conditions of effective preaching.

People like to be addressed in language that they can understand. When Jesus spoke, "the common people heard him gladly" (Mark 12:37). One reason was the simplicity with which He

---

[2]Gilman, Aly and Reid, *Speech Preparation*, p. 113.
[3]Luccock, *In the Minister's Workshop*, p. 189.
[4]*Principles and Practice of Preaching*, pp. 14, 36.

expressed the profound truths that He taught. In the Sermon on the Mount, approximately four-fifths of the words are of one syllable.

3. *Refinement.* Let the preacher draw heavily upon the simple vocabulary of "Basic English," as necessary; but let him not descend to the crudities of "Pidgin English" or gutter slang. Pure, dignified English, however simple the vocabulary, will reach the people on "both sides of the tracks." When the Apostle Paul spoke of being "all things to all men," that he might "by all means save some" (I Cor. 9:22), he was not suggesting departure from good taste or good grammar.

In ministering to children or to persons with a meager knowledge of English, such as our missionaries encounter in other lands, "Basic English" has proven itself an excellent medium of communication. This "Globalanguage" reduces the English vocabulary from 414,825 words to 850 words, which could be printed on a single page of paper.[5] *The New Testament in Basic English* makes use of only 1000 words, and has been remarkably successful in conveying the Christian gospel.[6]

If the language of the preacher is pedantic, or too flowery, or ungrammatical, it is likely to divert the attention of the hearer from the message to the messenger. In such case the messenger may become a hindrance to his own message and to the free operation of the Holy Spirit. The same is true if the preacher violates the rules of rhetoric as to redundancy, trite expressions, unpleasant combinations of sibilants, or other word combinations which are unpleasant to the ear. Like neatness and unobtrusiveness in dress and manner, the preacher's language must lend itself to the unhindered flow of thought from the heart of the preacher to the heart of the hearer.

"Let your style be such that the hearers will attend only to the thought, without considering that you have any style."[7]

---

[5]Lincoln Barnett, "Basic English: A Globalanguage," *Life* (Oct. 18, 1943), p. 57.

[6]Prepared under Direction of S. H. Hooke (New York: E. P. Dutton & Co., Inc., 1941).

[7]Griffin, *On the Art of Preaching.*

# 18

# The Systematic Filing of Materials

An adequate filing system may make the difference between a meager and an abundant pulpit ministry. But the system must be so simple as to insure lasting perseverance in its use. The unhappy experience of many ministers has been to establish a system, to become bogged down in its use, then to abandon it and have no system at all. Deterred by the elaborateness of systems proposed, young ministers have often muddled through their early years without any system. And when a simple, efficient, adequate system was finally developed, the familiar lament has been, "If only I had begun years ago!"

The time to begin is when the candidate for the ministry begins his college and seminary training. The system here recommended, which takes into account the experience and counsel of many ministers and excellent writers on the subject, might begin with relatively few folders, and be developed over the years to any degree of elaborateness desired. Nothing needs ever to be wasted or undone.

An excellent discussion of filing and indexing, of both bound and unbound materials, is that of L. R. Elliott in *The Efficiency Filing System*.[1] This system is presented in sufficient detail for an extensive library, and may need some adaptation and simplification for the beginner. Dr. Elliott suggests standard size folders, with extra creases at the bottom, to provide for expansion. Each memorandum or clipping, as it is inserted, is to be identified as to subject and as to source. Small fragments may be mounted on sheets, 8½ by 11 inches, with paste or Scotch Tape.

---

[1] (Nashville: Broadman Press, 1959).

Another excellent plan, long in use by ministers, is that of Andrew W. Blackwood, in *Planning A Year's Pulpit Work*.[2] He proposes the use of standard size folders, and a filing cabinet providing the four categories: *Bible, Subjects, Letters, Sermons.* In addition, he suggests a card index file, with cards of 4 by 6 inches, for indexing materials contained in books.

A synthesis of the most helpful ideas from many sources might take the following form, streamlined for simplicity and practicality for the average minister:

1. Set up a file of standard size folders (9½ by 11¾ inches), to carry memoranda up to letter size sheets (8½ by 11 inches). Provide alphabetical folders for filing letters. For the rest of the file, folders with "third cut" tabs (1/3 of the width of the folder) are usually the most practical. Select folders with reinforced tabs, and creased at the bottom so as to allow for expansion as the folder fills up.

2. Provide one category of folders for *Administrative* materials (such as Deacons, Trustees, Choir, Sunday School, Women's work, Youth work); and separate categories for the following classifications of *sermonic* materials:

(1) Occasions. This classification would include scarcely more than a dozen folders, for materials of seasonal interest, related to special days, such as the following:

| | | |
|---|---|---|
| New Year | Pentecost | Father's Day |
| Palm Sunday | Mother's Day | Labor Day |
| Good Friday | Memorial Day | Thanksgiving |
| Easter | Children's Day | Christmas |

(2) *Subjects.* In the course of time there would be several dozen separate folders for subjects which would vary with the special interests of the individual preacher, such as:

| | |
|---|---|
| Assurance | Character |
| Baptism | Christ |
| Bible | Christian Graces |
| Bible Persons | Church |

---

2 (New York: Abingdon-Cokesbury Press), 1942, pp. 225-231.

| | |
|---|---|
| Civics | Influence |
| Comfort | Judgment |
| Conscience | Lord's Day |
| Consecration | Lord's Supper |
| Crime | Love |
| Denominations | Ministry |
| Discipline | Missions |
| Evangelism | Prayer |
| Faith | Prophecy |
| Fellowship | Righteousness |
| Forgiveness | Salvation |
| Funerals | Science |
| Happiness | Sin |
| Heaven | Spirit World |
| Hell | Stewardship |
| Historic Persons | Sunday School |
| History | Temperance |
| Holy Spirit | Truth |
| Home | War |
| Humility | Work |
| Humor | Worldliness |
| Hymnology | Youth |
| Immortality | Unclassified |

There will inevitably be some overlapping. The subjects should therefore be kept rather general; else, materials might be difficult to find when needed. Someone has defined filing as "systematically burying material beyond the probability of recovery."

(3) *Bible.* Ultimately, as materials accumulate, this section would grow to 66 folders, one for each book of the Bible, and probably more than one folder for certain books.

(4) *Sermons Preached.* In filing these outlines, take care to record on the back side of each one the date and place where the sermon was preached.

File the sermons chronologically, with the most recent sermon in the front of the folder. Ultimately there should be one folder for each calendar year. If a sermon is preached repeatedly, re-file it each time according to the date of its most recent use. The question may be raised, Why not file it alphabetically according to title? Because the preacher may change the title when the sermon is used again. Why not file it according to subject? Because there are so many sermons that might be filed under any one of several subjects, such as salvation, grace, repentance, faith, forgiveness, reconciliation, etc. Why not file it by text? Because there may be several passages prominently involved; and cognate passages may appear in each of the four Gospels, or in each of the historical books of Samuel, Kings, and Chronicles. Besides, many passages are quoted by later writers in the Scriptures.

Keep a chronological record of every sermon preached, in a book wide enough so that one line (across the two opposite pages) can carry the full data: (1) Date, (2) Title of sermon, (3) Scripture passage, (4) Place where the sermon was preached, (5) Attendance, and (6) Comments on the service. For quick reference, the value of this simple, concise, streamlined record can scarcely be overstated. A plain, stiff-backed class roll book of about 8 by 10 inches, 72 to 100 pages, ruled and cross-ruled, will serve admirably; and, with about 26 lines to a page, one book will carry the record of years of preaching.

3. File immediately, in the appropriate folder, any helpful material that comes to hand, whether the particular item covers a full page, 8½ by 11 inches, or a small memorandum of any size or shape, or a clipping from a magazine or newspaper, taking care to identify in the margin of the item the subject and the source, including author, publication, and page. Whether the memorandum carries an idea or a quotation or only a reference to a book or other publication, place it in the same folder with all other memoranda under that subject or text or seasonal classification. Where no separate file is maintained for references to books and magazines, provide in the back of each folder one full size sheet for recording these references to bound materials. If there is a multiplication of small pieces, these can be mounted on full page sheets, with paste or Scotch Tape. Let no good idea be lost for want of proper note paper. Wherever the idea strikes, record it on any kind of paper available; save this memorandum; and file it!

As material accumulates under a given classification, sermonic treatments will suggest themselves; and by further additions to the file these ideas gradually ripen for full sermonic development.

Let nothing delay the starting of such a file, with at least 100 folders, obtainable at about 4 cents each. Where a student has no filing cabinet immediately available, it would be better to temporize with the use of a cardboard carton (12 inches wide and of suitable depth) than to put off the beginning of a systematic filing procedure.

4. As material is withdrawn from the folder, and embodied in a sermon, the memoranda are discarded. Unused material is returned to the folder, together with any new ideas that have come, including possible titles for further sermons on the same subject or Scripture passage. The files should of course be kept clear of materials that have become useless.

5. Add new folders only as additional material comes to hand, requiring such additional folders.

6. In addition to the file, there may be need for a cabinet with drawers for tracts and pamphlets, or for other materials which have become too bulky for the regular folders, or for sermons in process of preparation.

\* \* \*

"With joy shall ye draw water out of the wells of salvation" (Isa. 12:3). This is the normal experience of the faithful minister of Jesus Christ. And among the facilities for adequately ministering there is none that will give him deeper satisfaction than a well ordered file, in which the treasured gleanings from his own experience and reading are ready for instant use. What ministers generally do not realize is that the file can be so simple — as indicated in this chapter — that there is no danger of becoming bogged down in its operation. Then, what a joy when the time comes for a sermon on a particular *occasion,* or *subject,* or *Scripture,* to find in the appropriate folder the valuable materials that have been collecting!

# Appendix
## An Expository Sermon

# The Family of Christ

Scripture — I John 3:1-3.

1. Behold, what manner of love the Father hath bestowed upon us, that we should be called the sons of God: therefore the world knoweth us not, because it knew him not.

2. Beloved, now are we the sons of God, and it doth not yet appear what we shall be: but we know that, when he shall appear, we shall be like him; for we shall see him as he is.

3. And every man that hath this hope in him purifieth himself, even as he is pure.

\* \* \* \* \*

"Behold, what manner of love the Father hath bestowed upon us, that we should be called the sons of God!"

In this exclamation, the Apostle expresses an intermingling of amazement, humility, and exaltation. In the preceding chapter he has been solemnly warning against the frailties and blunders to which the saints of God are subject. And now he exclaims, how wonderful it is that we, with all our spiritual deficiencies and imperfections, our shortcomings and inconsistencies, should be so honored and privileged of God as to be called the sons of God! Look at us! What a poor, shuffling, blundering, stumbling lot we are at best! And yet, we are "the sons of God," born to a high destiny.

In its upward look, this passage has much in common with the communion hymn which we love to sing at every observance of the Lord's Supper:

> Blest be the tie that binds
> Our hearts in Christian love;
> The fellowship of kindred minds
> Is like to that above.

The tie that binds us together in holy brotherhood with one

another and with Christ, the firstborn of many brethren (Rom. 8:29), and the tie that binds us in holy sonship to the Heavenly Father, are one and the same tie.

The experience by which we become the sons of God, and the experience by which we become brothers to one another, are one and the same experience. The Lord Jesus calls it the new birth. When we are born again, born of the spirit, born into the family of Christ, into the household of God, we have become not only the sons of God; but by the same token we have become brothers to one another. It follows, that the brotherhood of man, in so far as it is ever to be attained in this world, must be attained by way of the Fatherhood of God. It is of course true that, creationally, all the sons of men are the sons of God. "He hath made of one blood all nations of men for to dwell on all the face of the earth..." (Acts 17:26). But in the prevailing New Testament sense, not all the sons of men are the sons of God, by any means. Only "As many as received Him, to them gave He power to *become* the sons of God..." (John 1:12) And as the sons of God, we become "heirs of God, and joint heirs with Christ" (Rom. 8:17).

The unique inheritance of the family of Christ includes privileges, graces, and assurances which are reflected in many inspiring passages of Scripture; but there is probably no one passage which spells out more beautifully the *distinctions* which are part of this family inheritance than does the passage here marked for our attention.

I. THE FAMILY NAME — the "Sons of God" (v.la).

1. *The sons of God are sharply distinguished, in the Holy Scriptures, from the rest of humanity.*

To a mixed company of believers, including the very opposite extremes of human society, Jesus declared, "All ye are brethren ... one is your Father, which is in heaven ... one is your Master, even Christ" (Matt. 23:8-10). Surely the Lord Jesus never performed a greater miracle in the days of His flesh than when He welded together into one holy, harmonious brotherhood those rugged and diverse individuals who made up that early disciple group. Of all the creatures that walked or crawled on the earth, probably none was more deeply despised or more bitterly hated by the average Jew than was the Publican. Quite often he was himself a Jew, usually not very scrupulous, a hireling of Rome, whose function it was to collect taxes which the Jews never felt that they should have to pay. And of those who hated the Publican, there was probably none who hated with greater fury and venom than did the Zealot. He was that fanatical agitator who never ceased clamoring for freedom from the obnoxious Roman yoke. Yet, whom do we find in that disciple band — Matthew the Publican and Simon the Zealot!

To the unbelieving, Jesus denied the Fatherhood of God. "Ye are not of God . . . if God were your Father, ye would love me . . . ye are of *your* father the devil . . ." (John 8:47, 42, 44). This distinction between the "children of God" and the "children of the devil" crops out in other New Testament passages (I John 3:10; Acts 13:10). Thus the fatherhood of the devil is no less a Scriptural doctrine than the Fatherhood of God.

The half brothers of Jesus, who became such staunch believers and witnesses after the resurrection, were ruled out, in the time of their unbelief, from any relationship of true brotherhood with Jesus. "Thy mother and thy brethren stand without, desiring to speak with thee," someone had said. To this, Jesus replied, "Who is my mother? and who are my brethren?" And he stretched forth his hand toward his disciples, and said, "Behold my mother and my brethren! For whosoever doeth the will of my Father which is in heaven, the same is my brother, and sister, and mother" (Matt. 12:47-50). In another connection Jesus had said, "That which is born of the flesh is flesh; and that which is born of the Spirit is spirit" (John 3:6). And infinitely more important than the ties of the flesh, which are severed at the grave, are the ties of the Spirit, which unite everlastingly the family of Christ.

The unpedigreed outcast, if "born again," is hailed by the Lord Jesus as one of the sons of God, a brother beloved. At the same time, the highly pedigreed Pharisee, in his unbelief, with all his moral excellences, is disowned as none of His. The household of God is for the sons of God, and heaven is attained, not by merit, but on the basis of relationship.

2. *The "Sons of God" have another family name, no less to be*

*cherished than their designation as "Sons of God."* "The disciples were called Christians first in Antioch" (Acts 11:26). Antioch was in Syria; and the name "Christian" is typical of many Syrian names, being compounded of two parts — "Christ," the head of the family, plus the characteristic Syrian ending "ian," meaning "of-the-family-of." Originally, the term "Christian" seems to have been merely a term of convenience to identify the followers of Christ, as the term "Herodians" identified the supporters of the dynasty of Herod. But Syrian Christians have given to the term "Christian" a more intimate rendering: "of-the-family-of-Christ." The term means immeasurably more to us when we realize that every time we call ourselves "Christians," we are declaring, "I am of-the-family-of-Christ."

II. THE FAMILY LIFE — "Every man that hath this hope in him purifieth himself, even as he is pure" (v. 3).

1. *The Apostle John wisely emphasizes the earthly consequences of our heavenly hope,* the practical bearing of our spiritual relationships, the visible proof of that invisible reality to which we bear witness every time we declare, "I am a Christian."

First, he lifts us into the radiance of heavenly altitudes, reminding us that we are the sons of God, born to a high destiny (v. 2); then he brings us back down to earth, as does the ancient Prophet Isaiah — "They that wait upon the Lord shall renew their strength; they shall mount up with wings as eagles; they shall run, and not be weary; and they shall walk, and not faint" (Isa. 40:31). The proof of the genuineness of our relation to God lies not only in those "glory-hallelujah" moments which are such a precious experience and such a cherished memory to the believer. A more convincing evidence of the heavenly inflow of grace and strength may be in the ability to persevere in godly living and service when others are dropping out or breaking down from sheer exhaustion.

"As many as are led by the Spirit of God, they are the sons of God" (Rom. 8:14). "By their fruits ye shall know them" (Matt. 7:20). "The fruit of the Spirit is love, joy, peace, longsuffering, gentleness, goodness, faith, meekness, temperance" (Gal. 5:22-23). Thus there is a world-wide family resemblance among the true sons and daughters of God. Whatever one's race, color, language, or cultural level, when the Holy Spirit comes into that life, the same nine-fold fruitage of the Spirit makes its appearance. And a family resemblance is one of the most convincing proofs of a family relationship.

2. *The Apostle Paul, in a similar challenge to the Christians in Philippi, refers to the group as a "Colony of Heaven"* (Phil. 3:20, Moffatt). Thus they were a colony *within* a colony, since Philippi was a Roman colony planted in a vast non-Roman area. One of the most powerful considerations with which to inspire or restrain the Philippian was to remind him that he was a Roman citizen and must conduct himself accordingly, before an alien world. Similarly, the Apostle appeals to the Christian minority in Philippi to conform to the highest citizenship of all, their citizenship in heaven. This challenge has a perpetual relevancy for the sons of God. We are colonizing for Christ; we hold citizenship in heaven; we are in daily personal communication with the Sovereign of heaven Himself. When this consciousness is kept alive, we can not let down and live a shabby Christian life.

During slavery days, some Northern visitors in New Orleans were watching a company of slaves wearily shuffling along the dock, returning to their work. Spiritless, apparently indifferent to life itself, they were dragging thmselves along. But one, in striking contrast, with head erect and with unbroken spirit, strode among them with the dignified bearing of a conqueror. "Who is that fellow?" someone asked. "Is he the *straw boss;* or the *owner* of the slaves?" "No", was the answer; "that fellow just can't get it out of his head that he is the son of a king." And so he was. He had been dragged into slavery as a small child, but had already been taught that he was no ordinary person; he was the son of a king, and must bear himself accordingly, as long as he lives. Now, after half a lifetime of hardship and abuse, which had broken the spirit of the others, he was still the son of a king! Such is the inspiration and the strength of the sons of God!

III. THE FAMILY HOPE. A three-fold hope is set before us (v. 2).

1. *"He shall appear."* It is not as though the Lord Jesus had

withdrawn Himself from the affairs of His kingdom. "Lo, I am with you alway, even unto the end of the world" (Matt. 28:20). This promise has sustained the servants of Christ through innumerable crises, reverses, discouragements, and persecutions. The immortal George W. Truett was asked at a time when the world outlook was particularly threatening, "Is the task of evangelization hopeless?" "If it were not for the divine element," replied Truett, "I would quit now." Of course, he did not quit, but persevered with all his God-given powers, in reliance upon the divine presence and the promise of the ultimate return of the Savior of the world.

2. *"We shall see him."* In the early church there were those who feared that death might rob them or their loved ones of the supreme experience of witnessing the glorious return of the Lord Jesus. Therefore, this assurance from the Apostles John, and similar assurances from the Apostle Paul (I Thess. 4:13-18).

3. *"We shall be like him."* This is perhaps the highest "shouting ground" for the believer in all Scriptural revelation. When we become utterly discouraged with our sinfulness, our inexcusable blunders, our miserable failures in Christian living, we are assured that in the fullness of time we shall stand before our Lord in the unmarred likeness of the Son of God — pure, unblemished, with the beauty of holiness upon us. At last we shall be what in our better moments we have always dreamed and hoped and prayed that we might become.

This will not be achieved through our own effort, but by the grace of God, having been settled before we were born. In eternity past, when we wre "foreknown" as those who would open their hearts and lives to the Saviorhood of Christ, we were "predestined to be conformed to the image of his Son" (Rom. 8:29-30). God will not drop the believer along the way, but will bring him to that glorious fulfillment. "Eye hath not seen, nor ear heard, neither have entered into the heart of man, the things which God hath prepared for them that love him" (I Cor. 2:9).

\* \* \*

As the family of Christ, we are a favored family indeed, with a high destiny and a rich inheritance — the family name, the family life, the family hope. To the sons of God, this is a message of cheer, to put a song in every heart. To our uncommitted friends and loved ones, the Head of the family beckons and says, "Come" — with all the attractiveness that divine grace can put into the invitation. And when Christ becomes Lord of one's life, he becomes Savior of the soul and Guardian of the destiny.

# Index

Part 2

# Sermons Preached
without Notes

# Contents

# Introduction

This volume of sermons has a two-fold purpose. First, there is the obvious purpose of communicating Biblical truth to bless the lives of the readers. Beyond this, it is hoped that ministers of the gospel will find these sermons helpful from a structural point of view, and for illustrative material.

For the minister, this is a companion volume to *Expository Preaching without Notes*, by the same author and publisher. These sermons have been preached *without notes,* and are presented in demonstration of the principles, procedures, and homiletical devices discussed in the earlier volume. The structure of each sermon is reflected in the use of Italics and capital letters, and the numbering and indentation of paragraphs, corresponding to the outline by which it was prepared. Wherever practical, the phraseology of the outline is carried into the sermon.

Ordinarily, a carefully prepared outline, handwritten, on one side of one sheet of paper (8½ x 11), is adequate if the preacher's preparation has been adequate, from the standpoint of organization *and "saturation."* For a thirty minute sermon, there might be from thirty to thirty-six lines, or approximately one line to a paragraph. This calls for conciseness and every possible abbreviation of words. The outline is carried into the pulpit for possible use *in case of emergency,* but with the hope that such emergency will never arise. Such an outline is shown on page 12, facing the opening page of Chapter 1.

Each of these sermons is in the "Basic" or "Propositional" pattern (as distinguished from the "Narrative" pattern, the "Problem Solution" pattern, the "Homily," and the "Bible Reading"). In the "Basic" pattern, the Introduction leads to a thesis or proposition, and the body of the sermon is the elaboration of that thesis or proposition.

Four of these sermons are "Topical," four are "Textual," and seven are "Expository." The emphasis on "Expository" preaching is based on the feeling that "Expository" preaching will, in the long run, yield larger dividends to both the preacher and his hearers. There is no particular merit in holding to one type of preaching, so long as all the messages are Biblical in content. Indeed, there is merit in variety. And it is not necessary for a sermon to be always strictly "Expository" or strictly "Textual" or "Topical." As ministers endeavor to "feed the flock" with a balanced diet, they may find many of their sermons difficult to classify as between the three types indicated.

A "Topical" sermon is usually rather easy to classify. It is merely the elaboration of a *topic.*

A "Textual" sermon may at times be quite difficult to classify. Simply stated, it is the elaboration of a *text.* But just how long is a text? Is it a *verse* of Scripture; or is it a *sentence,* which might include two or more verses? A further problem arises. A *text* can be fairly interpreted only in the light of its *context;* and the preacher might draw rather heavily upon the latter. The resultant sermon might then be "Expository" in that it illuminates the entire context; but it would still be "Textual" in that it is primarily a development of the *text* upon which the emphasis is focused.

An "Expository" sermon, though illuminating the entire passage or chapter or book of the Bible, must of necessity select the high points and omit much of that which is incidental. Judicious discrimination is essential. The thesis or proposition may reflect either the major thrust of the passage or one of its minor thrusts or implications. In any case the "Expository" sermon will pick up the material that is relevant to the thesis, and judiciously omit the rest, or give only passing notice to it. Thus a single sermon on a given passage of Scripture can seldom be exhaustive.

Rules of structure, though indispensable, could be applied too rigidly. This might take an unjustifiable amount of time; and too much precision could make a sermon seem stilted. It might require the sacrifice of some particularly apt and forceful phrasing which cannot be brought neatly into the structural pattern. A bit of flexibility, therefore, is good in the application of homiletical rules, as in other areas of life.

It would be too much to hope that every sermon will present material that is entirely new to the hearers. To a large degree, the aim of the preacher is as the Apostle Peter expressed it: "to put you always in remembrance of these things, though ye know them . . ." and to "stir up your pure minds by way of remembrance" (II Peter 1:12; 3:1).

The messages in this book are sent forth with the prayer that every message will bring some lasting spiritual benefit to the reader.

*  *  *  *  *  *  *  *

The sermon entitled "The Living Plus Sign" appeared in the Select Sermon Series of *Christianity Today*, January 2, 1961.

The sermon "Slightly Soiled, Greatly Reduced in Price" was preached before the North American Baptist General Conference in Detroit, Michigan, August 30, 1931, and was published in the *Baptist Herald* and later distributed in tract form by the Conference.

The sermon "Living with Your Frustrations" was preached at the Bethel College and Seminary, St. Paul, Minnesota, during Founders' Week, February 18, 1958, and was published with other addresses of that week.

Permission to include these sermons in the present volume is gratefully acknowledged.

Charles W. Koller

# "Topical" Sermons

The handwritten outline on page 12 emphasizes the visual advantages of handwriting, underscoring, and the numbering and indentation of points. The handwriting and abbreviations may be a bit difficult for others to decipher, but would be quite intelligible to the minister who prepared the sermon and outline, and who is adequately "saturated" with the subject matter. Being familiar with his own handwriting and his own peculiar abbreviations and "shorthand," he would have no real difficulty in getting the thought; and he would find such an outline, prepared by himself, not too difficult to carry in memory.

## The Living Plus Sign
### 2 Cor. 5:14-15, 17-20.

Intro.: "On a hill far away stood an old rugged cross ...."

1. We have not really seen cr. of Christ until we see it as a great plus sign ....
   - Above: loving Hv. Father bendg. down fr. throne, offerg. hand of reconcil.
   - Beneath: confused mass, blundrg., sinning, suff. hum., alienated, lost, divided.
   - Upon cr., in form of livg. plus sign, body of Son of G., great "Reconciler", Eph. 2:14,16.

2. We have not really seen Christ until we have seen Him as christ of cr.
   - Thus, three eyes of Peter, who emph. not flawless life but atoning death.
   - Thus, Paul ... not Christ of wayside, seaside, synag., but cross, 1 Cor. 2:2.
   - Thus, Christ desires to be rem.: "This is my bl. ... this do in rem. of me, Lk. 22:19 ro.

3. We have not really seen entirely miss., hv. dest. until ... in light of pl. sign on skyline.
   - There, emp. thr. hv. & earth, outstr. form, hands uplifts in pr. of reconcil., Lk. 23:34.
   - Beyond, gates of Par. swing open, angels wele., returng. Son of G., redm. mult. follong.
   - All around us, lost, unrec. ... "We are amb.," 2 Cor. 5:20; pl. sign spks., 2 fold msg.:

## I. What does it say to the unreconciled?

1. The atong. wk. of Christ is "finished," chasm. bridged, way open to throne of grace.
   - Cf.: Completion of trans-cont. railway ... "It is fin.!"

2. The plus sign is still adding ... souls to household of G.
   (1) Makes men bro. thru fatherh. of G., Jno. 1:12; not all are "sons," Mt. 23:8,9; Jn. 8:44.
   (2) Unites hostile elements by only tie th. truly binds.
      - Cf.: Eng. soldier & Arab warrior meet at tomb of Jesus.

3. The reconcils. Christ is still at wk.; ancient invit. stands: "Be ye recone. to G.!"
   (1) He purifies as He recone.; sinner not lifted in filthin. to holy bosom of Hv. Father.
      - Cf.: Dr. Samuel Chadwick meeting w. infidels.
   (2) He pays as He recone.; gave life "a ransom for many." Mk. 10:45.
      - Cf.: Pastor hopelessly in debt finds bills pd. ... "Jesus pd. it all ...!"

## II. What does it say to the reconciled?

1. "He hath rec. us" (Paul); we are "redeemed," 1 Peter 1:18; "cleansed," 1 Jn. 1:7.
   - P. borrows fr. vocab. of slave mkt. -- not "agorazo" but "ex-ag.," Gal. 3:13.

2. "He hath committed unto us the wd. of recone."
   (1) Our supreme task: interp. "Livg. Pl. Sign," introd. unres. to recone. Christ.
   (2) Our motive, th. of Apost.: "We can not but speak," Ac. 4:20.
   (3) The great divine embarr.: shortage of dedic. m. & w. to bear witn.
   (4) The most rewardg. hum. endr. ... "wise," Prov. 11:30; "shine forever," Dan. 12:3.

Concl.: Somethg. intensely pers. about th. cross, demandg. resp. fr. each.
   1. To the unrec. it says, "Come, be recone.!"
   2. To the recone.: "Go, tell others!" Of 31,102 vs. in Bible, none more urgent than 2 Cor. 5:20.

# 1

# The Living Plus Sign

II Corinthians 5:14-15, 17-20

*Now then we are ambassadors for Christ, as though God did beseech you by us: we pray you in Christ's stead, be ye reconciled to God.—II Corinthians 5:20*

> "On a hill far away stood an old rugged cross,
> The emblem of suffering and shame.
> But I love that old cross, where the dearest and best
> For a world of lost sinners was slain."

1. *We have not really seen the cross of Christ, until we have seen it as a great plus sign* by which God and man are drawn together in holy reconciliation.

*Above* that cross, a loving Heavenly Father is bending down from His throne and offering the hand of reconciliation to an estranged human family. *Beneath* that cross is the great, confused mass of blundering, sinning, suffering humanity, alienated from God, lost in ways of its own choosing, and divided by those innumerable barriers which sin sets up. *Upon* that cross, in the form of a living plus sign, is the quivering, bleeding body of the Son of God, the Great Reconciler, who has "broken down the middle wall of partition between us . . . that He might reconcile both unto God in one body by the cross" (Eph. 2:14, 16).

2. *We have not really seen Christ until we have seen Him as the Christ of the cross.*

It is thus, primarily, that we see Him through the eyes of

13

Peter, who knew Him so well and loved Him so devotedly,
and who emphasizes, not His prepossessing personality, His
superior mind, His magnificent character, His lofty ethics, or
His flawless life, but His atoning death! It is thus, primarily,
that we see Him through the eyes of Paul, who emphasizes, not
the Christ of the wayside, the seaside, the synagogue, or the
market place, but the Christ of the cross (I Cor. 2:2). It is
thus, primarily, that Christ Himself desires to be remembered.
How did He spend that last evening with the disciples before
His death? Significantly, He did not devote those briefly precious moments to a review of His life, but to a preview of His
death; not to the Sermon on the Mount, but to the *Sacrifice*
on the Mount. "This is my body which is given for you: this
do in remembrance of me. . . . This cup is the New Testament
in my blood, which is shed for you" (Luke 22:19-20). Thus it
is the Christ of the cross, primarily, whom we memorialize
in the Lord's Supper "till he come."

3. *We have not really seen our earthly mission or our heavenly destiny until we have seen it in the light of the cross,* that
great plus sign on the sky line of Calvary.

There, suspended between heaven and earth, is the Living
Plus Sign, the throbbing, outstretched form of the Son of God,
with hands uplifted in that holy prayer of reconciliation,
"Father, forgive them, for they know not what they do" (Luke
23:34). Beyond the cross, behold the gates of Paradise swinging
open, while the angels sing their welcome to the returning,
thorn crowned, crucified, but resurrected and glorified Son of
God! And who are those that follow in His train? They are
sinners all, but sinners cleansed, forgiven, reconciled! To such
a high destiny we move, as the people of God; but all around
us are the lost, the unreconciled, in whom we have a great
uncompleted mission to fulfill. Nowhere is the earthly mission
of God's people more perfectly expressed than in the words
of the apostle, "Now then we are ambassadors for Christ, as
though God did beseech you by us: we pray you in Christ's
stead, be ye reconciled to God" (II Cor. 5:20). To all alike,

the reconciled and the unreconciled, the great plus sign speaks. Its *twofold message* is the hope of the world:

### I. WHAT DOES IT SAY TO THE UNRECONCILED?

1. *The atoning work of Christ is finished.* The chasm between the sinfulness of man and the holiness of God has been bridged. The way is thrown open for the lowliest of sinners to come to the throne of grace and receive cleansing and forgiveness.

It was a great day in American history, when the first transcontinental railway was completed. A memorable occasion was planned for the laying of the last rail and the last tie, and the driving of the last spike, out on the western frontier where the project was brought to completion. On the appointed day, after elaborate preparations, with due publicity, a large crowd gathered for the concluding ceremonies. When the last spike had been driven, the assembled crowd broke into applause, while reporters who had tapped the telegraph wires flashed the good news to the world. The great feat had been accomplished, spanning the continent from coast to coast! That was indeed a great day. But it was a far greater day when the reconciling Christ, with cruel spikes driven through His hands and feet, cried out from the cross, "It is finished!" Now angels could flash the news to the ends of the earth, and sinners can forever rejoice, "It is finished!"

2. *The great plus sign is still adding!* Unceasingly it is adding souls to the household of God.

(1) It makes men brothers through the only means by which the brotherhood of man is ever to be achieved, namely, through the fatherhood of God. There is a sense in which all the sons of men are the sons of God; but in the prevailing New Testament sense not all the sons of men are the sons of God, by any means. Only "as many as received *Him,* to them gave he the power to *become* the sons of God" (John 1:12). And when, through the new birth, two men have become sons of

God, they have by the same token become brothers to one another. To a mixed company of believers, Jesus said, "All ye are brethren . . . one is your Father, which is in heaven" (Matt. 23:8-9). To a group of unbelievers, Jesus said, "Ye are of *your* father, the devil" (John 8:44).

(2) The Living Plus Sign unites hostile elements by the only tie that truly binds. After the first World War, the Arabs in Palestine and the British soldiers of the army of occupation generally regarded one another as mortal enemies. One of the British soldiers, a devout Christian, visited the reputed tomb of Jesus. As he approached the tomb he was startled to note, just inside the opening, a tall swarthy Arab warrior, with hands folded in deep meditation. The British soldier waited, not wishing to intrude, and not knowing what might happen next. When finally the Arab warrior turned to leave the tomb, their eyes met. The Englishman extended his hand and uttered one word, "Jesus!" The Arab took his hand and responded with the Arabic equivalent of "Jesus." It was a warm, lingering handshake. Not one further word was spoken, but both men realized that they were brothers, sons of the same Father, servants of the same Master.

3. *The reconciling Christ is still at work;* the ancient invitation still stands: "be ye reconciled to God!"

(1) He purifies as He reconciles. The sinner could never, in the filthiness of his unforgiven state, be lifted to the holy bosom of the Heavenly Father. Helpless and hopeless, he must look to the reconciling Christ. Samuel Chadwick of Leeds, England, once announced a service for infidels only. A large crowd came. They would not sing or join in prayer, and the preaching was under constant heckling. After the service, Dr. Chadwick invited any who were interested in further discussion to meet him in the vestry. Nineteen men followed. After long and apparently fruitless discussion, Dr. Chadwick said, "Suppose we grant your philosophy to be sufficient for the man who has moral character, social position, economic sufficiency and domestic happiness; what will you do for the man who has none of these, whose life has been wrecked by the ravages of

wrong living, and from whom all hope has departed?" The lawyer who had become spokesman for the group arose, offered his hand to the minister, and said, "I would bring him to you, Dr. Chadwick; for you have his only hope." What a tribute to the redeeming, reconciling Christ!

(2) He pays as He reconciles. What the sinner in his bankrupt state could never do for himself, Christ does on his behalf. He gave His life, "a ransom for many" (Mark 10:45). A pastor came to a new realization of this fact through an almost fatal illness. When he had recovered to the point where he could barely walk again, he became concerned about the staggering bills that had been piling up. There had been two nurses and two or three doctors, costly prescriptions, and other extraordinary expenses. But in all those weeks of illness he had, of course, paid nothing. He walked to the nearby business district of his little town, and stopped first at the druggist. When he asked about his account, the druggist opened the old fashioned ledger and showed him a long list of items. "You see, it's a big bill," said the druggist. "Yes," said the preacher, weakly, "I was afraid of that. I can't pay now, but I will pay just as soon as I can." Then the druggist removed his hand from the bottom of the page, and the preacher saw in big, red letters the word PAID. His deacons had paid the bill. He went to two other places where huge bills had been accumulating. Every debt had been paid. As he walked home, overwhelmed with gratitude, he began singing in his heart, "Jesus paid it all, all to Him I owe; sin had left a crimson stain, He washed it white as snow."

The great plus sign on the skyline of Calvary speaks again.


### II. WHAT DOES IT SAY TO THE RECONCILED?


1. *"He hath reconciled us,"* says the Apostle Paul. We are "redeemed," says the Apostle Peter, not "with corruptible things, as silver and gold . . . but with the precious blood of Christ, as of a lamb without blemish and without spot" (I Peter 1:18-19). We are "cleansed," says the Apostle John, not by the

exemplary life of Christ, but by his sacrificial death, not by
His lofty teachings, but by "the *blood* of Jesus Christ" (I John
1:7).

In speaking of our redemption, the apostle Paul borrows
from the vocabulary of the slave market of his day. Some of us
have vivid memories of the old market place of horse and
buggy days. The first Monday of each month was the traditional
"Trade Day," when every farmer with livestock to sell or trade
would bring it to the public square in the county seat. Here,
a mule offered for sale would be tied to the hitching rail,
where he might stand for hours in the broiling sun. Prospective
purchasers might open his mouth to determine his age, prod
him in the flanks, drive him around in a gallop to make sure
that he was sound of wind, and then perhaps decide that he
would not do. This might be done repeatedly before a purchaser was found, and next year the mule might be returned
to the same place, and subjected to the same experience. In
the slave traffic of Paul's day, the usual word for such a
purchase was *agoradzo* (from *agora,* meaning "market place").
But, in speaking of our redemption, Paul uses the much
stronger term *ex-agoradzo,* which suggests the finality of our
redemption, our permanent removal *out of the market place*
(Gal. 3:13).

2. *"He hath committed unto us the word of reconciliation."*
Our supreme task is to interpret that Living Plus Sign and to
introduce our unreconciled, unforgiven friends to the reconciling Christ. Our motivation is that of the first century, "We
cannot but speak the things which we have seen and heard"
(Acts 4:20). The great divine embarrassment is the prevailing
shortage of dedicated men and women to bear witness. How
shamefully casual we often are! "I don't want to be tied down."
How familiar that sounds! Our Lord was willing not only to
be tied down, but to be *nailed to the cross,* for our redemption.
"Love so amazing, so divine, demands my soul, my life, my all!"
The most rewarding of all human endeavors is that of introducing others to the reconciling Christ. "He that winneth
souls is wise" (Prov. 11:30); and "they that be wise shall shine

as the brightness of the firmament, and they that turn many to righteousness, as the stars for ever and ever" (Dan. 12:3). Without a doubt, the sweetest music in heaven will be reserved for those who have directed others into the great heavenly chorus of the redeemed.

There is something intensely personal about the cross. From each of us it calls for a response. To the unreconciled, it says, "Come—be reconciled!" To the reconciled, it says, "Go—tell others!" There are said to be 31,102 verses in the Bible. Not one could be more important than this: "Now then we are ambassadors for Christ, as though God did beseech you by us: we pray you in Christ's stead, be ye reconciled to God" (II Cor. 5:20). For the unreconciled, nothing could be more urgent than to heed this invitation. For the reconciled, nothing could be more urgent than to convey the invitation to others. It is the world's only hope.

# 2
# Slightly Soiled,
# Greatly Reduced in Price

*Who shall ascend into the hill of the Lord? or who shall stand in his holy place? He that hath clean hands, and a pure heart. . . .—Psalm 24:34*

1. On the bargain counter of the department store we sometimes find merchandise of the finest quality marked down to incredibly low prices. We pause and wonder. Such quality, such beauty of design, such workmanship—and so cheap! But closer examination reveals the truth, or perhaps a modest cardboard sign tells the story: "Slightly soiled, greatly reduced in price."

In the market of life we find much human material similarly marked down. Many of these people are gifted, cultured, and of high potential, but slightly soiled—in speech, in character, in reputation—and drastically reduced in worth. They are not ruined; but they are disqualified for the highest achievements; they are defeated in their noblest aspirations. The best to which they can ever attain is only second best to that which might have been, had they kept their hands clean and their hearts pure.

2. In the loss accounts of a department store there are items of merchandise which have been completely ruined or hopelessly damaged in handling; but far greater in the aggregate are the losses on merchandise which has become slightly soiled, and so greatly reduced in price as to turn a potential profit into an actual loss.

In the loss accounts of the Kingdom of God there are many reflections of the same principle. The great losses of the church do not come through the falling of its members into some foul, flagrant, shocking iniquity, but through the subtle intrusion of the sin that slightly soils. We have seen young people, and older people, who at first impression thrill the soul. Spontaneously, you exclaim, they are the finest ever! But on closer acquaintance you discover, they are slightly soiled—in the ways of the world—just enough to dim their Christian radiance, to muffle their Christian testimony, and to impair their Christian influence, so that singly or collectively they are a total loss to the Kingdom of God.

The suggested theme—"Slightly Soiled, Greatly Reduced in Price"—carries *warnings* to which the believer needs to be constantly alert.

### I. TO BECOME SLIGHTLY SOILED IS A REAL DANGER

1. *The sin that slightly soils is deadlier than it appears.*

(1) It is not the sin that completely destroys, but the sin that slightly soils, that we must learn to fear. It is not sin in the ugliness of its grosser forms, but sin in the attractiveness of its milder forms; not sin identified and labeled as to its true character, but sin in the guise of sweet innocence, like sugar-coated poison with its deadliness concealed.

(2) It is not Satan like "a roaring lion" (I Peter 5:8) with his hideousness revealed, but Satan in the guise of a good fellow who is going to show us how to have a good time. It is not the lions, the tigers, and the rattlesnakes, that we must learn to fear, but those tiny disease germs of which we have been victims again and again, and which carry thousands of persons to premature graves every year.

2. *The sin that slightly soils leaves no life unmolested.*

(1) There is no person so noble, so pure, so completely consecrated as to be beyond its reach. There is no profession so sacred or so sheltered as to be secure against its intrusion. Even the min-

istry is not without its pitfalls. Indeed, one minister declared that he had never been seriously tempted to profanity until he became pastor of a certain church and had to work with some of its difficult members.

(2) There is no environment so wholesome as to be secure against the stealthy infiltration of the sin that slightly soils. Even the Garden of Eden was not secure. As a teen-age boy growing up in a bakery, I was perfectly sure that the hardest place in which to live a consistent Christian life was the bakeshop. Further experience, on the farm and in the large cities, made it clear that there are no areas of safety. Every environment has its own peculiar temptations.

(3) There is no place so remote as to be beyond the reach of the baited hook. A friend returning from a fishing trip brought his pastor a beautiful specimen weighing between five and ten pounds. "Wonderful!" the pastor exclaimed, delightedly. "Where did you catch him?" "You would not believe me if I told you," the friend replied. "Try me!" said the pastor. "That fish," said the friend, "was caught about fifty miles out from Long Island, and brought up with a hook from a depth of about three hundred feet." It seems fantastic that this unwilling victim hiding in the depths of the sea, sheltered by a covering of three hundred feet of water, fifty miles from the normal habitation of man, should not have been safe. Again one is reminded, there are no areas of safety. "My soul, be on thy guard!"

3. *The sin that slightly soils often finds us unprepared for successful resistance.*

(1) Perhaps it is because our spiritual vitality is low. To live a pure, godly life in an impure, ungodly world is no small undertaking. The testing to which a Christian life is subjected is like walking down a long corridor in an atmosphere saturated with countless billions of invisible disease germs. If the lungs are sound, and the heart is strong, and the blood stream is healthy, the germs may be thrown off without serious consequences. But if the lungs are unsound, and the heart is weak, and the blood stream is without vitality, the outcome is likely

to be disastrous. And how does one develop a strong spiritual physique? The formula is much the same as for developing a strong body: plenty of good nourishment—the Word of God; plenty of wholesome exercise—Christian service; plenty of pure air—the atmosphere of prayer.

(2) Perhaps it is through want of spiritual discernment that we go down in defeat. Some are inclined to count as wrong only that which is inherently wicked, vicious, or degrading. Some can distinguish between white and black, but not between white and the varying shades of gray. This is particularly true in regard to border line pleasures.

The proper test is not whether it offends my conscience, which may be unillumined, or dulled from long neglect or abuse; not whether it violates my understanding of Scripture, which may be altogether too meager; not whether I am able to place my finger on the wrongness of it; not whether others are doing or condoning it: the majority is more often wrong than right on fine moral and spiritual discriminations.

More properly, let us apply the following tests to the questionable amusement: Would its free indulgence on the part of your pastor lower, ever so slightly, your regard for him as your spiritual teacher and leader? Would its free indulgence lessen your appetite for spiritual things, and dull your enthusiasm for participation in spiritual service and testimony? Would its free indulgence impair the tenderness of your conscience or the clearness of your spiritual discrimination? Would it weaken, ever so slightly, your possible influence as a soul-winner? If it offends in any of these points, however slightly, it has no proper place in the Christian life. Character will become slightly soiled, and usefulness heavily discounted. "Be ye clean that bear the vessels of the Lord" (Isa. 52:11).

### II. TO BECOME SLIGHTLY SOILED
### WILL CERTAINLY REDUCE OUR WORTH

1. *Slight soiling may leave an indelible stain.* One may lose what one can never fully recover. A damaged reputation is hard to repair.

Years ago it became known of a certain beautiful and popular young lady that sometimes under provocation she would use profane language. With those who knew, she lost something of that dainty feminine charm that they had idealized in her, and which no young lady can afford to lose. One wonders, does she still use that kind of language when under provocation?

A brilliant student, in his zeal to maintain an A-plus standing, cheated on examination. The teacher never knew, and the student received a high grade as usual. But several fellow students had seen what was taking place at the examination, and have found it difficult to forget what they saw. The disturbing question remains, did that student carry into his professional life the disposition to cheat whenever the pressures were sufficiently strong?

A little group of soldiers, off duty, were standing on a street corner in the nearby town, exchanging yarns and having a good time, when a ministerial student came along. Being known to one of the soldiers, he joined the group and entered into the fun. Presently he contributed to the merriment with a little jingle which was clever and humorous, but as vulgar as it was clever. Ten years later, at a large convention, one of the soldiers was among the audience, and it happened that the man reading the Scripture lesson was that former ministerial student, now an honored pastor. As the former soldier recognized him, he instantly remembered that vulgar little jingle, and could not quite put the words out of his mind as he tried to listen to the Scripture reading from a minister who was "slightly soiled" in speech.

2. *Slight soiling may involve outright defeat.* Trifles often fix the course of human destiny, and trifles may make or break an individual who is living with a high purpose.

A young preacher with a fine personality, popular, capable, and well trained had just one objectionable habit. He had spent seven long, hard years in college and seminary preparing for his life work. Now he was graduating. An attractive pastorate was open to him. A large, strong church was asking for confidential references concerning him. The whole truth had to be told. All was favorable, except the unfortunate fact that he smoked. He did not get the call. He wondered why. Some of the church members, who did not wish their growing boys to become addicted to smoking, were unwilling to call a pastor who would set the wrong example. "Let us lay aside every *weight*," as well as "the *sin* which doth so easily beset us" (Heb. 12:1). No one is so gifted, so strong, so capable, that he can afford to encumber his Christian life with so much as one unnecessary "weight."

One of our national heroes, who thrilled our nation as it has rarely been thrilled, was the young aviator Charles Lindbergh. Suppose he had been at less than his best when he undertook that memorable flight across the Atlantic by which he became world famous! In the terrific strain of those thirty-three and one-half hours alone day and night maneuvering that frail airplane through space, suppose his mind had been dulled, or his heart weakened, or his physical endurance depleted by dissipation! An ordinary Lindbergh, with ordinary powers and an ordinary airplane, could never have borne the strain, but would have come to an untimely end in the depths of the sea. Extraordinary achievement is only for the *extraordinary* person, with *extraordinary* powers, grounded in *extraordinary* purity.

Suppose the Virgin Mary had been just slightly soiled! When God was searching the whole world over for that one young woman who was most pure, most worthy to become, on the human side, the mother of the Son of God, would he have chosen such a one? Never! There were lesser things to which she might have attained, but the supreme honor would never have been hers.

### III. TO RESIST BECOMING SLIGHTLY SOILED
### CALLS FOR POWERFUL DEFENSES

1. *One powerful defense is in strong affirmative living.* Every vice is but the absence of some virtue. Cultivate the virtues, and the vices fall away, like dead leaves falling before the oncoming growth of new leaves. Learn to say "yes" to Christ in all things, and it will not often be necessary to say "no" to the world. A life filled with the right things is fairly secure against the intrusion of the wrong.

Christianity is not a pale-blooded system of negatives, but a red-blooded challenge to join a great Leader, to take up a great cause, and to fill the life with a great program. "I am come that they might have life, and that they might have it more abundantly" (John 10:10). This "abundant life" is a life filled to overflowing with the privileges, responsibilities, and compensations of godly living.

The goodness which is required of us is not the goodness of the wooden Indian, who stands out in front of the store the year round, in every kind of weather, and never does a wrong thing, and never does anything else. Our defense is in positive, outgoing, achieving goodness which leaves no room, no time, no thought, and no energy for that which slightly soils.

2. *A further defense is in the cultivation of worthy friendships.* To a remarkable degree we mold and are in turn molded by our friends.

Great men and women are usually produced in clusters. A common ideal binds them together, and they grow together—inspiring, strengthening, and building one another. Thus, at the heart of every church and every Christian institution, in its golden years, there is a small cluster of dedicated men and women standing together, and encouraging one another to good works (Heb. 10:24). And at the source of all great forward movements in Christianity we find a cluster of spiritual giants. One person may start a movement, but he can not carry it through without the enlistment of a cluster of kindred spirits.

Friendships develop on the basis of congeniality. The fellowship of like-minded believers is one of the richest gifts of God and a mighty source of strength in times of testing. Many a Christian has been saved from falling by being in the right crowd. But "be not conformed to this world" (Rom. 12:2). The secret of popularity is conformity. To be popular with that great unwashed, worldly-minded majority which predominates in high school and college, in factory and office, our purest and finest young people would have to adopt the unspiritual ways of the crowd, drink its cocktails, and share in its dubious pleasures, pastimes, and practices. But thank God, in every city, every town, every community, there is a precious minority, like flowers growing among the rocks, with whom one may be exceedingly popular without the necessity of becoming slightly soiled. Choose your crowd!

3. *Our ultimate defense is of course the resourceful partnership of Jesus.*

(1) In the hour of crisis, when our own defenses break down, and other helpers fail, one hope remains. "I need Thee every hour; stay Thou near by; temptations lose their power when Thou art nigh." Truer words were never put in rhyme or set to music. Not only in the hour of conscious temptation is He our refuge, but in those crucial hours of suffering, sorrow, and danger which have swept so many off their feet.

(2) Before the hour of crisis, the decisive steps are taken and the outcome of the crisis predetermined. In quiet moments of unhurried contemplation, the heart and life are thrown open to the Lordship and Saviorhood of Christ and his everlasting partnership. "I will never leave thee, nor forsake thee" (Heb. 13:5). Thus reinforced, the soul is made ready for emergencies, and begins laying up spiritual reserves for the unknown future.

General Stonewall Jackson did not choose the name "Stonewall," by which he is known in history; but he earned it. He was a deeply spiritual man; he never went into battle without prayer; he never failed to thank God publicly for victory. In one of the great battles of the Civil War, when the battle line was wavering, General Bee rallied his South Carolinian troops with that memorable challenge, "Look at Jackson—there he stands like a stone wall!" His serenity in battle was almost incredible. How did he secure it? His Negro attendant who took care of his horse and the related chores declared, he could always tell when the General was "going on an expedition," by the added time which he spent in his prayer hideout. Thus the battle may be won before the battle begins!

The King's business requires clean hands.

The surgeon would not think of putting unclean hands in the vitals of his patient. The believer who would attain to his highest and best must pay the price in terms of dedication and purity of life. The Psalmist David, toward the close of his life, had one great ambition—to build a magnificent temple unto his Lord. But David was denied the fulfillment of his dream, as God said, in effect: "No—not you, David—there is blood on your hands" (I Chron. 22:8). Unfortunately, there was a stain which time had not erased from his record.

The Lord Jesus, the strongest of the strong, the purest of the pure, remains our incomparable ideal. From beginning to end he was as a "lamb without blemish and without spot" (I Peter 1:19). He could not have lifted the world with unclean hands, nor inspired the world with an unclean tongue, nor ennobled the world with an unclean life. In loving reference to his disciples, he said, "For their sakes I sanctify myself" (John 17:19). And the hands which he laid upon the blind, the lame, the leper, the deaf and the speechless, tenderly restoring them, were clean hands! The hands which he gently laid upon the little children, and with which he broke the bread and blessed the multitudes, were clean hands! The hands with which he stilled the sea and with which he beckoned Lazarus from the grave were clean hands! The hands which he lifted up in prayer, calling down the power of heaven, were clean hands! And finally, the hands which were nailed to the cross for the sins of the world, were clean hands!

> "See, from His head, His hands, His feet,
>     Sorrow and love flow mingled down:
> Did e'er such love and sorrow meet,
>     Or thorns compose so rich a crown?
>
> "Were the whole realm of nature mine,
>     That were a present far too small;
> Love so amazing, so divine,
>     Demands my soul, my life, my all."

# 3
# Living above the Snake Line

Isaiah 40:9-11, 28-31

1. *Naturalists tell of an invisible line—real, definite, unchangeably fixed, at a given altitude above sea level—known as the "snake line."* We are told that in certain mountainous areas in New England one of the first questions of a prospective purchaser of a farm is likely to be: "Is this farm above the snake line?" Below that line there may be deadly reptiles, imperiling man and beast; above that line no snake can live. Below that line an unsuspecting child or an unwary adult might fall victim to one of these deadly reptiles; above, they may move about in untroubled security.

The upper altitude is kept securely inviolate not by visible defenses or man-made barriers but by an immutable mandate of the living God, dating back to the creation of the reptile world, in which God said in effect, "Hitherto shalt thou come, but no further!" Security is purely a matter of altitude: pitch camp below the snake line, and invite possible disaster; pitch camp above the snake line, and be safe!

2. *Scripture suggests a line similar to the "snake line" of the naturalists,* which marks the division between a lower and an upper *spiritual* altitude. Below, the soul is never secure against the molestations of Satan, that wily reptile, that deceiver and destroyer of souls; above, Satan can not come. Below, there is spiritual depletion, spiritual poverty, weariness, exhaustion, and

29

collapse; above, there is spiritual replenishment, spiritual abundance, security and endurance.

The upper altitude is suggested in Paul's reference to the blessedness of sitting "in heavenly places in Christ Jesus" (Eph. 2:6); and in his exhortation, "If ye then be risen with Christ, seek those things which are above, where Christ sitteth on the right hand of God. Set your affections on things above, not on things on the earth" (Col. 3:1, 2).

Similarly, the Prophet Isaiah speaks of God as dwelling "in the high and holy places with him also that is of a contrite and humble spirit. . ." (Isa. 57:15). There, near to the heart of God, "they that wait upon the Lord shall renew their strength; they shall mount up with wings as eagles; they shall run, and not be weary; and they shall walk, and not faint" (Isa. 40:31). This text is an invitation not merely to spend a holy hour in the upper altitude, above the spiritual snake line, but to pitch camp and abide. "Waiting upon the Lord" means more than an occasional climb to the upper altitude for a fleeting visit, an occasional coming up for air, or an occasional flight to the upper altitude for refuge. Instead, it calls for trustful abiding like that of the babe nestled in its mother's arms. The text suggests that there are two levels on which the Christian life may be lived or attempted, and draws attention to the *results* to be expected:

### I. THE SECURITY OF THE UPPER ALTITUDE

"They that wait upon the Lord shall renew their strength . . . mount up with wings as eagles . . . run, and not be weary . . . walk, and not faint."

1. *Here is the promise of more strength to endure the strains, temptations, and irritations of life.*

(1) Those inclinations of the flesh, those creeping things—like fear, hate, envy, wrath, impurity—which thrive in the lowlands, disappear in the open sunlight of the divine presence. One of the vivid recollections of my boyhood is that of walking barefooted with others along the banks of the creek and finding a

large, flat rock on the warm, soggy ground near the water's edge, and discovering the fantastic aggregation of tiny wriggling creatures that stirred underneath. There, hidden from the sunlight, the slimy surface of the muck was alive with innumerable creeping things. But when the stone was lifted there was a frantic scurrying for cover, and in a moment every creature had burrowed into the darkness beneath the surface. To catch these creatures and dispose of them one by one would have been unthinkable; yet, to dispose of the whole aggregation required only a moment of open sunlight.

The way to deal with our many sins is not to struggle with them singly, but to let the light of heaven into the soul. The way to acquire the Christian graces is not to strive for them one at a time, but to open the heart and life to the Holy Spirit. Then, simultaneously, the nine-fold "fruit of the Spirit" makes its appearance: "love, joy, peace, longsuffering, gentleness, goodness, faith, meekness, temperance" (Gal. 5:22, 23).

(2) Those breakdowns which are so common in the lowlands are no problem in the upper altitude. "They shall run and not be weary," though others are falling exhausted by the wayside. "They shall walk and not faint," though others are breaking down. Those who lived through the great depression of the early thirties know something about hard times and fainting spirits. New York papers reported that on a single day, on Manhattan Island alone, eighty-eight persons had taken their own lives. In dark despair some had taken poison, others had turned on the gas, still others had leaped from tall buildings, or cast themselves in front of on-rushing subway trains. But in the midst of the human misery of those days there were those who bore their losses and sorrows without breaking under the load.

One prosperous business man in the metropolitan area had lost his business, his home, and his liquid assets, and was left deeply in debt besides. He was a deacon in his church, also a Sunday School teacher, and head usher. On Sunday mornings he continued in his place with the usual cheerful greeting, and again on Sunday evening, and at the midweek services. Casual acquaintances would never suspect that he had suffered financial reverses, and close acquaintances never ceased to marvel at the fortitude with which he faced economic disaster. How could he do it! The answer lay in his close fellowship with his Lord and the daily renewal of his strength. He was like that spring in the desert valley which never ceases to flow, even through the longest drouth, because it is mysteriously fed by the inexhaustible waters of some distant mountain lake.

2. *Here is the promise of more calmness of soul in the time of trial.* The strong do not tremble. Fortified by continuous "renewal," the soul is adequate. "The Lord is the strength of my life; of whom shall I be afraid?" (Ps. 27:1).

"In quietness and in confidence shall be your strength" (Isa. 30:15). But how can a person be quiet and confident walking in the fog of the lowlands, out of step with God, alone in his struggles, conscious of the disapproval of God, and apprehensive of His descending judgments! Is not our want of serenity the index to our spiritual altitude, the reflection of our unbelief and want of commitment?

In total commitment, and nothing less, is complete serenity to be found. "I beseech you therefore, brethren, by the mercies of God, that ye present your bodies [present yourselves bodily] a living sacrifice, holy, acceptable to God, which is your reasonable service" (Rom. 12:1). Accept the total pattern of godly living. Live by principle—not by impulse, convenience, emotion, or the mood of the moment. No commitment means no serenity; partial commitment means partial serenity; full commitment means full serenity.

3. *Here is the promise of more freedom from struggle.* The strong do not struggle.

(1) Most of our struggles and consequent failures are due to low altitude. The outcome of our testings is determined not by latitude but by altitude. There were saints in the wicked city of Ephesus (Eph. 1:1), and there were sinners in the Garden of Eden (Gen. 3). In a given environment one person finds serenity, while another is kept in constant agitation and struggle. The one lives on the high altitude where "it is well with my soul"; the other is living below the "snake line." A little girl coming

in from the flower garden with soiled hands, dress, and shoes, made this refreshing observation: "Mother, I know why flowers grow; they want to get up out of the dirt." Saints grow spiritually tall by stretching toward higher and higher altitudes.

(2) Most of the characteristic triumphs of believers are achieved not in combat, but in the avoidance of combat. Even the Archangel Michael would not venture into combat with Satan, but said, "The Lord rebuke thee" (Jude 9)! Occasionally an unseasonable frost will strike when fruit orchards are in full bloom. Fruit farmers may struggle day and night to save the crop, by means of smudge pots and smoke screens. But, as one experienced fruit farmer pointed out, the freeze that kills the fruit in the valley will often leave the blossoms on the uplands completely unharmed. The "freeze line" and the "snake line" seem to have something in common.

There is a better strategy than the strategy of struggle. One of our famous airmen, about the close of World War I, landed his frail craft at Kobar, Arabia. Here a large rat managed to get into his airplane. The airman became aware of its presence when he was in mid-air and heard the sound of gnawing behind him. Alarmed by the threat of disaster, he remembered that rats can not live in high altitudes. Accordingly, he nosed his plane upward until breathing was difficult; and when at length he descended to a lower level the gnawing had ceased, and upon landing he found that the rat had died.

There is a better place to win our battles than in the area of combat with the enemy. Rarely has a trial judge been put to so severe an ordeal as that to which Judge Harold R. Medina was subjected in the famous trial of eleven Communists in 1949. By every conceivable device, the defense attorneys and the defendants and their Communist sympathizers tried to wear the judge down and to goad him to some intemperate remark or judicial error that might bring about a mistrial or an ultimate reversal of the verdict. Daily, for the duration of the trial, which lasted nine months, picket lines paraded before the court house, shouting abuse at the judge. At home he received threats of violence. And in the court room the defendants refused to cooperate; and the defense lawyers, working in relays, kept up a bombardment of unreasonable questions and objections. At times the uproar was so great that the judge abruptly recessed the court. Throughout the trial, the judge maintained, with incredible patience, his judicial dignity. What was the secret of his serenity? Besides his customary daily prayer life, the judge bears eloquent testimony to those moments of refuge behind the scenes—away from the arena of battle—where he communed with his Lord. In regard to one of those crises, he declared, "That brief period of communion with my Maker saved my life and saved the trial."

Truly, "they that wait upon the Lord shall renew their strength." But what about those who do *not* "wait upon the Lord," and do *not* "renew their strength," and do *not* mount up with wings as eagles?" There is a grim alternative:

## II. THE INSECURITY OF THE LOWER ALTITUDE

1. *The eagle is well aware of the perils of the lowlands.* While he may have to forage for a living in the lowlands, he builds his nest in the high cliffs beyond the reach of invasion from the reptile world. He does not needlessly expose himself, and does not spend his leisure time defending his life against hazards from which the upper altitudes are free.

2. *The aviator is constantly warned against the peril of low flying.* Want of alertness at this point has accounted for many disasters. An army bomber, flying over fog-shrouded New York City at about four miles a minute, crashed into the 79th floor of the Empire State Building. Thirteen persons were killed, and in addition to the destruction of the airplane there was property damage of about half a million dollars. After an exhaustive inquiry into the cause of the crash, there was only one answer: The plane was flying too low! There was no adverse weather condition, and no malfunctioning on the part of the plane; but the required altitude of at least five thousand feet above the city had not been maintained.

3. *The Christian needs to realize the peril of low altitude.*

(1) A man's associations generally reveal his spiritual altitude. Kindred spirits gravitate together, and on each level a person will find himself in associations congenial to his own spirit. Wholesome associations raise favorable presumptions as to what a man is, while *un*wholesome associations raise correspondingly *un*favorable presumptions. Although such presumptions are not always valid, and "guilt by association" has been rightly condemned as a basis of judgment, unwholesome associations often provide important clues in the detection of crime. "Blessed is the man that walketh not in the counsel of the ungodly, nor standeth in the way of sinners, nor sitteth in the seat of the scornful" (Ps. 1:1).

(2) A man's associations may determine his conduct, his character, and his destiny. Those are our best friends in whose presence we can be our best selves. And when a good man gets into bad company, he generally ceases to be a good man. A heartbroken mother, appealing to the judge on behalf of her son who had been convicted of crime, kept repeating, "He is such a good boy; he just got into bad company!" She did not realize that when a good boy gets into bad company, he ceases to be a good boy; and when a good girl gets into bad company, she ceases to be a good girl. "Evil communications corrupt good manners" (I Cor. 15:33). Even so stalwart a saint as the Apostle Peter could not maintain his spiritual integrity while sitting among the enemies of Christ, but shamefully denied his Lord (Mark 14:66-72).

(3) A man's associations may be his making or his undoing. For the aspiring Christian who has moved up to high ground, the fellowship of kindred spirits is one of the choicest gifts of God, and one of the most powerful safeguards to Christian living. But the old associations, below the "snake line," must be forever broken. One man who had been redeemed from a life of drunkenness and sin, and who had set an inspiring example of Christian living for more than a year, fell back into his former loathsome state, to the astonishment and dismay of his Christian friends. They would not have been surprised if they had known that he was still parking his car every day in the same old place,

and walking past the open door of the same saloon which had been his downfall before. One moment of weakness, one more drink, and he was back in the old life!

There is something highly suggestive in one little phrase, often overlooked, in the Biblical account of the shipwreck of the Apostle Paul by the Island of Melita (Acts 28:1-6). Because of the cold, a fire was built for the comfort of the shipwrecked. As the Apostle Paul was laying a bundle of sticks on the fire, a deadly viper sprang out and fastened itself on his hand. By a miracle, Paul escaped harm; and he shook off the viper *"into the fire!"* There was finality in that gesture, and that viper would never jeopardize another life. Only by such finality can the defeated Christian move up from his precarious existence to the security "above the snake line." He cannot *drift* to higher ground; there must be finality in his break with the old and his commitment to the new.

The appeal of our text is not an appeal to make a few minor adjustments, to improve our manners, to lay aside a few vices which can be conveniently spared, or to develop a few minor virtues, but to move the whole of life to higher ground. Thus in one sweeping gesture a thousand problems are solved. Near to the heart of God there is one decisive principle: "Lord, what wilt thou have me to do?" Life built around this principle is life at its best. The divine imperative is not merely to "lay aside the *sin* which doth so easily beset us," but to lay aside "every *weight*" as well (Heb. 12:1). The "weights" may often be as damaging to the Christian life as the "sins."

Some boys climbing in the high cliffs along the shore of Nova Scotia came upon an eagle's nest. In it were some tiny baby eagles. One of these, they took home with them and placed it with a mother hen and her tiny chicks. Here the little pet grew; but, becoming more and more unlike the chicks, he began to stand alone in the barnyard looking up toward the sun. In the course of time he would try his wings, flopping along the ground. One day as he was standing in the sunlight as usual, another eagle flew over the barnyard. The pet eagle became strangely agitated. Standing on tiptoes, he unfolded his wings, and with a strange cry he rose from the ground, higher and higher, and presently disappeared from sight. It was a great day in the life of that eagle when he discovered that he was not made to be an ordinary barnyard fowl, to spend his life scratching in the dirt, but that his place was up there in the heavenly blue. And what a day for the defeated Christian when he comes into his true inheritance and takes his place in the intimate fellowship of the Heavenly Father, in the sweet security of those who truly "wait upon the Lord—" living above the "snake line!"

# 4

# The Hope of the Home

Ephesians 6:1-9

*Except the Lord build the house, they labor in vain that build it.—Psalms 127:1*

1. Except the Lord build the home, it becomes another little "Tower of Babel," a place of frustration, confusion, and disappointed hopes.

(1) Happy weddings do not insure happy homes. The sweetness of wedding bells, with a profusion of lovely gifts and showers of good wishes, is not enough.

(2) Sincere love on the part of the bride and bridegroom is not enough. Love may be misdirected, unsanctified, unblessed, and of uncertain duration.

(3) Pious mottoes placed by undedicated hands on undedicated walls of an undedicated house are not enough.

2. If the Lord build the home, it becomes a little bit of heaven. This is not too much to expect.

(1) Many centuries ago, as the wandering people of Israel were preparing to move into the Promised Land and set up housekeeping on a permanent basis, God gave them a clear pattern of procedure, and directed that they be diligent in compliance, "that your days may be multiplied, and the days of your children . . . as the days of *heaven upon the earth*" (Deut. 11:21). What more could He have said to encourage godliness and insure the stability of the home!

(2) Jesus, the Bringer of joy who honored with His presence the wedding of Cana in Galilee (John 2:1-11), always comes to the wedding when properly invited; He never comes empty-handed; and He does not lose interest in the bridal pair when the wedding is over. Happy is the home that is made congenial to His presence, and in which the family can truthfully declare: "Christ is the Head of this house, the unseen Guest at every meal, the silent listener to every conversation."

3. A home of divided allegiance is a "house divided against itself" (Matt. 12:25).

(1) Such a home is never congenial to the presence and operation of the Holy Spirit, and the development of the "fruit of the Spirit," which is "love, joy, peace, longsuffering, gentleness, goodness, faith, meekness, temperance." The most casual visitor can sense the spiritual atmosphere of the home. This is particularly true if the visitor is making a call with a spiritual objective. A young pastor in his first pastorate was calling on all the families of his church, with a special concern for uncommitted members of the household. One of his first visits was made at a home in which the husband was not a professed Christian. When the pastor came to the door the husband promptly disappeared. The wife was embarrassed and ill at ease; the visit was fruitless and extremely brief, the pastor having quickly sensed that the Lord could do no "mighty works there because of . . . unbelief" (Matt. 13:58).

(1) Such a home is always subject to the descending judgments of God, and when one member suffers the whole family suffers. In our vernacular there is a familiar concession about people of dubious merit: "Yes, he is a good man—*when he is asleep.*" This appraisal can not possibly be true if the man is not a good man while awake. The presence of Jonah, whom God was chastening, was no less dangerous to the ship and the seamen when Jonah was asleep than when he was awake. Indeed, Jonah "was fast asleep" when that terrifying storm descended.

4. A home united in Christ is a house of hope. No tie so binds together the members of a family as for the household to be

anchored in Christ, the family united in the bonds of the Holy Spirit, worshiping the same Lord, cherishing the same faith, and moving to the same high destiny. No cleavage is so deep, so wide, and so tragic, as for one member to be traveling the high road of faith that leads to the heavenly home while the other is traveling the low road of unbelief that leads to a Saviorless, hopeless eternity. No Kingdom task is so urgent and so rewarding as to unite the family in Christ. And no safeguard is so effective to make the family hearth secure as are those two ancient God-given *safeguards*: the family altar and the family pew.

### I. THE FAMILY ALTAR

"These words, which I command thee this day, shall be in thine heart; and thou shalt teach them diligently unto thy children, and shalt talk of them when thou sittest in thine house, and when thou walkest by the way, and when thou liest down, and when thou risest up" (Deut. 6:6-7).

1. *The idea of a family altar has come down to us from the earliest days of recorded history.* In Old Testament times there was a literal altar built of stone. Upon this altar sacrifices were offered to God. Around this altar the family was taught the Word of God; here family prayers were offered. The divine intent was that the household should be saturated with the consciousness of God, as suggested in the text and the context of Deuteronomy 6:6-7. Worship and instruction in the things of the Lord was to be a family affair.

Today, in the well ordered Christian home, family worship answers to the same divine commandment. Since the atoning sacrifice of Christ, there is no sacrifice of burnt offerings, and therefore no literal altar of stone. But all the atmosphere and spiritual values of the old family altar are carried forward. The Word of God is taught and discussed, family prayers are held, and the things of the Lord are normal topics of family conversation. This means more than a brief, perfunctory saying of grace at the table. A small boy was asked whether in his home there were family prayers. The most that he could say was, "Yes, whenever we have company Daddy says grace at the table." What that household needed was a family altar.

2. *The value of the family altar has been confirmed by centuries of blessing.*

(1) The child is more likely to come to a saving knowledge of Christ, more likely to be "born again." He is likely to be better born and better nourished in the things of the Spirit. He is likely to be better prepared to live clean in the midst of delinquency, vandalism, cheating in school, and those adolescent escapades which break the hearts of parents.

A chaplain in an Arkansas penitentiary declared: "Out of 1700 convicts I found only one who was brought up in a home where they had an old-fashioned family altar. I have heard since that he was pardoned, as he was found innocent of the crime with which he had been charged."

(2) The family life is purified by the family altar. This is reflected not only within the four walls of the home, but in many outward manifestations as well. Family ideals will inevitably find expression. A public school teacher was making conversation with two little boys, twin brothers, who were enrolled in the first grade. "How old are you?" she asked. One of the boys naively replied, "When we are in school we are six years old; when we ride on the street car we are only five." The explanation, which the teacher immediately sensed, was this: They could not be enrolled in school if they were under six; and they could not ride free on the street car if they were over five. Their home was not a Christian home, and there was no family altar.

(3) The parents rise to nobler living around the family altar. Abraham was a godly patriarch, a "friend of God" (Isa. 41:8), a confidant of the angels (Gen. 18). Pioneering in the wilderness, he built altars "and called upon the name of the Lord" (Gen. 12:9). Five times, as he settled down with his household, he built an altar. But there seem to have been two serious lapses; twice there is no reference to an altar. The first instance

occurred in Egypt. Here, instead of being spiritually helpful to Pharaoh, as a spokesman for God, Abraham resorted to deceit, and as a result was virtually thrown out of Egypt with all that he possessed (Gen. 12:10-20). The second lapse occurred at Gerar (Gen. 21). Here, in the household of Abraham, there occurred a family row which has had bloody repercussions down to the present day. Abraham's wife, Sarah, who had been responsible for his taking a secondary wife, Hagar, the Egyptian handmaid of Sarah, now demanded that Hagar and her son Ishmael be expelled. Hagar and Ishmael went, but apparently they never forgave and never forgot. Today, after all the intervening centuries of bitter hatred, warfare, and bloodshed, the descendants of Ishmael, the son of Hagar, and of Isaac, the son of Sarah, are still in conflict. And all is traceable to a family row in the altarless household of Abraham at Gerar, nearly four thousand years ago!

3. *The urgency of the family altar could not be greater than in the present decade* of spiritual deterioration and shallowness, the commercialization of everything sacred, the wicked secularization of the Lord's Day, and the virtual banning of God from the public schools.

(1) No command of God is more emphatic than that of providing spiritual training in the home. "These words . . . shall be in thine heart; and thou shalt teach them diligently unto thy children. . . ." This command establishes the right of the child to receive instruction from his parents in the things of the Lord. Here is a responsibility which can not be evaded or set aside or delegated to others. "Bring them up in the nurture and admonition of the Lord" (Eph. 6:4). It is a fearful responsibility, for the body and mind and soul of the child, which a man or a woman assumes in choosing to become a parent. A recent survey drew attention to the tens of thousands of irresponsible fathers who each year, in utter unconcern, abandon their unborn children. As a footnote to these appalling statistics it might be pointed out that when the wrath of God breaks in judgment upon these unprincipled reprobates, it will be a terrible day of reckoning!

(2) No other institution can match the importance of the home as a means of bringing heaven to earth. Even the church, which did not come into existence until centuries later, can not relieve the home of its spiritual task. The church, at best, can command only a tiny fraction of the child's time, while the home's opportunity for access and influence is almost unlimited.

(3) No prospect could be more inviting than that of a dedicated Christian home with the favor of God upon it. Suppose each of the four million children born in our country every year could be born in a home like Joshua's—"As for me and my house, we will serve the Lord" (Josh. 24:15)! Suppose every home had a family altar, with every family praying daily, "Lord, what wilt Thou have me to do?" Truly, "the family that *prays* together *stays* together!"

Inseparably linked with the family altar is another safeguard of the family hearth:

## II. THE FAMILY PEW

"Let us consider one another to provoke unto love and to good works, not forsaking the assembling of ourselves together, as the manner of some is; but exhorting one another . . ."(Heb. 10:24, 25).

1. *An indispensable supplement to the family altar is the family pew.* Good men are largely "home made," having been brought up in homes of dedicated parents, generally with the support of the church. The home needs the church, and the church needs the home. Like heredity and environment, each plays a vital part; and the parent is largely responsible for both. The supreme evangelism is *family evangelism,* and this involves three elements:

(1) Family worship at home comes first. Family evangelism begins early—before the child reaches the age of accountability, and before the child understands what he learns. Scripture passages learned in early childhood are like money placed in

the bank at compound interest. Throughout life, these Scriptures will come up from the subconscious, and the person so trained will remember in critical moments that "it is written" (Matt. 4:4, 7, 10). The prayers heard and learned in childhood likewise become an imperishible resource. And the example of godly parents is often decisive in the life and destiny of the child. The parent is teaching even when he is unaware of it. The headmaster of a school in New England was telling about one of his students who apparently did not know a thing about grammar but who spoke excellent English. The student, when asked for an explanation, said he simply talked the way his parents did.

Let fathers and mothers be encouraged to begin early in acquainting the child with the Holy Scriptures. Let a Bible be given to the child before he is able to read it, with the explanation that it is something to read later and to love and treasure forever. Let parents be reminded that even the small child has an amazing capacity for reverence. "Except ye . . . become as little children, ye shall not enter into the kingdom of heaven" (Matt. 18:3).

(2) The Sunday School, traditionally paired with the family altar, gives powerful support in bringing up the child "in the nurture and admonition of the Lord." The godly parent finds in the Sunday School teacher a natural ally; and for the child the Sunday School is often decisive in leading to salvation and church membership. No memory of childhood is more gratefully recalled than that of being taken to Sunday School by godly fathers and mothers.

(3) The family pew is the ultimate step in family worship. The blessing of regularly sitting together as a family in the Lord's house, on the Lord's Day, with the Lord's people—under the illumination, stimulation, and discipline of the Word of God—can scarcely be exaggerated. For such a family there is no occasion for uneasiness on the part of the pastor. But for the home from which only a part of the family attends, there is reason for deep concern, in our generation of juvenile delinquency and broken homes. Let the family begin the Lord's Day with the family altar, then proceed to Sunday School, and

finally to the family pew. In many churches the saddest five minutes of the week are the five minutes just before the Sunday morning worship service, when the Sunday School is over and some misguided parents and teachers go home instead of leading the children to the crowning spiritual benefit of the morning, in the family pew.

2. *The family pew opens an additional channel of blessing, for which there is no substitute.* There are blessings which come through individual personal devotions and in no other way. Other blessings come only through family devotions. No plan of personal devotions, however diligently maintained, can compensate for the omission of family devotions. And no combination of personal devotions and family devotions can possibly compensate for the omission of public worship. All three channels must be kept open. All three are vital to the spiritual health of the individual, the exercise of his stewardship, and the ongoing life of the church.

3. *The family pew proclaims with convincing eloquence the spiritual state of the individual.* With the family regularly in place, it speaks of unity, faith, spiritual aspiration, and a receptiveness which says, "Speak, Lord; for thy servant heareth" (I Sam. 3.9). The empty pew speaks no less eloquently. Much more is involved than the neglecting of "the assembling of ourselves together" and the ministry of sharing to which we are called. The empty pew speaks of an undernourished, meagre Christian life, neglected prayer, Scripture, stewardship, and testimony. A neglected pew is almost never found in combination with faithfulness in these other areas.

*When do we begin with setting up these safeguards upon which the hope of the home so largely depends?* When two lives are joined in the holy bonds of marriage, how long should they wait before inviting the full blessing of God upon their home? Obviously, the first day together is the day to begin reading the Scriptures together and praying together as a team—audibly. To defer this beginning even one day is an error, and to wait longer is to set a pattern which may be difficult to correct. But suppose there is an embarrassing sense of inadequacy or unworthiness on the part of one or the other! And suppose a parent realizes that his life is not always consistent with his Christian profession, and the family knows it! Is silence the answer? By no means! Fortunately, the power to "bring up" the child spiritually is not dependent so much upon spiritual attainment and flawless conduct as upon the evidence of sincere endeavor on the part of the parent. The child quickly discerns the difference between sham and sincerity, and is not without some realization of his own deficiencies.

*How do we begin when one of the partners is unwilling?* A Christian young woman was married to a husband who was not a Christian. He was not a churchgoer, and he was engaged in a business that was incompatible with the things for which the church stands. The wife became deeply concerned about being "unequally yoked together" with an unbeliever (II Cor. 6:14), and about the future of their home. She tried to establish family prayers, but of course her husband was not interested. Finally, under much persuasion and because of his great love for her, he consented to read the daily Scripture passage if she would do the praying. This arrangement was followed for years; then he came to a transforming experience of saving grace. He was happy to tell what brought him to the Lord. It was nothing but this daily reading of the Scriptures, coupled with the prayers of his wife, backed by her example of consistent Christian living. In short, it was the "family altar!" And now he was ready for the family pew also!

"Textual" Sermons

# 5
# Looking toward the Light

II Corinthians 3:1-6, 17, 18

Text: *We all, with open face beholding as in a glass the glory of the Lord, are changed into the same image from glory to glory, even as by the Spirit of the Lord.—II Corinthians 3:18*

When we see ourselves in the mirror of God's Word, we become immediately aware of our spiritual imperfections and deficiencies. And when we compare our own likeness with that of the Son of God, the contrast is such as to humble the spirit and prompt us to cast ourselves afresh upon the mercy of God.

What we have so often felt, was dramatically expressed by a Negro soloist whom we heard some years ago at a convention. A Negro choir of about one hundred voices was singing, and this soloist was standing alone by the microphone, well to the front, and was filling in, again and again, with one fixed refrain: "Lord, God, forgive, and try me one more time!" When he had sung this refrain a few times, we knew his spiritual biography without needing to be told. We knew that he could not have sung what he was singing, with such deep feeling, without a background of profound spiritual experience. We knew that here was a man who realized what it was to be lost—without God, without hope—and to experience the saving, lifting, cleansing grace of God. But we knew that there were further chapters in his spiritual life—of falling again, and experiencing again the forgiveness of God. Humble and repentant, he pleads, "Lord, try me one more time!" Like that

49

soloist, we are without excuse, and our only appeal is to the grace of God. With all the light that we have, how poorly we do, even at best!

The Apostle John, apparently feeling as we have so often felt, exclaims: "Behold, what manner of love the Father hath bestowed upon us, that we should be called the sons of God" (I John 3:3)! Here is amazement, and humility, but exaltation as well. The Apostle does not leave us in a mood of discouraged introspection, but carries us to the pinnacle of inspiration as, in the following verse, he points to the glorious fulfillment of our destiny. "We shall be like him" (I John 3:2), conformed to the image of His Son (Rom. 8:29). But for the glory of this fulfillment, we must wait till "He shall appear." What about the meanwhile, with its weaknesses, inconsistencies, and short-comings?

The Apostle Peter, in the very last verse of his last epistle before his martyrdom, challenges the believer to "*grow* in grace, and in the knowledge of our Lord and Savior Jesus Christ" (II Peter 3:18). Be not content with smallness of spiritual stature, meagerness of spiritual understanding, mediocrity in spiritual service; but aim to "grow"!

The Apostle Paul is sounding a similar note in our text: "We all, with open face beholding as in a glass the glory of the Lord, are changed into the same image from glory to glory, even as by the Spirit of the Lord." That Christ-likeness which is the birthright of every true child of God, and that radiance which is the hallmark of mature Christian sainthood, are not attained by one quick, simple transaction, but by the progressive operation of *two simultaneous processes,* distinct and yet inseparable from one another:

### I. THE PROCESS OF BEHOLDING
("We all, with open face beholding . . .")

1. *Our text implies that we have the means of "beholding . . . the glory of the Lord."* God "left not himself without witness" (Acts 14:17) or without means of self-revelation.

(1) "Holy men of God spake as they were moved by the Holy Spirit" (II Peter 1:21), and thus we have the Holy Scriptures. Whatever else they may contain, of truth, beauty, and inspiration, they are given us primarily as a *revelation of God*. As such, they are to be read and studied and shared with others.

One of the most helpful testimonies that I ever heard from a brother minister was on this point. This aged minister, perhaps eighty years old, was addressing a group of us preachers, and said, "I've had a long and happy ministry; and, as some of you know, I have had large congregations. I was given of God a vivid historic imagination, and I made the most of it in my preaching. I would preach on Abraham, and the people would compliment me and declare that I had made Abraham so real that it was as though they had seen him in physical presence and had heard him speak and had seen his gestures. Thus encouraged, I would prepare a sermon on Isaac and receive the same compliments; then on Jacob, and they would tell me the same. And when I preached on Mary, Martha, and Lazarus, they would tell me that it was as though they themselves had made a Sunday morning visit in that little home in Bethany. All along, I thought I was doing the very utmost of which I was capable. But when I had been preaching for many years, by the grace of God I came to realize fully that the Bible was not given us as a revelation of Abraham and Isaac and Jacob, but as a revelation of the God of Abraham, of Isaac, and of Jacob; not as a revelation of Mary and Martha and Lazarus, but as a revelation of the *Savior* of Mary, Martha, and Lazarus. Now, when I am through preaching I want to know above all else that my people have seen the *hand of God* in the life of Abraham, or Isaac, or Jacob. And when I have preached on Mary and Martha and Lazarus, I want to be assured that my people have seen the *Savior* of Mary and Martha and Lazarus."

The perfect approach to the Scriptures, in the light of our text, is that of the devout carpenter who led his family every morning in family devotions, and who was overheard saying to himself audibly, as he reverently opened the old Book,

"Speak to me, Word of God, and tell me what my Lord has to say to me today."

(2) Besides the Holy Scriptures, we have another means of "beholding . . . the glory of the Lord." The Prophet Isaiah pointed the way many centuries ago: "They that *wait upon the Lord* shall renew their strength . . ." (Isa. 40:31). The fullness of blessing comes not to those who rush into the presence of the Lord and pour out their hearts in a torrent of petitions and then rush out again, but to those who "wait" in a spirit of unhurried communion with the Lord. A certain pastor who was particularly fond of the hymn, "Take Time to be Holy," would at times ask his congregation to modify the wording and to sing, "Take time to *behold Him.*" This is in the spirit of our text.

2. *Our text fixes the manner of our "beholding . . . the glory of the Lord."* We are to behold Him "with open face." What does this mean? A beautiful symbol of worship at its best is the ordinary sunflower as known in the Southwest. When the blossom is in its full vigor it has this interesting characteristic: It begins the day with its face open toward the rising sun; all day long it faces the sun as it passes overhead; and at evening time its open face is still toward the sun as it drops behind the horizon.

(1) By "beholding with open face," the Apostle evidently means worshiping with a complete readiness to see what the Lord seeks to reveal, and to hear what the Lord has to say, and to understand what He aims to communicate—in order to respond with every fiber of one's being. "He that willeth to do His will shall know . . ." (John 7:17). But God does not reveal Himself to unwilling eyes; He does not speak to unwilling ears; He does not come with salvation and blessing into an unwilling heart. "If he call thee . . . thou shalt say, Speak, Lord; for thy servant heareth" (I Sam. 3:9). This good counsel of the aged Eli to the boy Samuel three thousand years ago is still good. *"If ye continue in my word,"* says the Lord Jesus, "then are ye my disciples indeed; and ye shall know the truth, and the truth shall make you free" (John 8:31, 32).

(2) "Beholding with open face" carries the suggestion of worshiping with that spiritual discernment which comes only with the new birth. "Except a man be born again, he cannot see . . ." (John 3:3). There are so many things that one can not see until he is "born again." The only way to acquire the vision of an eagle, is to be born an eagle. The only way to acquire the understanding of a sheep, is to be born a sheep. The only way to acquire the discernment of a child of God, is to be born a child of God. "The natural man receiveth not the things of the Spirit of God . . . neither can he know them, because they are spiritually discerned" (I Cor. 2:14).

(3) "Beholding with open face" carries the further suggestion of worshiping with unblinking clarity of conscience. Any known sin, so long as it remains unconfessed, unremoved, and unforgiven, dims the vision and disqualifies the soul for effective petition or intercession. And sins of omission are no less deadly than sins of transgression. There is a principle in law to the effect that the plaintiff who brings a case before the court must come "with clean hands." He must himself be without guilt. This principle holds true in the court of heaven. "Who shall ascend into the hill of the Lord? or who shall stand in His holy place? He that hath clean hands, and a pure heart . . ." (Ps. 24:3, 4).

## II. THE PROCESS OF BECOMING
("We . . . are changed into the same image . . . .")

1. *The change is inevitable.* As we keep open the eyes of the soul toward "the Light of the world," we inevitably reflect that light, as the moon reflects the light of the sun. The radiance is not our own, but a reflection of the glory of God. It is not to our credit, but has been wrought "by the Spirit of the Lord." Our goodness is not our own. The Christian graces (love, joy, peace, longsuffering, gentleness, goodness, faith, meekness, temperance) are "the fruit of the *Spirit*" (Gal. 5:22). When a notoriously wicked man becomes clean, decent, and honest, people instinctively exclaim, "Thank God!" But why

thank God? Why not thank the man himself? Because we know, without needing to read it in the Scriptures, that "It is *God* which worketh in you both to will and to do his good pleasure" (Phil. 2:13). In other words, we never did a good thing in our lives except as God gave the prompting and provided the enablement. At best, we are like the three year old child who presented her father with a lovely birthday gift. The father was lavish in his expression of appreciation, but he understood perfectly that it was the *mother* who had provided both the prompting and the enablement for the gift.

2. *The change may be unconscious on our part.* Our text has for its background those verses which refer to Moses, who spent a prolonged period of time on Mount Sinai communing with his Lord. When he came down from the mountain, there was such a radiance upon his face that his people were afraid to come near him. But Moses himself "wist not that the skin of his face shone" (Exod. 34:29). When the Apostles Peter and John were on trial before the Sanhedrin, for preaching the gospel, they probably did not realize the extent to which they were reflecting Christ; but their persecutors "took knowledge of them, that they had been with Jesus" (Acts 4:13). We are more transparent than we generally realize. We may not know whether we have gained ground or lost ground spiritually; but those around us know, because our attitudes, our words and actions, and our facial expressions reveal the soul within.

3. *The change is gradual.* The expression "from glory to glory" reflects gradualness. Growth in grace takes time; and the image of maturity is not quickly developed. Years ago, on the wall of an office in St. Louis, there were two striking portraits. The one was a portrait of a notorious criminal, in prison stripes, with closely cropped hair and a desperately evil countenance. The other was a portrait of a man with a heavy mop of gray hair and a face of extraordinary kindliness, understanding, and goodness. Both were portraits of the same man, with about thirty years between. The convict had been given a tract entitled, *How the Jailor Got Caught*, written by

D. L. Moody, dealing with the conversion of the Philippian jailor (Acts 16:25-34). With the help of this tract, the convict, in the solitude of his prison cell, found the Lord. His change of heart was complete, and led eventually to his parole; but the hard lines of his face were not quickly erased, and proved a real problem until there had been time enough for these lines to be re-written from within, to reflect the new life in Christ. As he struggled prayerfully through those early days of rehabilitation, his constant heart cry was, "Lord, make me better looking, so that people will trust me and give me a chance to make good." One look at his later portrait reveals the gracious fulfillment of this prayer.

4. *The change is true to pattern.* We are changed "into the same image." In the familiar story of "The Great Stone Face," by Nathaniel Hawthorne, a life is molded by the contemplation of that face. The story begins with a mother and her little boy sitting at the door of their humble cottage and talking about that face, which was a formation of rocks on the side of a cliff many miles across the valley but always in plain view. With the sunlight and shadows playing upon its features, the face seemed actually alive, reflecting unusual nobility, strength of character, wisdom, and warmth of heart. According to an ancient legend, some day there would be a man, born in this vicinity, who was destined to become the noblest person of his time, bearing the image of "the great stone face." The little boy, Ernest, grew up within sight of that benign face, often meditating upon it, and longing to see the fulfillment of the legend. From time to time, someone would appear who seemed at first to be the man of destiny; but each one fell short. As Ernest grew up, his waiting seemed in vain. It was not until his latter years that the fulfillment came: Ernest *himself* had become the living embodiment of the graces reflected in "the great stone face," and was so recognized and acclaimed by the people of the valley among whom he lived.

5. *The change is within reach of all.* Especially cheering are the opening words of our text: *"We all . . .* are changed.

. . ." The promise is not limited to people who are pleasant and agreeable. The meanest, ugliest, most un-Christlike person will find, as he perseveres in *"beholding,"* that he is also in process of *"becoming."* More than once we have seen the promise of our text beautifully fulfilled. The case of a certain young lady is particularly in point. In her early years she was quarrelsome, quick tempered, and sharp tongued. In her later years she was a person of such remarkable poise, serenity, and sweetness of disposition as to stand out in any group. How was the change brought about? The answer is found in that memorable occasion when she stood in the baptismal waters, in holy symbolism declaring that a new life in Christ had begun. As she steadily followed her Lord in worship and service through the years, ever "beholding," she was being gradually changed "into the same image."

> "I asked the rose as it sweetly grew
> Richer and lovelier in hue,
> What made its tints so rich and bright;
> It answered, 'Looking toward the light.'
>
> "Ah, cheerful, fragrant friend of mine,
> God meant my life to be like thine,
> Radiant, with heavenly beauty bright,
> By simply looking toward the light."

"We all, with open face beholding as in a glass the glory of the Lord, are changed into the same image from glory to glory, even as by the Spirit of the Lord."

# 6

# The Life Line
# from Heaven to Earth

Ephesians 2:1-10

Text: *By grace are ye saved through faith . . . .—Ephesians 2:8*

"Millions now living will never die!" This message, widely publicized, and confidently preached, following World War I, anticipated the second coming of Christ in our lifetime. One preacher, taking advantage of the widespread publicity, adapted the theme to a sermon of his own, entitled, "Millions now living *are already dead!*" The sermon was based upon the familiar Biblical concept: "dead in trespasses and sins" (Eph. 2:1). Death is separation from the source of life, as with a branch broken from a tree. Spiritual death is separation from God, "alienation from the life of God" (Eph. 4:18). But *"you hath he made alive, who were dead. . . ."* How was this accomplished?

One dangerous, unfortunate innovation which some are seeking to introduce into traditional Christian thinking is the doctrine of universal salvation. With incredible want of logic, the gospel is presented as the good news that God in Christ has already reconciled the world to himself, and that redemption is an accomplished fact whether recognized or not. Thus evangelism aims merely to inform the lost that they have been saved—"Be glad; acknowledge the fact; live accordingly." How different from the Apostolic thrust, with its zealous concern, and its impassioned appeal for response!

The Biblical way of salvation is clearly marked as a two-way transaction. It is grace reaching *down,* and faith reaching *up.* When the two meet, salvation takes place. *"By grace* are ye saved *through faith . . ."* (Eph. 2:8).

(1) God "would have all men to be saved . . ." (I Tim. 2:4); and so He takes the initiative: He formulates a plan; He reveals himself through his Son; He extends the invitation; and He awaits a response.

(2) God throws out the life line, but the lost soul, like a drowning sailor, must take hold of that life line.

(3) God lets down the ladder from the throne room of heaven to the place where Jacob, the lone fugitive, the homeless wanderer, lies on the ground, with a stone for a pillow. In the holy symbolism of that dream, Jacob sees the angels descending and ascending; and he must have caught the suggestion of the two-way communication which God was seeking to establish with him. So overwhelmed was he with the awesome realization of the presence and holiness of God, that he cried out, "This is none other than the house of God [*beth-el*], and this is the gate of heaven" (Gen. 28:17)! Here, in saving faith, he opened his heart to the living God. In token of his response, he set up and ceremoniously anointed the stone which he had used as a pillow, and it became a cherished memorial. So profound was this experience, that ninety-seven years later, at the age of one hundred thirty-seven, as Jacob was on his deathbed with his loved ones gathered around him, his first words were a testimony to that saving experience in which God came to him at Bethel (Gen. 48:3).

(4) God does not save a man in spite of himself. God will not break into the citadel of his soul; He will not override man's free will; He will not drag an unbelieving, unsurrendered, unregenerate sinner into His kingdom, like a rebellious child, kicking, screaming, and resisting. *"By grace* are ye saved *through faith."* Even *grace* must be *accepted.* A convict in the penitentiary may be offered a pardon, but he either *accepts* the pardon or he remains in his prison cell.

How does a man connect with that life line which reaches from heaven to earth? What is the saving response? How does the soul make the contact? Hear some of the *witnesses* through whom God has given the answer:

### I. WHAT SAYS THE LORD JESUS?—*"Believe!"*

"For God so loved the world, that he gave his only begotten Son, that whosoever believeth on Him should not perish, but have everlasting life" (John 3:16). Believe—or perish!

1. "He that believeth not . . . shall not see life" (John 3:36). "He that hath the Son hath life; he that hath not the Son of God hath not life" (I John 5:12). "Christ in you, the hope of glory" (Col. 1:27).

There are two gates, two ways, two destinies: "Wide is the gate, and broad is the way, that leadeth to destruction . . . strait is the gate, and narrow is the way, which leadeth unto life . . ." (Matt. 7:13, 14). Twice, Jesus draws the curtain aside, and allows a glimpse of eternity:

In the first instance, a judgment scene unfolds before us. "Then shall the King say unto them on his right hand, Come . . . inherit the kingdom prepared for you from the foundation of the world. . . . Then shall he say also unto them on the left hand, Depart from me, ye cursed, into everlasting fire, prepared for the devil and his angels. . . . And these shall go away into everlasting punishment: but the righteous unto life eternal" (Matt. 25:34, 41, 46). The judgment is final. There is no intimation of any reopening of the case at a later time.

In the second instance, we see *beyond* the judgment. Between the doomed and the redeemed, there is "a great gulf fixed," with no bridge across it and no passing from the one side to the other. One man finds himself on the wrong side of the "gulf"; the "gulf" is *"fixed"* (Luke 16:19-31); and there is nothing to suggest that the situation will ever be otherwise. The "rich man" has not changed—in identity, or in character, or in his separation from God; neither has there been any change in the relation of Lazarus to his Lord. Thus the miracle of continuity extends from the present life into the life to come.

2. "O Jerusalem, Jerusalem, which killest the prophets, and stonest them that are sent unto thee; how often would I have gathered thy children together, as a hen doth gather her brood under her wings, and ye would not!" (Luke 13:34). Why should Jesus weep over the sinners of Jerusalem, if in the end all are to be saved anyway? Clearly, He was not thinking in terms of universal salvation.

### II. WHAT SAYS THE APOSTLE PETER?—*"Repent!"*

"Repent, and be baptized every one of you in the name of Jesus Christ for the remission of sins . . ." (Acts 2:38).

1. Repentance is decisive in salvation. "Repent!" Change your attitude! Reverse your direction! "Turn ye, turn ye from your evil ways; for why will ye die . . . ? (Ezek. 33:11). "Repent . . . *for the remission of sins* . . . ." Without repentance, the guilt of sins unconfessed, unremoved, unforgiven, continues to pile up until the day of reckoning. Christ came not to circumvent the justice of God and to deliver unrepentant sinners from the guilt and the consequences of their wickedness, but "to call . . . sinners *to repentance*" (Luke 5:32), and to save them "from their sins" (Matt. 1:21).

"All have sinned" (Rom. 3:23): and all have need for repentance. The difference between the worst sinner and the "mildest" is purely a difference of degree—not a difference in kind. Sins of omission are no less real than sins of violence. In the sight of God there are no "mild" sinners, and sin does not come in pastel shades.

But more grievous than all the sins which may appear on the surface is the all-inclusive SIN which may lie beneath, and which says, "We will not that this one shall reign over us" (Luke 19:14). Sins are violations of the *laws* of God; SIN is resistance to the *sovereignty* of God, and rejection of His love.

It is ingratitude, lawlessness, rebellion, moral anarchy, such as would dethrone God if it could.

2. Repentance deals with the *cause* of alienation from God; and this cause, Peter insists, must be removed. An apt analogy appears in a recent editorial in Billy Graham's magazine, *Decision:* A child comes to its parent with a sliver in its thumb. What does the parent do? Quickly pour water on it? Or iodine? Or read a comforting Bible verse? Or hand the child a piece of pie to make it stop crying? No; he must get rid of the sliver! Without *repentance* there is no salvation—individual or universal.

### III. WHAT SAYS THE APOSTLE PAUL?—*"Be ye reconciled!"*

"Now then we are ambassadors for Christ, as though God did beseech you by us: we pray you in Christ's stead, be ye reconciled to God" (II Cor. 5:20).

1. Why this fervent appeal, if they are *already reconciled* to God? And why the continuing "ministry of reconciliation" (II Cor. 5:19)? And why that three-year ministry of tears at Ephesus—warning every one "night and day with tears" (Acts 20:31)?

2. Why this insistence upon reconciliation with God? There is no problem when we look at the alternative. Suppose God were to receive unreconciled sinners into the heavenly household —to profane the holiness of heaven with the attitude of indifference, disobedience, or rebellion toward the Head of the family! Heaven would immediately cease to be heaven!

Suppose God were to receive guilty, unclean, unregenerate sinners—to befoul the purity of heaven with the filthiness of unforgiven sin, and with every filthy inclination of the flesh! Heaven would be just another hell!

Suppose God were to receive sinners in their unchanged, unsanctified state into the same heavenly home with the redeemed, transformed children of God! How long would it be till the tranquillity  of heaven would be destroyed with the resumption of earthly hatreds and aggressions, and the brutal persecution of believers by unbelievers! In *Foxe's Book of Martyrs* we read that " . . . amidst the flames . . . the . . . martyr's heroic spirit ascended beyond the reach of man's cruelty." Would God expose His beloved children to a renewal of such cruelty?

Somewhere in the world there is a person, whose identity is known only to God, who is more desperately wicked, more depraved, more completely given over to Satan than any other person on earth—guilty of so much that any normal person would exclaim, "If there *is* no hell, there *ought to be!*" Somewhere else there is another person, whose identity is known only to God, who is the world's purest, noblest, kindest person, the most deeply devoted servant of Jesus Christ. To bring the world's best and the world's worst to the same destiny, without repentance and transformation, would not accord with the righteousness of God and the law of the harvest: "Whatsoever a man soweth, that shall he also reap" (Gal. 6:7).

### IV. WHAT SAYS THE APOSTLE JOHN?—*"Confess!"*

"If we confess our sins, he is faithful and just to forgive us our sins, and to cleanse us from all unrighteousness" (I John 1:9).

1. The alternative is to remain forever unforgiven and uncleansed, and thus to meet God in judgment, having spurned his gracious offer. The "mild" sinner, who has ignored God, and resisted the Holy Spirit, and rejected Christ, can still be saved—if he will "confess." The savage with the blood of many murders on his hands can still be saved; likewise, the human beast who has had all the benefits of civilization—if he will "confess."

2. The ancient invitation still stands—"Come now, and let

us reason together, saith the Lord: though your sins be as scarlet, they shall be as white as snow . . ." (Isa. 1:18). To each, the Holy Spirit speaks individually. Each is born individually; each one dies individually; and each one goes to his eternal destiny as an individual. Each one recognizes the voice of conscience, which is the voice of God speaking through the Holy Spirit to the soul. Each must individually come to terms with God: he must "believe," "repent," "be reconciled," "confess," in his own name, on his own behalf. There is no repentance by proxy, no group salvation, no tribal salvation, no salvation by families.

### V. WHAT SAYS THE HOLY SPIRIT?—*"Come!"*

"The Spirit and the bride say, Come. And let him that heareth say, Come. And let him that is athirst come. And whosoever will, let him take the water of life freely" (Rev. 22:17).

1. God the Father has spoken. Approximately two thousand times the Holy Scriptures declare, "Thus saith the Lord." God the Son has spoken. The Apostles have spoken. Now God the Holy Spirit presses the invitation: "Come!" "He will guide you into all truth," said the Lord Jesus, concerning the coming of the Holy Spirit (John 16:13). And how appropriate that the Holy Book, with its eleven hundred eighty-nine chapters, should conclude its final chapter with this invitation! In a voice that is clear, insistent, and familiar to each of us from early childhood, the Holy Spirit says in effect, "Come—accept the hand of reconciliation which God is extending; relate yourself to the source of life; open the heart for the life of God to flow in." Thus begins the restoration of the lost "image of God" (Gen. 1:26, 27).

2. "If the Spirit of him that raised up Jesus from the dead dwelleth in you, he that raised up Christ Jesus from the dead shall give life also to *your* mortal bodies through his Spirit that dwelleth in you" (Rom. 8:11, ASV). Thus, for the be-

liever, physical death is not the end of life, but only an incident along the way of everlasting life. The body is "sown in corruption . . . raised in incorruption . . . sown a natural body . . . raised a spiritual body" (I Cor. 15:42, 44). With the removal of the imperfections and limitations of the flesh, the believer is brought into full and final conformity with "the image of His Son" (Rom. 8:29). But *everything* depends upon the indwelling of the Holy Spirit.

Without the indwelling of the Holy Spirit, man's best is not enough. He remains "dead in trespasses and sins." A house, however beautiful and well equipped, and however excellently wired for lighting, heating, and the operation of its facilities, remains dark, cold, and lifeless till the connection is established with the source of light, warmth, and power. Though the power line be close at hand, with enough power to supply a million houses, this house will remain "dead"—until the roof caves in, and the beams disintegrate in their sockets, and the stones crumble—unless the *connection* is made. Similarly, the sinner remains forever "dead," unless he, by a definite, individual, voluntary act of faith, responds to the invitation of his Lord, and connects with the lifeline that reaches from heaven to earth.

God's witnesses have spoken: "Believe. . . . Repent. . . . Be reconciled. . . . Confess. . . . Come!" Each has insisted upon an individual response to the grace of God. It is the sinner's only hope of salvation. *"By grace* are ye saved *through faith."*

# 7

# Christ and
# the Golden Candle Sticks

Revelation 3:7-13

Text: *Hold that fast which thou hast, that no man take thy crown.—Revelation 3:11*

It is a solemn and sobering spectacle which unfolds before us in the opening three chapters of the Book of Revelation.

1. *There are the seven golden candle sticks, representing seven churches made up of people like ourselves.* They were fashioned of the same clay. They professed the same faith. They were a people of like aspirations, weaknesses, struggles, failures and successes.

2. *There, walking among them, is Christ*—resurrected, glorified, infinitely holy, almighty in power, before whom there are no secrets, before whom every soul is laid bare, before whom every church is as an open book. One by one the churches come under his divine scrutiny, which penetrates to the inmost depths. To each group he says, with solemn, heart searching emphasis, "I know thy works!" And to each he addresses some word of counsel, encouragement, or approval, or some word of correction, warning, or rebuke.

To one, he says, with sorrow in his heart, and sorrow in his voice, "Thou hast left thy first love." They were still going through the motions of worship and service, but these were largely motions without motivation. There was not that warm, outflowing devotion of earlier days. "Remember . . . repent . . . do the first works!"

To another, he says, in effect, "Thou hast lost thy purity of doctrine. Thou art harboring within thy fellowship the wicked heresies of Balaam and of the Nicolaitans. Repent, and set thine house in order!"

To still another, he says, in effect, "Thou hast lost thy purity of life. Thou art tolerating in thy midst the filthy sins of Jezebel, and art become partaker of her guilt. Repent! Purge thyself, and be clean!"

To another, he says, "Thou hast a name that thou livest, and art dead." The church was still coasting on the momentum of its earlier, better days; and there were "a few names" which had not "defiled their garments." Again, the challenge is, "Repent!"

To the church of Laodicea, he says, "Thou art lukewarm . . . thou sayest, I am rich and increased with goods, and have need of nothing; and knowest not that thou art wretched, and miserable, and poor, and blind, and naked."

To the church in Smyrna, the Lord speaks in an altogether different mood: "I know thy works, and tribulation, and poverty. . . . be thou faithful unto death, and I will give thee a crown of life."

To the church in Philadelphia, comes the happiest message of the seven: "Thou hast a little strength, and hast kept my word, and hast not denied my name. . . . hold that fast which thou hast, that no man take thy crown." For faithful servants of Christ, there is a perpetual timeliness in this brief message with its *implications:*

### I. IT IS POSSIBLE TO LOSE THAT WHICH WE HAVE
(of spiritual possession, spiritual power, and spiritual worth)

1. *This can happen on any level of spiritual attainment.*

Among the distinguished comrades of the Apostle Paul, was a man named Demas, whose name appears three times in the Epistles. In the first reference, Demas is affectionately included with Mark and Luke, "my fellow laborers" (Philemon 24). in the second reference it seems that Demas has lost something, so that the less said about him, the better: "Luke, the beloved physician, and Demas, greet you" (Col. 4:14). In the last reference, all is lost. "Demas hath forsaken me, having loved this present world, and is departed . . ." (II Tim. 4:10). Having companied with so illustrious a group, through whom the world has been immeasurably blessed, how could he ever be ordinary again!

From Paul, the Prince of Apostles, we have a legacy of one hundred chapters in the New Testament; from Luke, we have the next largest number of chapters, fifty-two in all (Luke and Acts); from Mark, we have the earliest of the four Gospels. And from Demas, what have we? Only a final rear view as he departs from that distinguished fellowship and returns to the unregenerate world out of which he had come—only a sad example of one who failed to "hold fast" that which he had.

2. *This can happen among the best of people.* Where would one ever find a nobler company of men than that dedicated group of disciples who walked with Jesus! There was Peter, there were John and James, Andrew, Philip, Matthew, Thomas, and other kindred spirits—and Judas. Eleven of the disciples held fast to their place of privilege, blessing, and opportunity. But Judas fell. When he left those sacred associations and went out, "it was night" (John 13:30). And in the darkness of despair which followed the betrayal of his Lord, Judas died a wretched suicide.

3. *This can happen in any kind of place.* The most beautiful, most wholesome, most inspiring environment ever provided for human habitation was the Garden of Eden. In this garden there lived two young people, Adam and Eve. Never since Adam has the world seen another so strong, so noble, so magnificent. And never since Eve has the world seen another so

pure, so lovely, so heavenly. But they fell. And the world has never recovered from the shock of that fall.

Coming to the Seminary twenty-five years ago, I found a student body of about two hundred of the finest young people I had ever seen. Individually born into the family of Christ, individually called and dedicated to vocational Christian service, motivated by the same spirit, they were an inspiring group. To see them growing together, working, singing, praying, strengthening one another, one would conclude that surely there could never be a casualty here. And yet there has probably never been a year without the loss of someone who failed to "hold fast." Perhaps it was someone who could not bring himself to match the whole of life to that high hour of dedication when he had said, "Here am I, Lord; send me!" Perhaps, like those Israelites who never lost their longing for "the flesh pots of Egypt," he could not forget about the money he might have made, the prestige to which he might have attained, or the easier path he might have chosen.

In every pulpit there stands a potential Demas; in every pew there sits a potential Demas. Let us not say, "It can't happen here." Rather, let us ask ourselves, in all seriousness: Is my life as pure as ever it was? Is my conscience as tender as ever it was? Is my devotion to my Lord as warm as ever it was? And is my zeal for the things of Christ as pronounced as ever it was? If so, let us thank God; and "Let him that thinketh he standeth take heed lest he fall" (I Cor. 10:12).

4. *This can happen to any kind of church.*

(1) Through complacency born of prosperity. This was the big concern of Moses as he led his people to the border of the Promised Land. "When thou shalt have eaten and be full, then beware lest thou forget the Lord, which brought thee forth out of the land of Egypt, from the house of bondage" (Deut. 6:11, 12). This was the concern of John Wesley, who had no fears for his people so long as they remained poor, but felt great uneasiness as to whether they could endure prosperity, "walking on carpeted floors, sleeping in soft beds, and sitting in cushioned pews." "Then, oh my people, beware lest thou

forget the Lord . . . !" The Baptist Executive Secretary of New York City, years ago, declared, "The great peril of the metropolis is not the degradation of its slums, but the godlessness of its wealthy suburbs." A minister holding a funeral service in a wealthy suburb of Chicago inquired about the church affiliation of each of the seventeen persons who had attended the service in the funeral home. He found that every one of them had been actively related to a church in Chicago, but had left the church behind, and had not established a church connection after moving out to the beautiful suburb.

(2) Through discouragement growing out of adversity, struggle, and exhaustion. A church in downstate Illinois lost many of its leaders during the depression in the early thirties, and finally gave up in sheer discouragement, and ceased to function. Apparently there was no hope. But two elderly women "held fast," and continued going regularly to the church house at church time on the Lord's Day. Even on the coldest days, through rain, snow, and sleet, they would come and unlock the door and kneel in the dismal chill of the abandoned sanctuary, and beseech the Lord to come again in power and grace. These prayers were answered; the Lord "revived his work in the midst of the years" (Hab. 3:2); and there was "joy in Jerusalem" (II Chron. 30:26), such as the people had not experienced since the original dedication of the church. Discouragement has been characterized as the most valuable tool in the Devil's workshop.

(3) Through living too much in the past. A church with a noble past is more vulnerable to this danger than a church that has always been ordinary. Such a church is too much like the fabled "floogee bird," which is said to fly backwards instead of forward, singing one monotonous refrain: "I don't know where I'm going, but just look where I've been!" A church without a clear aim is not a happy church. On the platform of a railroad station, for several days, there was a large crate with a big dog inside. He was the most melancholy sight imaginable. A passerby inquired about him and was told, "You would be sad too if you were in his plight. He has chewed the tag off the crate, and does not know where he's going . . .

*we* don't know where he is going; *nobody* knows where he's going."

But along with the somber implication of our text, there is a happy implication, to put joy in the heart of every believer:

II. IT IS POSSIBLE TO HOLD THAT WHICH WE HAVE
(of spiritual possession, spiritual power, and spiritual worth)

1. *We have the same spiritual resources and defenses which made the church in ancient Philadelphia invincible.* We have the same gospel, the same body of truth, the same doctrinal distinctives, the same Great Commission. The promise, "Lo, I am with you always," has not been withdrawn. The gospel still has its transforming power—to make the foulest clean, to make the meanest noble, to make the ugliest beautiful.

> "How firm a foundation, ye saints of the Lord,
> Is laid for your faith in His excellent word!
> What more can He say than to you He hath said,
> To you who for refuge to Jesus have fled?"

2. *We have the confirmation of nearly two thousand years of Christian history to validate our faith,* to undergird our labors, and to encourage our hearts.

Thank God for the testimony of those who have gone before us! There are the Apostles, the early Church Fathers, the Reformers, the martyrs whose labors and sacrifices through the centuries have kept the gospel alive in the world. In the Scriptures we read of that "great cloud of witnesses" (Heb. 12:1), who look down upon us from their place in glory. The challenge that comes ringing from the battlements of heaven is like the message of that soldier who fell in the War of Independence, and whose monument carries the appeal, "Oh, posterity, do not sell cheaply that which has cost us so much!"

Thank God for the example of great souls, towering in spiritual stature, who are still among us, as living monuments to the living God! A large Baptist congregation in Indiana was holding the last service in the venerable and beloved sanctuary which had served the church for eighty-one years. Just before the service, the pastor and the visiting speaker met in the pastor's study for prayer with the deacons. The pastor called on one of the deacons to lead in prayer. This deacon knelt in the middle of the floor, and the rest of us knelt in a circle around him. Never have I heard a more deeply moving prayer; surely, never has the presence of God been more real to a group of men. Under the spell of that prayer, in total silence, the group walked down the long corridor to the sanctuary. Entering the door to the sanctuary, I whispered to the pastor, "What a prayer!" Afterwards the pastor asked, "How old do you suppose this deacon is?" He was strong and well preserved, with a heavy head of iron-gray hair, and with a carefully trimmed full beard. I supposed that he was about seventy years old. "No," said the pastor; "he is ninety years old. When this church was built, eighty-one years ago, he was a nine year old boy, probably the youngest member. When, on that beautiful Sunday afternoon of the dedication, the whole church family marched ceremoniously down the middle of the main street, and for the first time entered the sanctuary, with the singing of the Doxology, this boy was among the marchers. He has been in the church ever since, and has never belonged to any other. He has seen the church weathering all sorts of storms—wars, financial panics, political upheavals, theological controversies—but moving steadily forward by the grace of God, with the serenity of a great, invincible ocean liner. Do you wonder that he could pray so eloquently about *'the grand continuity of the grace of God?'* "

3. *We have the same divine Overseer who encouraged the faithful Philadelphians.* He still walks among the "golden candle sticks." And to every soul that listens, he speaks—lovingly, understandingly, and with authority.

A chaplain in World War II relates as his most profound experience of the war a simple conversation with his commanding general at Corregidor. The chaplain had been greatly encouraged as he noted that in every service, whether the attendance was large or small, the commanding general was among those present. One day he called on the general at headquarters, and was warmly greeted: "Chaplain, what can I do for you?" "Nothing at all, sir," replied the chaplain; "I just came to thank you for your constant attendance at our services of worship. I could not possibly tell you how much it means to me, and what your good example means to the soldiers, as they see their General regularly in the place of worship." After a thoughtful pause, the general said, "Chaplain, let me show you something." He pressed a button, and some high ranking officer came, clicked his heels, saluted, and stood at attention, awaiting orders. Quietly, the general said something to the officer, and dismissed him. When two others had been similarly called and dismissed, the general said, "See, Chaplain, I'm a big shot around here. I press the buttons, and the high brass comes running; they stand at attention and await my orders. But, Chaplain, one of these days I shall not be here; I shall have gone the way of all flesh— here today, gone tomorrow! Chaplain, thank God, you are not serving that kind of a general; you are not serving an ordinary four star general, of short lived power and authority. You are serving that *seven star general* of whom we read in the Book of Revelation—'He that hath the seven stars, who is alive for-evermore, and whose Kingdom endureth forever' (Rev. 1:16, 18; 2:1). Never forget that, Chaplain!"

"Hold that fast which thou hast, that no man take thy crown!"

This challenge to the faithful is more than a call merely to hold their own. A defensive rear guard action, however brilliant, is not enough. There must be advance. And to the faithful, several promises are held out by Him who walks among the golden candle sticks: "An open door" that no man can shut (v. 8), a reverential response on the part of those to whom they minister (v. 9), an everlasting reward in the "new Jerusalem" (v. 12), and security through all the vicissitudes along the way to glory—"I will keep thee from the hour of temptation, which shall come upon all the world" (v. 10).

In the light of this divine challenge, let every believer examine his own soul. Every year of life should find us purer, stronger, taller in spiritual stature, more discerning, more deserving of commendation by Him who never ceases to walk among the golden candle sticks.

# 8
# God's Best for You

Romans 12:1-2

Text: *I beseech you therefore, brethren, by the mercies of God, that ye present your bodies a living sacrifice, holy, acceptable unto God, which is your reasonable service. And be not conformed to this world; but be ye transformed by the renewing of your mind, that ye may prove what is that good, and acceptable, and perfect, will of God.—Romans 12:1-2*

One of the vivid recollections of my youth is that of watching a baseball game between two teams of unsophisticated teen-age amateurs, who played for fun, but with a tremendous determination to win. When the batter came up for his turn at bat it did not matter what the situation was—how many scores, how many men on bases, how many strikes, balls, outs—he had only one thought; and that was to lose the ball in a grand home run over the back field fence. And so he would swing at the ball with all the power he could muster, putting every ounce of his being into the effort. That may not have been good baseball strategy, but it was a magnificent demonstration of aiming for the best.

The Christian who aims for the highest and best will find in the words of our text a powerful challenge to godly living, a ringing call to higher ground.

(1) Most Christians have never proven "what is that good, and acceptable, and perfect, will of God," but are living on something less than God's best.

(2) Many are living unhappily on spiritual lowlands only slightly above the level of the unregenerate world, without "the peace of God, which passeth all understanding" (Phil. 4:7), and without that heavenly lift which is the soul of happiness.

(3) Some are trying to be Christians in a mild sort of way, vainly trying to find happiness without holiness. Thus they live their pinched, meagre little lives, and die their little deaths, and are laid in their little graves, without ever experiencing the "abundant life" which is the unceasing concern of the Savior, who came "that they might have life, and that they might have it more abundantly" (John 10:10).

(4) All who seriously aspire to God's best will find help in the Scriptural statement which reveals the way and spells out God's *requirements*:

#### I. COMPLETE CONSECRATION

" . . . present your bodies a living sacrifice, holy, acceptable unto God, which is your reasonable service."

1. *It is required that we "present" the body, the instrument of every vice and every virtue.*

(1) How do we serve our Lord? We serve Him with the body —with the eyes seeing what He would have us to see, with the ears hearing what He would have us to hear, with the tongue speaking what He would have us to speak, with the hands doing what He would have us to do, and with the feet going where He would have us to go.

(2) How do we serve sin? Again, it is with the body—with the eyes, the ears, the tongue, the hands, and the feet choosing to engage in that which is repugnant to the Holy Spirit.

(3) How does one pay the penalty for sin? Here too the body is involved. Sin ravages the body as well as the soul. The judgment of God descends upon the body as well as the soul, in time and in eternity. The Bible declares that "there shall be a resurrection of the dead, both of the just and unjust" (Acts 24:15). The righteous are "raised incorruptible" (I Cor. 15:52),

with a body "like unto His [Christ's] glorious body" (Phil. 3:21). About the resurrection body of the wicked we are not expressly told; but there are Biblical intimations of a re-identification of the soul with some semblance of its former body.

Jesus repeatedly speaks of the destiny of the doomed, in terms of "hell fire," "outer darkness," and "weeping and gnashing of teeth" (Matt. 18:9; 22:13). Somewhat more articulate is His reference to the doomed man in the place of torment pleading for a few drops of water to cool his tongue (Luke 16:24).

Clarence E. Macartney, in his very stimulating book, *Preaching without Notes,* gives the substance of a dialogue between a lost soul and its resurrection body, in the judgment, as imagined by Samuel Davies, noted preacher of Colonial times. The soul curses the body, and blames the lusts of the body for the soul's eternal undoing, and cries out against the loathesome prospect of being reunited with the body. The body makes answer, bitterly accusing the soul of having prostituted the body to sin, forbidding the knees to bow before the throne of grace, and overruling every inclination of the eyes and ears to read and hear the Word of Life. In consequence, the body recognizes itself to be the just instrument of the soul's everlasting punishment, while crying out against the necessity of being bound together by chains which even the pangs of hell and the flames of unquenchable fire can not dissolve.

2. *It is "reasonable" that we "present" the body as a living sacrifice.*

(1) It is reasonable on the ground of our redemption. "Ye are not your own. . . . ye are bought with a price; therefore glorify God in your body, and in your spirit, which are God's" (I Cor. 6:19-20). "Ye were not redeemed with corruptible things, as silver and gold . . . but with the precious blood of Christ, as of a lamb without blemish and without spot" (I Peter 1:18-19). On the cross hangs Christ; beneath the cross lies a helpless sinner, "dead in trespasses and sins" (Eph. 2:1). What takes place is far more than a blood transfusion which revives the body; it is a transfusion which imparts everlasting life to the soul.

> "To Him I owe my life and breath,
> And all the joys I have;
> He makes me triumph over death,
> And saves me from the grave."

(2) It is reasonable on the ground of our participation in the life of Christ. A valid, saving faith is based not on *imitation* of Christ, but on *participation* in the life of Christ. "We are made *partakers* of Christ"—not mere *imitators* (Heb. 3:14). "I am the vine, ye are the branches" (John 15:5). "Christ in you, the hope of glory" (Col. 1:27). One of the renowned international statesmen of the past century was a rather consistent imitator of Christ; but, according to his own profession, he was not a Christian. He accepted the ethics of Christ, but not the Lordship of Christ. And it is only when Christ becomes our Lord that He becomes the Savior of the soul and the Guardian of our destiny.

(3) It is reasonable on the ground of our relation to the Holy Spirit. "Know ye not that ye are the temple of God, and that the Spirit of God dwelleth in you" (I Cor. 3:16)? This means that your eyes are the eyes of the Holy Spirit; your ears are the ears of the Holy Spirit; your tongue is the tongue of the Holy Spirit; your hands and feet are the hands and feet of the Holy Spirit. When we present ourselves bodily, "a living sacrifice," there is no conflict between the parts, but perfect co-ordination.

The problem of the defeated Christian is largely a problem of uncompleted consecration. There may be some lingering conflict of aims and desires. There may be tainted contacts which have not been broken, bridges that have not been burned, decisions that have not been pegged down with finality. And so there is want of co-ordination. Of King Amaziah we read that "he did that which was right in the sight of the Lord, but not with a perfect heart" (II Chron. 25:2). And Amaziah came to grief. Of the ancient Samaritans we read that they "feared the Lord and served their own gods" (II Kings 17:33). They too came to grief.

In college days I witnessed an unforgettable demonstration of a so-called "split personality." A young woman on the platform, with her arms behind her and her back against a curtain, was giving a highly dramatic reading. Behind the curtain stood another young woman, completely out of sight, with her arms extending through the curtain in such a way as to make them appear to belong to the young woman who was in view. While the one was giving her reading, with the utmost vocal and facial expression, the girl from behind was providing the gestures. The result was ludicrous beyond words. But the audience got the message. An unco-ordinated Christian is a defeated Christian. There is a better way, and that is *total consecration*, in the spirit of our text.

This text lays a further requirement upon us:

## II. COMPLETE SEPARATION

"Be not conformed to this world. . . ."

1. *Blessed is the man who does not do what the unregenerate world does.* "Blessed is the man that walketh not in the counsel of the ungodly, nor standeth in the way of sinners, nor sitteth in the seat of the scornful. But his delight is in the law of the Lord; and in His law doth he meditate day and night. And he shall be like a tree planted by the rivers of water, that bringeth forth his fruit in his season; his leaf also shall not wither; and whatsoever he doeth shall prosper" (Ps. 1:1-3).

(1) The happy man in the first Psalm was a non-conformist. It is not indicated what he may have endured, in terms of social pressures, ostracism, and ridicule on the part of the ungodly, the sinners, and the scornful. But it is made clear that he had chosen the better part. His prosperity was God-given. He was reaping the blessings of an ancient promise: "Them that honor me I will honor, saith the Lord" (I Sam. 2:30).

(2) Daniel, who "purposed in his heart that he would not defile himself" after the manner of the Babylonians (Dan. 1:8), was another non-conformist—a man of character, conviction, and determination. How easy it would have been to fall into prevailing patterns of conduct—"When in Babylon, do as the Babylonians do!" Daniel's "separated life" was no bed of roses, but by the grace of God he survived all the hazards of non-

conformity, in crisis after crisis. He powerfully influenced a succession of four reigning monarchs; and after three quarters of a century in Babylon he stood taller than ever, before God and man. "Be not conformed to this world"; there is a higher conformity!

(3) The young man in the armed forces today faces testings no less crucial than the testings of Daniel. He can go in clean and come out clean, but only as a non-conformist in his personal life. In the anonymity of a uniform, a thousand miles from home, unknown and without the strengthening presence of parents, pastors, and teachers, the easy way is to be "conformed to this world." When I wore the uniform I was appalled to find what happened to the morals and integrity of many who at home had been active front line Christians. But, thank God, there was always a precious minority who carried their convictions and dedication with them and who mightily fortified one another when the going was hard.

The young man who "conforms to this world" does not need to invite Satan to come in; the door is already open. He is like the boatsman guiding his little craft over turbulent waters. The boat is in the sea, but the sea must be kept out of the boat. If he keeps the water bailed out as quickly as it splashes over the sides, the boat is secure. But if he carelessly or consciously allows water to accumulate, a single unexpected wave, added to this accumulation, will sink the boat.

2. *Blessed is the man who does not know what the unregenerate world knows.* It might surprise us to discover in the Scriptures a case in which our Lord actually places a premium on ignorance. In the message to the church at Thyatira the Lord notes that the church is tolerating in its midst the filthy sins of Jezebel, and is becoming involved in her guilt. Divine judgment is about to descend, but not upon those "which *have not known* the depths of Satan" (Rev. 2:24).

Mother Eve was intrigued by the promise of Satan that her knowledge would be increased by eating of the forbidden fruit. And so it was. But how infinitely poorer she was with the consequences of this further knowledge! (Gen. 3). The Prodigal Son learned much through his "riotous living" in the "far country" (Luke 15:11-24). But,

> "Oh, that I never had gone astray!
> Life was all radiant with hope one day;
> now all its treasures I've thrown away!"

No, the increase of knowledge is not always the way to God's best. "Be not conformed to this world."

*3. Blessed is the man who lays aside "every weight" as well as "the sin which doth so easily beset us"* (Heb. 12:1).

Many who are not readily tempted with outright sin are defeated by these "weights"—these practices and indulgences which may seem harmless in themselves, but which at best tend to muffle or limit one's Christian testimony, and which may open the way to disaster.

Some years ago, in Newark, New Jersey, the front page of the newspaper carried the startling headline that ducks by the hundreds were drowning in one of the bays in the vicinity. What was the story? Great flocks of these migrating wild ducks were settling down upon the water as usual; but there was a new, unsuspected hazard. From a nearby refinery a large quantity of crude oil had spilled into the bay. The oil itself was not harmful; it was not poisonous; it had no hurtful acid content. But gradually and subtly it matted the feathers together; and before the ducks realized what was happening the icy waters had penetrated to the skin; the bodies became numb with cold, and the ducks perished. "My soul, be on thy guard!"

Along the way to God's best, there is still another requirement:

### III. COMPLETE TRANSFORMATION

"Be ye transformed by the renewing of your mind."

*1. We can not transform ourselves.*

"The natural man receiveth not the things of the Spirit of God . . . neither can he know them, because they are spiritually discerned" (I Cor. 2:14). However he might strain for vision and discernment, he is helpless until the transforming grace of God shines in. He can not change himself from a sinner to a saint, or elevate himself to higher ground. But he can open his heart and life to the One who "is able."

James L. Kraft, the renowned Christian layman, recalls as a great turning point in his life the day that a certain kindly eye doctor came into his life. James was a fourteen year old boy, one of a family of eleven children, living on a farm in Canada. In his book, *Adventure in Jade,* he relates that he had never been able to distinguish objects clearly. His nearsightedness was so acute and so distressing that he assumed everyone on earth suffered continuously from furious headaches, and that all the earth had the blurry image of a boat seen from under water. It happened that the oculist was vacationing in the vicinity, and young James was taking care of his horse and buggy. Noting his extreme nearsightedness, the oculist insisted that the boy go to the city with him to be fitted with a pair of glasses. In that gift of glasses, Kraft gratefully recalls, "he gave me the earth and all that was in it, completely in focus and beautiful beyond anything I could have dreamed. . . . I can not think of another act of human kindness in my lifetime which can compare with his." It was not possible for the boy to transform himself, but it was quite possible for him to *be transformed.*

2. *We can not have the "fruit of the Spirit" without the Spirit.*

"The fruit of the Spirit is love, joy, peace, longsuffering, gentleness, goodness, faith, meekness, temperance" (Gal. 5:22-23). This nine-fold fruitage grows spontaneously out of the heart that is indwelt by the Holy Spirit. A semblance of these graces might be achieved without the Holy Spirit, but such simulated graces would be rootless and superficial, like flowers pinned on a corpse. It is not in the nature of unregenerate man to bring forth such fruitage with the vitality to endure. At best, what is brought forth is like the sprouting of the seed that fell on stony ground—quick to come up, and quick to wither away when the sun became hot (Matt. 13:20-21).

A visitor from Norway told of two trees in the front yard of his home. In full bloom in the spring the two trees looked exactly alike; but year after year the one bore a bountiful crop of cherries, while the other, known as a "wild cherry tree," never once produced a cherry. It was not in the nature of that tree to bring forth more than the outward appearance of a genuine cherry tree.

3. *We can not have godliness without God.* "It is God which worketh in you both to will and to do of his good pleasure" (Phil. 2:13). There are those who have a "form of godliness" but not "the power thereof" (II Tim. 3:5). Faith has been defined as "the life of God in the heart of man." Man is not fully alive until he has that inflow from above. A familiar parting salutation of frontier days was: "I hope you'll really live until you die." Perhaps this was meant facetiously, but with the right interpretation it could be a noble and fitting salutation.

4. *We can not have God without Christ.* Christ, the Great Reconciler, "hath broken down the middle wall of partition between us . . . that he might reconcile both unto God in one body by the cross" (Eph. 2:14, 16). But "no man cometh unto the Father but by me" (John 14:6). This fact would account for something that can be seen daily in certain lands of the Near East. The adherents of one particular faith believe in God and in prayer, but emphatically reject the deity of Christ. At appointed times they hasten to the place of prayer, and go through all the ritualistic prostrations as prescribed. But one's heart goes out in deep sympathy to the many who return with facial expressions no less grim, tense, and distraught than before the prayers. To all appearances, there has been no experience of the mellowing, strengthening, transforming grace of God; and there is not that serenity which is the reward of real prayer communion with the Heavenly Father.

Our text assures us that we can "prove what is that good, and acceptable, and perfect, will of God."

> "But we never can prove the delights of His love
>   Until all on the altar we lay;
> For the favor He shows, and the joy He bestows,
>   Are for them who will trust and obey."

"Expository" Sermons

# 9
## Near to the Heart of God

*O Lord, how long shall I cry, and thou wilt not hear! even cry unto thee of violence, and thou wilt not save! . . . Thou art of purer eyes than to behold evil, and canst not look on iniquity: wherefore lookest thou upon them that deal treacherously, and holdest thy tongue when the wicked devoureth the man that is more righteous than he? . . . I will stand upon my watch, and set me upon the tower, and will watch to see what he will say unto me. . . . And the Lord answered me, and said, Write the vision and make it plain . . . .—Habakkuk 1:2, 13; 2:1, 2*

(Read the remainder of Habakkuk 2, one of the most quoted and least known chapters of the Old Testament.)

1. *The book of Habakkuk reveals the deepest gloom in Judah's long night of apostasy and peril preceding the Babylonian captivity.*

The world outlook was grim and threatening. It was a time of mighty upheavals. The great Assyrian empire was disintegrating; Babylon and Egypt were locked in a Titanic struggle for world supremacy. Caught between the two was the tiny kingdom of Judah. Israel had been conquered and her people carried into captivity; and Judah was on the way. It was a time of ruthless conquest, bloody suppression, and merciless tyranny.

The internal outlook of Judah was hardly less grim and threatening. There was widespread wickedness, violence, injustice, and idolatry. The masses were dulled in conscience, and calloused by long exposure to danger. Unmoved by the warnings and pleadings of the prophets, they showed the unconcern of a people living complacently on the slopes of a smoldering volcano. Habakkuk, agonizing over the delinquencies of his own people and the wicked expansionism of pagan empires, and sensing disaster in the offing, cries out, "O God, why don't you do something!"

2. *The prophet, in his perplexity and distress, finds the only way out of the dark, the only true refuge, near to the heart of God.* Symbolically, he speaks of ascending the watch tower and there waiting on God.

Here he sees, through the deep gloom, light beams from some of the brightest stars in God's heaven. God was speaking to him as He spoke to one of our missionaries at her lonely outpost during World War II. A night time bombing raid by enemy airmen was raining death and destruction from the sky. Helpless natives were trembling in the pitiable shelter of their huts. In the midst of panic and horror the missionary looked up, and saw, by the grace of God, the stars above the bombing planes. To her, in that desperate moment, they were the silent sentinels of the eternal, unchanging sovereignty of God, who never forsakes his own and never forgets a promise. Immediately she became quiet within, and her spirit was fortified for that harrowing ordeal.

Habakkuk, from his vantage point near to the heart of God, gains new *insights* for the warning of the wicked and the encouragement of the righteous.

### I. THE WOES OF THE WICKED

Five times he hears the voice of God in thunderous denunciation.

1. *Woe to the aggressor who, with insatiable greed, "increaseth that which is not his"* (v. 6). Here the primary reference is to the Babylonian empire, drunk with power, steadily enlarging itself through conquest, irresistible in its advances and seizures. The descending judgment of God falls in the familiar pattern, "They that take the sword shall perish with the sword" (Matt.

26:52). How consistently this has been true, the history of kingdoms and empires abundantly demonstrates.

2. *Woe to the covetous plunderer, who craftily "sets his nest on high," to make his spoils secure* (v. 9). The primary reference is to the Edomites, who lived among the cliffs in the semi-desert area south of the Dead Sea. From their lofty fastnesses they made raids upon the neighboring lowlands, and stored their plunder in the almost inaccessible cliffs. To the Edomites, the Lord speaks through the prophet Obadiah: "Though thou exalt thyself as the eagle, and though thou set thy nest among the stars, thence I will bring thee down, saith the Lord" (Obad. 4). The emphasis of Habakkuk is upon the fact that the plunder will not remain hidden. "The stone shall cry out of the wall," and the beams and timbers shall echo the accusation. Sooner or later every dishonest dollar will avenge itself, as the prophet Ezekiel points out: "They shall cast their silver in the streets and their gold shall be removed. Their silver and their gold shall not be able to deliver them in the day of the wrath of the Lord" (Ezek. 7:19).

3. *Woe to the destroyer who builds upon the destruction of others* (v. 12). The judgment is of the Lord, and not of man. "Except the Lord build the house, they labor in vain that build it" (Ps. 127:1), whether it be the tower of ancient Babel (Gen. 11:4-9), or the wall of modern Berlin. The Judge Himself has been an eye witness to every crime, every tear, every drop of blood that has been shed. What He said to Cain, the first murderer, He will say again to every mass murderer or individual killer, "Thy brother's blood crieth unto me from the ground" (Gen. 4:10).

4. *Woe to the debaucher "that giveth his neighbor drink"* (v. 15). Surely no greater menace threatens the moral and spiritual life of our nation than the rising tide of alcohol which is sweeping across the land. "Drink" has proven itself the arch enemy of everything that is essentially Christian, and is probably the greatest single destroyer of the souls of men. Recent

statistics indicate approximately five million drunkards, both men and women, with all that this means in lives wrecked, homes broken, crimes committed, and souls doomed. And the end is not yet; the frightening increase of drinkers and drunkenness continues. The percentage of drinkers has risen from 33% to 63% in our generation; 50% more men are drinking; 174% more women are drinking; and 74% of all college students are drinking.

Surely no greater outpouring of the wrath of God will take place on the day of judgment than upon the makers and sellers of alcoholic beverages, and upon the false friend "that giveth his neighbor drink," thus placing the deadly reptile at his neighbor's bosom.

One of the saddest aspects of the problem of alcohol is the easy tolerance into which so many otherwise sensible and discerning people have been lulled. Once, the corner saloon was the menace to be feared. Now, with the expenditure of two hundred fifty million dollars a year to glamorize social drinking as an element in "gracious living," the homes are being invaded with this unholy propaganda, by every known means of publicity. If all professed Christians became abstainers, with the courage of Daniel of old, this would be a staggering blow to the alcohol traffic and to alcoholism. Drunkards are not recruited from the ranks of abstainers, but from moderate drinkers.

One of the most devastating arraignments of alcohol is Upton Sinclair's book, *The Cup of Fury*. It records the tragic story of seventy-five victims of alcohol whom he has known. All had attained to fame and fortune; they were "men of distinction"; but alcohol became their undoing. The book makes clear the wisdom and moral necessity of total abstinence. A comparable book is that of the American Business Men's Research Foundation, entitled *What's New about Alcohol and Us?* Actually, there is nothing new. Alcohol is what it always was, and does what it always did, whether served in cocktails or in some other form, whether one drinks alone or in a group. It is the same whether served in the sacred vessels profaned by King Belshazzar centuries ago, or from dainty goblets in some elegant living room, or from an uncorked bottle passing from one dirty mouth to another in the foulest dive in the underworld. "Woe unto him that giveth his neighbor drink!"

5. *Woe to the idolator* (v. 19). The pagan Assyrians, Babylonians, and Egyptians were not the only idolators. Among Habakkuk's own people, as in the days of Moses, Joshua, Elijah, and Isaiah, there were those who practiced idolatry. This was not because they knew no better, with their long tradition of godly training, but apparently because at times it seemed expedient and was the sophisticated thing to do. Political considerations and status seeking are not of modern origin.

It would be pleasant to assume that the pronouncement against idolatry is no longer relevant. We do not worship "the golden image" or "the molten image," but how often profit, pleasure, prestige, or public opinion are placed ahead of God! And perhaps we are closer to ancient Israel than we realize. We do not bother to fashion an image; we just worship our gold without melting it, and our greenbacks, without taking them out of the bank.

The prophet Habakkuk was not left in a spirit of depression. Near to the heart of God, he gained new insights into the woes of the wicked; but there were further insights, into the blessedness of the righteous.

## II. THE COMFORT OF THE RIGHTEOUS

Three stars of hope never cease to shine in the believer's firmament.

1. *The just shall live by faith* (v. 4). His reliance is not upon defensive armaments, but spiritual defenses and resources from Almighty God. "Some trust in chariots, and some in horses: but we will remember the name of the Lord our God" (Ps. 20:7).

Faith is the life of God in the heart of man. "Christ in you, the hope of glory" (Col. 1:27). Besides this hope, there is none other. Salvation is not by merit, but by relationship. The household of God is for the children of God. In the Scriptures, the children of God are sharply distinguished from the rest of humanity. To unbelievers, Jesus denied the fatherhood of God. "Ye are not of God. . . . If God were your father, ye would love me. . . . Ye are of *your* father, the devil . . ." (John 8:42-47). No less clear is that further reference: . . . "the *children of God* . . . and the *children of the* devil" (I John 3:10). Thus the fatherhood of the devil is no less a Scriptural doctrine than the fatherhood of God.

Faith guarantees the survival of the soul through the most perilous night. "The Lord knoweth them that are his" (I Tim. 2:19). "He calleth his own sheep by name, and leadeth them out" (John 10:3). He identifies his own even in the largest flock; he finds his own even in the darkest night; he reads the fine print of the soul when all the lights are out.

2. *The truth shall prevail.* "The earth shall be filled with the knowledge of the glory of the Lord, as the waters cover the sea" (v. 14). Here is an assurance to treasure in the dark days when all the trends and appearances are running to the contrary, as in the days of Habakkuk.

The Satanic zeal with which false religions and philosophies are being propagated fills the thoughtful believer with dismay, and seems destined to win the world. With the closing of mission fields, the suppression of the truth, and the persecution of believers in many areas of the world, surely the world does not appear to be in process of being "filled with the knowledge of the glory of the Lord." As a matter of fact, the growth of the non-Christian population of the world is so outstripping the growth of the Christian population as to make Christianity, percentagewise, a steadily dwindling minority. Only the long look can sustain the believer's faith; without it he might well despair.

The destructive teaching of many educational institutions is producing skeptics and agnostics, and threatening to undo the work of our Christian homes and churches. Religion must not be taught; but religion can be undermined, at will. One minister, telling of his own experience in one of our great universities, recalls that he was one of thirty-three candidates for the ministry in the freshman class with which he entered. At graduation, four years later, thirty-one of the group had "lost their call"; and only two went on to seminary training. But "truth crushed to earth will rise again; error, writhing in pain, will die among its friends."

3. *The Lord is in his holy temple* (v. 20), with something to say to every listening heart. However dark the night, He is always accessible, ready to bless, responsive to those who seek him. "Here bring your wounded heart, here tell your anguish; earth has no sorrow that heaven can not heal"—no problem that heaven can not solve. Habakkuk was not the first, nor the last, to cry out in agony of soul, "Why . . . ? O Lord, how long . . . ?" And he was not the only one to find his answer in the holy temple of his Lord.

The Psalmist Asaph, centuries before, had been grieved and perplexed by the prevalence of evil and the prosperity of the wicked. "It was too painful for me, until I went into the sanctuary of God; then understood I their end." In the holy quietness of the sanctuary, God spake to his heart; there he saw what he had not seen before. As a result, his spirit was revived, his soul was fortified, and he closes that beautiful Psalm on a high note of grateful praise. "It is good for me to draw near to God . . ." (Ps. 73:3, 16-17, 28).

Every believer will find, like Habakkuk, and like Asaph, that "it is good to draw near to God." Private devotions are indispensable; likewise, the family altar; but let not the believer forget that "the Lord is in his holy temple," with further blessings not otherwise to be attained. It is in the Lord's house, on the Lord's Day, with the Lord's people, that a man is most likely to see himself as he is, and to hear the call of God to higher ground. In the Lord's house we are reminded that our problems, perplexities, and distresses are not unlike those of previous generations. The world outlook is filled with forebodings of disaster; and in the homeland, with sickening monotony, the statistics on all forms of evil are rising from year to year. How long will God forbear? "Take courage," Habakkuk is saying to the believer. "Draw near to the heart of God, and be assured, the just shall live; the truth shall prevail; and God is ready at this very moment to fortify the believer and to save the lost."

Near to the heart of God, Habakkuk saw the light.

Coming from the presence of God, Habakkuk reflected that light, like Moses, who came from prolonged fellowship with his Lord with such a radiance upon his face that people were actually afraid to come near him (Exod. 34:29-30). Similarly, the mother of John Wesley had learned the secret of spiritual replenishment near to the heart of God. With her large family of children, there were times when the atmosphere of the household became tense and difficult. At such times she would quietly slip away. When she returned, it was with a serenity and poise which the children did not understand until years later. "They that wait upon the Lord shall renew their strength" (Isa. 40:31).

A traveling man brought his wife a little souvenir—a phosphorescent match box which was supposed to glow in the dark. When he turned out the light to demonstrate its use, there was not even the faintest glow. Disgustedly, he concluded that he had been cheated. The next day his wife examined the gift more closely, and found an inscription in tiny letters, "If you want me to shine in the night, keep me in the sunlight through the day." She did as directed; and that night after dinner it was a pleasant surprise for her husband when she turned out the light and the match box shone with a brilliant glow. Thus only can believers "shine as lights . . . in the midst of a crooked and perverse generation" (Phil. 2:15).

# 10
# In the World, but Not of the World

John 17:11-23

1. *Judging by the facial expressions of downtown pedestrians, life, for the majority of people, must be pretty grim.* A roving photographer took snapshots of a sampling of the tense, troubled, unhappy faces that seemed to predominate. Some of the pictures were published; and a commentator raised the question, "Is sadness a disease . . . and has it become an epidemic?" What is wrong with us?

Times were never better. Living standards have never been higher since the Garden of Eden. Our generation has comforts, conveniences, labor-saving devices, and recreation facilities of which no previous generation has ever dreamed. And yet—

The strain of living has probably never been greater than in this day of struggles, anxieties, tensions, and tranquilizers. Statisticians declare that the American people are consuming approximately fourteen million pounds of aspirins a year; over fifty percent of our hospital beds are occupied by mental patients, while heart attacks and nervous breakdowns continue to increase.

2. *Judging by our newspaper headlines, life must be pretty grim.* Indeed, it can be quite an emotional experience to read of all the unpunished crimes, juvenile delinquency, the ravages of alcohol and narcotics, corruption and racketeering, inflation

and confiscatory taxation, threats of depression, international tensions and threats of global catastrophe.

Someone has counseled, "Don't read the morning newspaper if you want to be happy during the day!" Another has added, "Don't read the *evening* paper if you want to sleep without nightmares!" And, of course, "Don't look at T.V. or listen to the radio!"

The unbeliever, looking with sin dimmed eyes into a poorly lighted world, might well despair. But the believer, instructed in the Word of God, and illumined by the Holy Spirit, should be able to read what comes, as it comes, and still experience happy days and restful nights.

3. *Viewed in the light of Scripture, ours is a brighter prospect than that of the Apostles whom Jesus left behind.* Their world, like ours, was a world of many woes. Worse than all their conscious woes was the fact that the masses of people were out of joint with God. Their greatest need was not what they thought —the need for higher wages, better markets, the elimination of slave labor competition—but forgiveness of sin, and reconcilation with God. It was with them as with the woman who was complaining to her physician about her aching hands. Anxiously she asked, "Doctor, can't you do something for me?" He listened carefully; then, to her amazement, instead of going to work on her hands, he said, "Let me see your teeth." There he found the real cause of her trouble, and there the problem had to be met.

The world of the Apostles, like our modern world, was not organized for holiness, but was motivated in the main by "the pride of life" and "the lusts of the flesh" (I John 2:16). Into this unfriendly world, the Apostles were sent, as unwanted aliens, as homeless wanderers, like the Son of God himself. "The foxes have holes, and the birds of the air have nests; but the Son of Man hath not where to lay his head" (Matt. 8:20). Into a world that had registered its attitude toward Christ, and was not less ready to nail them to the cross also, they were sent as sheep among the wolves (Matt. 10:16). "In the world ye shall have tribulation; but be of good cheer: I have overcome the world" (John 16:33).

For such a world, the Lord Jesus fortified the souls of the Apostles by that memorable prayer in which we all are included, and from which the believers have drawn strength in all the intervening centuries. There are four expressions of concern, *four petitions* to the Heavenly Father on their behalf:

### I. THAT THEY MAY BE "KEPT"

"I pray not that thou shouldest take them out of the world, but that thou shouldest keep them from the evil one" (v. 15).

1. *The prayer of Jesus emphasizes what must have been to the disciples a heart breaking omission.* Jesus had warned them of the sorrow, tribulation, and persecution that awaited them; and had told them of his own impending crucifixion, resurrection, and departure. Peter, voicing what must have been in every heart, had asked, "Why can not I follow thee now" (John 13:37)? Those must have been moments of overpowering solemnity when Jesus began to pray for that deeply troubled group. As they listen, in breathless suspense, the prayer of Jesus anticipates their ultimate homegoing, but excludes any thought of that immediate deliverance for which their hearts were yearning. Perhaps they gasped and groaned in dismay. But their work was not done; and they needed to learn a further lesson about prayer. They were not to pray, "God, save me from this trouble," but "strengthen me for it." And this is what Jesus was asking on their behalf.

2. *The prayer of Jesus carried a note of assurance more powerful than their fears.* They were to be "kept from the evil one." Closely related is the Great Commission, which likewise throbs with a mighty assurance: "Lo, I am with you always!" Their spiritual defenses and resources were adequate. They were not promised a calm passage, but a safe landing. No boat ever sank with Jesus on board. Among the golden promises in the Word of God, there are said to be three hundred sixty-five "fear-nots"—one for every day of the year—each one addressed to

believers. For the unbelieving there is no such comfort. He has every reason to tremble. His soul is in mortal jeopardy every day of his life, with stark terror awaiting him at the end.

However deep the darkness, the true believer sings, "It is not night if Thou be near." And at the journey's end he is not alone. In *Pilgrim's Progress*, the glory of the "Celestial City" beckons, but between the pilgrim and his goal there is a deep river; and there is no bridge. He must pass through the troubled waters. Appalled and dismayed, he pleads, "Is there not some other way?" The answer is "No." But he hears the voice of his Lord, "When thou passest through the waters I will be with thee. . . . they shall not overflow thee" (Isa. 43:2). Soon this last obstacle is overcome, the river is crossed, and the pilgrim comes to his rest in the heavenly home. The prayer of the Lord Jesus is fulfilled—"that they whom thou hast given me, be with me where I am" (v. 24). Stephen, in the moment of his homegoing, saw "The heavens opened" and the Lord Jesus waiting to receive him (Acts 7:56, 59). Paul looked with eager longing to the time of his departure, when he would be "with Christ, which is far better" (Phil. 1:23). "Weeping may endure for a night, but joy cometh in the morning" (Ps. 30:5).

## II. THAT THEY MAY BE "SANCTIFIED"

"Sanctify them through thy truth" (v. 17).

1. *To "sanctify" means to make holy; to purify or free from sin; to separate; to set apart for divine use.* This is the purpose of the coming of Jesus, "who gave himself for us, that he might redeem us from all iniquity, and purify unto himself a peculiar people. . ." (Titus 2:14). "As he which hath called you is holy, so be ye holy . . ." (I Peter 1:15). "I beseech you . . . that ye present your bodies a living sacrifice, holy, acceptable unto God, which is your reasonable service. And be not conformed to this world . . ." (Rom. 12:1, 2). This means separation—from sin, selfishness, and worldliness. The terms "holiness," "saint," and "sanctify" are derived from the same Greek root, signifying "separation."

"Come ye out from among them, and be ye separate, saith the Lord, and touch not the unclean thing . . ." (II Cor. 6:17).

This is not—as sometimes interpreted—an exhortation to separate oneself from brethren who are spiritually or doctrinally immature, but to separate oneself from the seven evils enumerated in the context: "unbelievers . . . unrighteousness . . . darkness . . . Belial . . . infidels . . . idols . . . unclean." The believer, surrounded with evil, is *"in* the world, but not *of* the world," like the boatsman, who is *in* the sea, but not *of* the sea. In foul weather and troubled waters, he may have to bail out much water, but to relax would be to invite disaster. A boat kept constantly clear of water might survive many unexpected waves; but a sudden wave breaking over a boat with an accumulation of water in the hold might well sink the boat.

2. *To be "sanctified" is implied in church membership.* The church, the *ecclesia,* is "that which is called out." The members are the "called out ones," those who have been called out of the world and joined to the body of Christ. But too often the implied separation or sanctification is not real. Our generation has a larger percentage of church members than any previous generation, and a larger percentage of church attendance. But we are less distinguishable from the unregenerate world, that "crooked and perverse generation" among whom we are to shine "as lights in the world" (Phil. 2:15). What we have gained in numbers we have largely lost in depth. We have become shallower and poorer in conviction. We are like that fabled river which was said to be three miles wide and only three inches deep. There are too many superficial "cocktail Christians." Too many have lost the sense of sin, and the capacity for indignation. There is a tolerance of evils which should evoke holy horror, a widespread coddling of criminals, and a woeful unconcern for the laws of God and man.

We have become poorer in stewardship. The percentage of our national income given to religion and benevolence has been on a steep decline for over thirty years. In 1921 our giving amounted to 1.2% of our national income; in 1953 it had dropped to .4%; and the ratio continues to decline.

We have become less discerning in moral and spiritual values. Someone has suggested that the most fitting symbol of our moral and spiritual ambiguity would be some of those meaningless blobs, blurs, and smudges which, in certain quarters, pass for "modern art." Sharp discernment and deep convictions are basic to that sanctification for which Jesus prayed, and which is the mark of true discipleship.

### III. THAT THEY MAY BE "UNITED"

"That they may be one, even as we are one" (v. 22).

1. *This unity is the unity of a common devotion.* Love for the Savior has been likened to the thread which holds together the beads of a precious necklace: Break the thread, and the necklace falls apart. Love for the Savior has been likened also to a magnet: The nearer the particles are to the magnet, the nearer they are to one another. There is something in every true believer which enables him to sense his spiritual kindred, and inclines him toward them, in spite of human barriers and regardless of external differences. There may not be organic union, but there is the unity of a living organism, as the devoted believer recognizes himself and his fellow believers as belonging to the living, breathing, functioning body of Christ —the church—of which Christ is the Head (Col. 1:18). "Behold, how good and how pleasant it is for brethren to dwell together in unity" (Ps. 133:1).

Devotion to Christ is the common denominator that reaches across all barriers and outlast all other bonds. The sharing of lesser interests is not enough. Some people are drawn together by the fact that they like so many things in common; and persons have been known to become "fast friends" by the discovery that they *disliked* so many things in common. A common enemy brought the allied nations together in a mighty compact; but after the victory was won, certain allies turned into outright enemies. During World War II, the suffering in "concentration camps" seemed to bind victims into a solid unity; when the war was over and certain "concentration camps" became "*displaced persons* camps," some of the most fantastic feuds broke out among the liberated persons.

2. *This unity is the unity of a common motivation.* At Pentecost, in that beautiful fulfillment of the prayer of Jesus, the believers were "all with one accord in one place"; all were "filled with the Holy Spirit"; all were speaking "as the Spirit gave them utterance." Welded and wielded by the Holy Spirit, they were completely untroubled by diversities of culture, tastes, and temperament. Like one hundred and twenty electric clocks wired to the same current, they were in perfect rhythm, all speaking the same message. The unity of a common motivation was demonstrated in a remarkable display of two clocks, said to be the world's largest and the world's smallest, functioning side by side, giving the same true reflection of the time of day. Size made no difference; unity of motivation meant everything!

But as light can not be communicated through broken wires, the Holy Spirit can not work through a broken fellowship. The spiritual consequences of disunity can hardly be exaggerated. Worship languishes; evangelism loses its thrust; the effectiveness of the church is crippled. The Apostle Paul, in his appeal for the "unity of the Spirit," sees the "whole body fitly joined together" by the Lord, "and compacted by that which every joint supplieth." By the Lord's design, the body is "fitly joined together," but *every joint must supply its own cement* (Eph. 4:3, 13, 16). In our oft divided fellowship, with so much of doctrinal error and spiritual immaturity, we need to be constantly challenged by that time honored formula ("China's gift to the church universal"): "Agree to differ; resolve to love; unite to serve!"

### IV. THAT THEY MAY BE "PERFECTED"

"That they may be made perfect" (v. 23).

1. *Jesus was dealing with a group of imperfect people.* His

concern, when he chose the Apostles at the beginning of his ministry, was reflected in the challenge, "Be ye perfect, even as your Father which is in heaven is perfect" (Matt. 5:48). "Be ye spiritually mature," He is saying; and the aspiration to absolute sinlessness is at least implied. To aim for anything less is not worthy of a true believer, however poorly he may succeed. The disciples were dedicated to a high and holy calling; but they were immature, unripe, incomplete. In certain respects they were like Israel coming out of Egypt: It took only a short time for God to get Israel out of Egypt, but it took forty years in the wilderness to get Egypt out of Israel. Spiritual maturity is not wrought by miracle, but by discipline and persistent stretching toward the highest ideal. No Christian is so good, so gifted, so effective in service that he can afford the encumbrance of even the slightest "weights" or sins which "so easily beset us" (Heb. 12:1).

The concern of Jesus at the close of his ministry was still "that they be made perfect." They had come far, yet how immature they proved themselves in Gethsemane and in the testings of that fateful Friday of the crucifixion! The prayer of Jesus was nevertheless in process of fulfillment. The Epistles of Peter, written in old age, reflect a rare maturity. Especially significant is the closing line of his last recorded message, the appeal to "grow in grace" (II Peter 3:18). This was about thirty years after the prayer of Jesus, which was still in process of fulfillment. And when another thirty years had passed, the last of the Apostles, John, pointed confidently toward its ultimate fulfillment: "When he shall appear, we shall be like him" (I John 3:2).

2. *Jesus is still dealing with an imperfect people.* The trouble with the church is that it is made up of *people.* And so long as people are imperfect, we shall have an imperfect church. But who can wait for a flawless church to join! When the church ceases to be imperfect—after the Rapture—it will be forever too late to join. And if there were a flawless church to join, who could qualify to become a member! But the imperfections of the church and its members could never jus-

tify living with a lower aim than the perfection of our Lord. The familiar testimony of a certain member, often repeated at prayer meetings, was: "Brethren, pray for me. I am not what I ought to be; but thank God I am not what I used to be." Perhaps he was *aiming* too low.

The hope of the church lies not in human goodness, but in disciplines established by the Head of the church. "All Scripture is given by inspiration of God, and is profitable for doctrine, for reproof, for correction, for instruction in righteousness, that the man of God may be *perfect,* thoroughly furnished unto all good works" (II Tim. 3:16, 17). In addition, the Head of the church appointed *teachers,* "for the perfecting of the saints" (Eph. 3:11-13). But even this is not enough. There must be chastisement as well. "Whom the Lord loveth he chasteneth. . . ." The chastening may be grievous, "nevertheless afterward it yieldeth the peaceable fruit of righteousness unto them who are exercised thereby" (Heb. 12:6, 11).

Too many of us are like the bottle of medicine with the familiar label: "Shake well before using." We are agreeably, comfortably, complacently useless till "shaken" or chastened of God. An extensive survey revealed that, with school children, the threat of punishment was far more potent as an incentive to good work than was the promise of reward. A loving Heavenly Father will not withhold from his child that which is needful to bring him to maturity.

The Disciples were *"in the world, but not of the world."* How fortunate for the world that Jesus did not give them their heart's desire and let them depart with Him! That would have been like removing all the physicians in a time of epidemic; there would have been no Pentecost, no Gospels, and no Epistles.

This is a complicated world, bristling with problems, yet glorious with possibilities—and a good world for the purpose for which it was made. Therefore the prayer: "I pray not that thou shouldest take them out of the world"; but that they may be kept . . . sanctified . . . united . . . perfected!

# 11
# Something Better Than Gold

Acts 3:1-11

1. *Like Peter and John, we probably pass men and women on our way to church every Sunday whose need for help is no less real and urgent than that of the lame man at the beautiful gate.* There may not be poverty or physical infirmity, but needs that lie far deeper. The most obvious need of the lame man was for silver and gold. His deeper needs were not mentioned as he made his appeal for alms. And it was in terms of silver and gold that people were responding. Yet this was the kind of help with which the afflicted man might well dispense if given something better. Silver and gold, he had been receiving for forty years; but it left him as he was—a helpless, hopeless cripple, carried by others, begging for alms to hold body and soul together. Silver and gold, anybody could give him; but it remained for Peter and John to provide him with something better.

2. *Like Peter and John, we have resources for meeting the deepest need of every man that breathes.* These resources are spiritual. They are ours by the grace of God, and to share them is no less a divine imperative for us than for those faithful apostles.

(1) The apostles went "up into the temple at the hour of prayer" (v. 1), like the Lord Jesus, who "went into the synagogue on the Sabbath day . . . as his custom was" (Luke 4:16). Church-going Christians are the hope of the world. A solicitor

for a charity drive in a large city was asked by a generous churchman whom he had approached for a substantial contribution, "Why do you come to the church people who are already giving up to capacity through their churches? Why not look to the large untapped resources of the non-church-goers?" "Those who are already giving through the churches," said the solicitor, "are our main support; without them all our benevolences would collapse." A familiar observation, easy to confirm, is that the person who neglects church attendance (Heb. 10:25) is usually leaving undone just about everything else that a Christian ought to be doing. He is not praying; he is not reading the Bible; he is not witnessing to others; he is not giving. The lame man had good reasons for choosing to station himself near the door of the house of worship around the hour of prayer.

(2) The apostles looked with compassion upon the lame beggar. They had learned from the Lord Jesus, who "saw the multitude" and "was moved with compassion on them," and who wept over the city of Jerusalem, and in his compassion prayed even for those who nailed him to the cross. Peter and John knew the story of the good Samaritan, and had seen the Lord Jesus again and again healing the sick and restoring the blind, the lame, the lepers, the deaf and the speechless. Through long association with the Lord Jesus, they had absorbed his spirit, and were now reflecting it. Like their Master, who did not stand aloof and write the plan of salvation in the sky, but entered into the griefs and sufferings of lost mankind, the apostles put themselves in personal contact with the lame man, and "lifted him up."

By their Christ-like example, the apostles have left us three simple *rules of Christian sharing:*

### I. THEY SHARED WHAT THEY HAD

"Silver and gold have I none; but such as I have give I thee" (v. 6).

1. To share what they had was indeed all they *could do*.

(1) How poor they were; and yet, how rich! For three years they had walked with Jesus, who warned a would-be disciple, "The foxes have holes, and the birds of the air have nests; but the Son of Man hath not where to lay his head" (Matt. 8:20). Once, when there was need for one shekel, the equivalent of about sixty cents in American money, it was necessary for Jesus to perform a miracle to meet the need (Matt. 17:27). The disciples lived by faith, carrying no purse as they went about their labors at the bidding of their Master. Yet, as they testified on the night before the crucifixion, they had never lacked for anything (Luke 22:35). Their *visible* resources were virtually nil; but their *invisible* resources were unlimited. They had that with which the poorest is *rich,* and without which the richest is *poor*.

(2) How poor we sometimes feel when we are rich indeed! A young woman, feeling a bit sorry for herself, exclaimed, "I don't have looks; I don't have wealth; I don't have talent; I don't have position; I don't have anything! Thomas Jefferson said, 'All men are born equal.' He did not know what he was talking about! Men are not born equal; and there is no way of *making* them equal." While she was not altogether wrong, she was overlooking something. In the providence of God there is a grand impartiality in this friendly universe and in the distribution of its true riches—the beauty of nature, the glory of the sunset, the access of every soul to the Savior. He communes as freely with the pauper as with the millionaire. "Behold, I stand at the door, and knock; if *any* man hear my voice, and open the door, I will come in to him, and will sup with him, and he with me" (Rev. 3:20).

One of the poorest women I ever knew was also one of the richest and happiest. It was over forty years ago. She lived in a tiny cottage belonging to my employer, who had large real estate holdings and occasionally acquired, in his trading, properties like this, which he was not at all proud to own. This woman, an elderly widow, living alone, was not destitute; but even the modest rent which she had to pay was burdensome at times. Once when she was unable to pay on the due date, instead of coming to the door with a sad face and a prosaic explanation, she greeted me as brightly as ever. "Silver and gold have I none, she said; "but I have something far better! Young man, are you a Christian; and do you have the joy of the Lord in your heart?" Like Peter and John, she had something to share, and was eager to share it.

2. To share what they had was no more than they *should have done.*

(1) Much had been entrusted to them, with the intent that it should be used. "Freely ye have received; freely give" (Matt. 10:8). It was never intended that Christians should live for themselves alone, and having lived their meagre little lives, should die their little deaths, and be laid in their little graves without having tasted the "abundant life" (John 10:10). In the divine economy we are called not only to be "blameless and harmless . . . without rebuke," but to *"shine* as lights in the world" (Phil. 2:15). To live inoffensive, unblemished lives is not enough; our lives are to be *outgoing* as well. "To him that knoweth to do good, and doeth it not, to him it is sin" (James 4:17).

(2) "To whomsoever much is given, of him shall much be required" (Luke 12:48). And the Giver of all good gifts (James 1:17) remembers where all his resources are. In the parable of the talents (Matt. 25), Jesus makes it clear that there will be an accounting, and that we are responsible for all the knowledge, powers, and resources which we possess—and for all the knowledge, powers, and resources which we *ought to possess!* "Mine own *with interest"* (Matt. 25:27)—this is the basis of the final accounting. And the Lord will not deal lightly with those who have neglected their opportunities and ignored their responsibilities. In the New Testament pattern there is no place for passive discipleship. Every Christian is to be a *full time Christian,* concerned, alert, vocal, and outgoing in spiritual helpfulness.

The example of the apostles reflects a further rule of Christian sharing:

II. THEY GAVE WHAT THEY HAD IN THE NAME OF CHRIST

"In the name of Jesus Christ of Nazareth rise up and walk" (v. 6).

1. *"In the name of Christ"—Herein lies the merit of the gift.*

(1) Even so small a thing as a cup of water given "in my name," says the Lord Jesus, shall not fail of its reward (Mark 9:41). The same is true of major sacrifices which are made "for my sake and the gospel's" (Mark 10:29). It follows that if the motive is otherwise, the most generous giving is without merit in the sight of our Lord.

(2) Philanthropy which leaves Christ out, and which aims only to benefit the recipient or to bring honor or benefit or satisfaction to the philanthropist is without promise of heavenly reward. Like the Pharisees who prayed on the street corners "that they may be seen of men," they *have* their reward (Matt. 6:5). There have always been those who "loved the praise of men more than the praise of God" (John 12:43).

(3) Benevolence extended in the name of an organization unrelated to the cause of Christ would, of course, be without merit in his sight. And a million dollars given to charity in the name of the Association for the Advancement of Atheism would not only be without merit in the sight of God, but would constitute an act of war against the living God and would be judged accordingly. The most productive salesman in the metropolis can expect reward only from the firm that he serves, and would not think of receiving pay from firms with which his employer is competing. The ultimate test of our gifts, our services, and our virtues is quite simple: Were we seeking thereby to serve and honor our Lord; or was there some lesser motive? Did we give or serve *for Christ's sake;* or because of social pressure? Were we honest *for Christ's sake;* or because "honesty is the best policy"? Were we morally clean *for Christ's sake;* or for the sake of family or friends? Were we kind to others *for Christ's sake;* or because kindness pays such pleasant dividends?

2. *"In the name of Christ"—Herein lies the power of the giver.*

(1) The sincere use of the name of Christ, in the service of Christ, is honored according to promise. "Whatsoever ye shall ask in my name, that will I do, that the Father may be glorified in the son" (John 14:13). The disciples were not without previous experience. Long before, returning from one of their missions, they were jubilant as they reported to the Master, "Lord, even the demons were subject unto us *in thy name*" (Luke 10:17). In their own name, as they well realized, they were without power to cast out demons or to give strength to a man who had never walked.

(2) The idle utterance of the phrase, "in Jesus' name," at the conclusion of a prayer does not give power to the prayer. "They that worship Him must worship Him in spirit and in truth" (John 4:24). A prayer of "vain repetitions," perfunctorily recited, can not be redeemed by adding the phrase, "in the name of Christ," and will not bring down the answering fire of heaven.

(3) The dishonest use of the name of Christ, by imposters, has the judgment of God upon it. "Many will say to me in that day, Lord, Lord, have we not prophesied in thy name . . . ? And then will I profess unto them, I never knew you; depart from me, ye that work iniquity" (Matt. 7:22-23). The seven sons of Sceva, having seen the Apostle Paul casting out evil spirits in the name of Jesus, devised a scheme to capitalize upon that which they had witnessed. They found a man possessed of an evil spirit; they sought to cast out the evil spirit "in the name of the Lord Jesus . . . whom Paul preacheth" (Acts 19:11ff.); and they came to grief. "The evil spirit answered, Jesus I know, and Paul I know; but who are ye?" Thereupon the possessed man "leaped on them, and overcame them . . . so that they fled out of the house naked and wounded."

The third rule of Christian sharing follows naturally upon the first two:

III. THEY GAVE SOMETHING FAR BETTER THAN SILVER AND GOLD

"The lame man . . . was healed" and was "praising God" (vs. 8, 11).

1. *Silver and gold are quickly spent.* Health fails, sooner or later. The undertaker always wins out over the physician in the end. Only that which is done for the *soul* is eternal. To send an astronaut to the moon and bring him back alive would be, in the light of eternity, a far lesser achievement than to direct a soul to the heavenly home.

(1) If a parent should provide the child with everything that is good, *except spiritual care,* that parent would be, in the sight of God, a tragic failure. The most comfortable home, the most wholesome food, the finest in medical care, and discipline, and education would not compensate for neglect of the soul.

(2) If we could provide hospitalization, doctors, nurses, and medication for all the afflicted, shelter for the homeless, clothing for the destitute, and food for the hungry, this could not compensate for neglecting to give them the gospel of Christ. In 1793 William Carey was sent as a missionary to India. If, instead, the world's largest ocean liner had been loaded with silver and gold for India, such a gift would have been small compared to the gift of that lone missionary who brought the gospel to that sub-continent.

After the disastrous earthquake which occurred in Iran, Christians from around the world were sending relief, and the desperate need for spiritual help was again demonstrated. Bob Pierce tells of seeing an aged woman sitting among the ruins and looking off into space. She had lost her four sons and all that she owned. She had not eaten for five days, though food was available. Asked why she did not eat, she replied, with infinite sadness, "I cannot eat. My hunger is deep within my heart where no bread can ever reach it." Yes, there is a deeper need than that which can be met with bread or with silver and gold.

(3) If we could lift every filthy, drunken derelict out of

the gutter and clean him up, sober him, feed him, clothe him, move him from skidrow to a pleasant home on the boulevard, and provide him with a bank account, all this would leave him poor indeed if he has not been helped to a knowledge of the Savior.

2. *The gospel which is entrusted to us does what silver and gold could never do.*

(1) The aim of the gospel is to *save*—not merely to make the flock or the individual more comfortable on the way to the slaughter, but to save them *from* the slaughter. It aims to save *now*—not "by and by." Every day is the last day of opportunity for someone; the need is immediate. Like the thief dying on the cross, the sinner needs more than the promise of betterment through slowly evolving changes in the social order. And finally, the gospel aims to save *"to the uttermost"*—not just till the present life ends and the undertaker comes. "He that believeth" shall have *everlasting* life.

(2) The story of the lame man leaves us with the happy feeling that he was healed not only in body, but in soul as well. He was "walking, and leaping, and *praising God.*" Whatever his spiritual state had been previously, he was now in contact with the living God. He had received that which was far better than silver and gold.

Peter and John lived on a spiritual altitude congenial to dedicated believers. In their spiritual concern they were alert, vocal, and outgoing. They were never off duty. They shared what they had; they gave what they had in the name of Christ; and they gave that which is better than silver and gold!

# 12

# Plains of Peace and Hills of Joy

Philippians 4:4-9

*Rejoice in the Lord alway: and again I say, rejoice.*
*—Philippians 4:4*

1. *Some of us cannot stand in the light of this text and feel entirely comfortable.*

We are rebuked by the fact that we are not always rejoicing, radiant, serene, like true sons and daughters of God. To be sure, we are living in an unideal world, among imperfect people. The weather is not always fair. Times are not always good. Circumstances are not always conducive to cheerfulness. People are not always kind, thoughtful, and helpful.

We are reminded, nevertheless, that we must be a great disappointment to our Lord, who said, "Ye are the light of the world" (Matt. 5:14). He did not say, "Ye are the *clouds* of the world." A cloud behind the counter never attracted a customer. The wailing wall in Jerusalem never won a convert to Judaism. A cheerless Christian is no adornment to "the doctrine of God" (Titus 2:10). We shall never be spiritually effective until we have first become spiritually attractive.

2. *All of us are caught up in the admonition of Paul, the Apostle of good cheer.*

He indicates, by emphasis and repetition, the importance of rejoicing in the Lord. "Rejoice in the Lord *alway*"—there is the emphasis; "and *again* I say, rejoice"—there is the repetition.

112

He suggests the impossibility of being joyful apart from the Lord. "Rejoice *in the Lord.*" This joy is not a pumped-up emotion, such as the orator might seek to induce apart from the Lord as he challenges his hearers, "Stand erect! Stretch to your full height! Rise to your tip-toes! Reach up! Press forward . . . !" This joy is not self-induced. It is not the product of clever devising or strenuous exertion, but the simple by-product of godly living on the higher levels.

The Apostle traces the joy of the Lord to "the peace of God" and "the God of peace." But peace comes before joy. One of the most beautiful birthday cards I ever received carried this message: "May the years that lie ahead lead you o'er plains of peace and hills of joy!" First, the "plains of peace," then the "hills of joy"!

The Apostle supplies the formula by which the believer may attain to "the peace of God," which in turn leads to the joy of the Lord. Three *elements* make up the formula.

### I. THE SPIRIT OF MODERATION

"Let your moderation be known to all men" (v. 5).

1. *The meaning of the term here rendered as "moderation" has long puzzled the commentators.* It seems to mean far more than a mere balance between obsession and omission, or between exaggeration and under-statement. Various renderings have been suggested, such as "forbearance," "gentleness," and "magnanimity." Perhaps the nearest approach to the original idea is that of the commentator Matthew Arnold. Finding no single word to express the meaning exactly, he coined a phrase which has been gratefully borrowed by other commentators ever since: "the sweet reasonableness of Christ." It is really a composite virtue. It is holiness coupled with humility; loathing for sin coupled with love for the sinner; conviction coupled with forbearance; zeal coupled with discretion. It allows for indignation without vindictiveness; anger without sin.

2. *The incentive to "moderation" is the sobering, humbling sense of the presence of Christ.* "The Lord is at hand."

(1) How easy it is to practice moderation in *speech* when we have a lively awareness of the presence of our Lord! How easy to give the "soft answer" that "turneth away wrath!" There was beauty and merit in the old dining room motto which was once so familiar in our Christian homes: "Christ is the Head of this house—the unseen guest at every meal—the silent listener to every conversation."

An elderly Negro servant was asked by her mistress, "How do you manage to keep such a pleasant disposition with all the irritations that you have to endure?" She had a good answer: "When I remember that the Lord is at hand, I always taste every word before I let it pass my lips." But we do not always remember. Perhaps there have been times when our conversation had drifted to lower and lower levels and could no longer pass through "the three golden gates"—"Is it true? Is it kind? Is it necessary?" Then someone who was held in high and reverential regard entered the room. A moment later, as if by a miracle, the conversation had taken such an upturn that the ripest of saints would have found the atmosphere congenial to his presence.

(2) How easy it is to show moderation in *feeling* when we are mindful of the presence of our Lord! In frontier days, a father who could neither read nor write received a letter from his worthless son who, like "the prodigal son," had gone to "a far country." There he had run into trouble, and needed help. The father took the letter to his nearest neighbor to have it read. When the neighbor had finished, the father gritted his teeth and said, "It serves him right; he brought it on himself; let him take his medicine!" But the father could not forget. Next day he took the letter to another neighbor to have it read to him again. When this neighbor finished, the father, with tears in his eyes, said, "My boy is in trouble; I must help him;" and so he did. What made the difference? Both neighbors knew the son, his rebellious spirit, and the unworthy manner of his leaving. But the second neighbor, a very godly man, had, along with his sense of justice and indig-

nation, the spirit of moderation, a loathing for sin coupled with love for the sinner.

(3) How easy to maintain moderation in *behavior*, even under provocation, when remembering that "the Lord is at hand!" A pastor was having trouble with a pair of shoes he had recently purchased. When he returned to the shoe store, he found the salesman quite difficult. The longer they talked, the more tense the atmosphere became. The preacher was becoming exasperated; his temperature had risen; his pulse had quickened; and he was about to explode. But just as he was about to "lose his halo," the shoe salesman said, vehemently, "But Dr. . . . . , don't you see . . . ?" In a moment the preacher realized that he was known here—as a pastor, and as spokesman for Christ in the community. Instantly his temperature returned to normal, and his pulse likewise; and he resumed negotiations in a spirit compatible with his Christian profession. In a remarkably short time everything was worked out, to the satisfaction of all concerned.

Beyond the spirit of moderation, there is a further element in the Apostolic formula.


## II. THE DISCIPLINE OF PRAYER

"Be careful [anxious] for nothing; but in everything by prayer and supplication with thanksgiving let your requests be made known unto God" (v. 6). Effective prayer depends upon two qualities:

1. *Prayer must be trustful.*

(1) When times are normal there is no problem; our faith is like that of the Psalmist who declared, in perfect trust, "The Lord is my Shepherd; I shall not want. He maketh me to lie down in green pastures; He leadeth me beside the still waters. He restoreth my soul . . . ." In faith we echo the further testimony, "I will lift up mine eyes unto the hills, from whence cometh my help" (Ps. 121:1).

(2) When times are hard, a fitting symbol of persevering

faith is the tree at midwinter waiting for the spring. Stripped of its leaves, half buried in snow, caked in ice to the tips of its twigs, exposed to the fury of the blizzards, it continues lifting its bare hands toward the God of Heaven who has promised, "While the earth remaineth, seedtime and harvest, and cold and heat, and summer and winter, and day and night shall not cease" (Gen. 8:22). Yes, spring will come again; the snow and ice will melt away; there will be leaves, and blossoms, and fruit, as in other years.

(3) When times are desperate, we have a pattern of perfect trust in Psalm 27:1: "The Lord is my light and my salvation; whom shall I fear? The Lord is the strength of my life; of whom shall I be afraid?" In a dark hour of desperate peril the Psalmist turned to God for help; God turned on the light; and the Psalmist discovered that with God on his side he was more than equal to the situation. His defenses were stronger than the perils that threatened; his resources were greater than his need; his strength was greater than any strain that he would have to bear. He had found the only rational escape from fear. He did not need to be brave; he had something far better. All honor to the brave! Our hearts go out to the man who stands his ground and with trembling knees, and quaking heart, and pallid face, holds on until victory is achieved. But bravery at best is only the poor refuge of unfortunate persons who have nothing better. That better thing is simple fearlessness.

### 2. *Prayer must be thankful.*

Thankfulness is one of the graces by which the believer reveals the state of his spiritual health. "In everything give thanks: for this is the will of God in Christ Jesus concerning you" (I Thess. 5:18). The outlook may be grim and threatening, but the believer has learned from the Lord Jesus, who "gave thanks" (Matt. 26:27) even on that darkest night of all, just before the crucifixion. A thankful spirit does not reflect the state of the world in which we live, but it does reveal our nearness to our Lord.

Thankfulness adds a new dimension to all our blessings. Our

food tastes better when we have given thanks; our common blessings loom larger; our eternal destiny shines ever more brightly; and life becomes correspondingly more serene.

We are now well on the way to that "peace of God, which passeth all understanding." But there is still another element, not to be omitted, in the Apostolic formula.

### III. THE PRACTICE OF SELECTIVE LIVING

"Whatsoever things are true . . . honest . . . just . ... pure . . . lovely . . . of good report; if there be any virtue, and if there be any praise, think on these things" (v. 8).

1. *Selective living reflects wisdom of a high order.* In the worst of environments, however sordid and depressing, there is something good. In the ugliest of people there is something worthy of appreciation. In the most unideal situations there is something worth discovering. Selective living finds the good that is hidden away in the heap, and rejects what is unwholesome or unhelpful.

One of the memorable experiences of my brief time on the farm was that of hay baling. One man was bringing up the hay on the buck rake, another was piling it on the platform, and my job was to thrust the hay, in measured portions, into the baling chamber. I was a teen-ager, a green, uninitiated "town dude"; the others were experienced farm hands. At one point there were weeds mixed with the hay, and I was meticulously separating them and pitching them aside. One of the men became impatient and yelled at me, "What are you doing there? You're slowing up the works!" Meekly I explained; and he yelled back, "Don't bother about the weeds; leave that to the old cow!" That winter I understood, as I saw the cows nuzzle the weeds aside and feed upon the sweetly fragrant hay. The "old cow" showed greater wisdom than some of us who have not learned the fine art of selective living.

2. *Selective living reveals our taste and affinity for the good.*

A man sees the world not as it is, but as *he* is. In a given church or community, one person sees, absorbs and reflects that which is lovely, virtuous, and praiseworthy. Another seems particularly gifted in sensing scandal and sordidness. By revealing what we *see,* we often reveal what we *are.*

A country preacher was chatting with one of his deacons on the front porch, as they waited for the call to dinner, following the Sunday morning service. The porch was partly enclosed with honeysuckle vines in full bloom. The air was filled with a delightful fragrance. A wild canary was darting in and out among the blossoms, chirping merrily as he flitted about. After a while the farmer noted, across the field, the movements of a flock of buzzards which were evidently feeding upon something dead which they had found. What was it that attracted the canary to the fragrance of the honeysuckle, and the buzzards to the rotting carrion in the field? Each was merely expressing his own peculiar taste.

3. *Selective living develops character in keeping with the diet upon which we feed.* When the significance of vitamins first came to be appreciated, a fascinating exhibit appeared in one of our museums. There were eight white rats, all from the same litter, which had served in an experiment and were now suitably mounted for display. Above each specimen eight essential vitamins were listed. The first specimen was large, well rounded, fully developed; he had been brought up on all the eight vitamins. The second specimen was a bit smaller and less well favored; on his list, one of the vitamins was crossed out. Each specimen had been brought up on one vitamin less than the previous specimen, and was correspondingly less well developed, down to the eighth specimen, with only one vitamin on his list. It was a pitiable specimen, scrawny, dwarfed, misshapen, but an eloquent witness to the need for all the vitamins. Spiritual growth demands all the eight vitamins in the Apostolic formula—"Whatsoever things are true . . . honest . . . just . . . pure . . . lovely . . . of good report . . . virtue . . . praise. . . ."

4. *Selective living finds values to feed the soul in any environment.* The thoughtful Christian who earnestly seeks the good in his environment may find inspiration in the selective processes of the sun as it passes overhead doing its day's work. Where does the sun collect that pure, heavenly vapor which comes down in the form of rain and snow to bless the earth? Some indeed is drawn from sparkling lakes and mountain brooks, but by no means all. Some is drawn from polluted streams, and some from the foulest gutters in the filthiest slums. The sun is selective, and draws from every environment only that which is pure, leaving all the filth and stench behind.

"Those things . . . do: and the God of peace shall be with you" (v. 9). Here is the heavenly formula: the spirit of moderation, the discipline of prayer, the practice of selective living. Thus, having fellowship with the "God of peace," and having the "peace of God" in our hearts, we are prepared to experience the joy of the Lord.

# 13

# Living with Your Frustrations

Philippians 1:12-21

*I would ye should understand, brethren, that the things which happened unto me have fallen out rather unto the furtherance of the gospel. . . .—Philippians 1:12*

Like a light beam out of the dungeon, comes this cheering message from the Apostle Paul in his Roman imprisonment. You may put an eagle in a cage, but he will soon make his way to the highest perch and there he will spend his enforced leisure looking out toward the sun. You may put a great man in prison and chain him to the floor between armed guards, but his soul remains free; his spirit cannot be imprisoned.

Imprisonment never was a matter to be lightly taken, and particularly in the experience of a man like the Apostle Paul. Not only was he a refined, sensitive soul; but he was also an athlete in every fiber of his mind and spirit, a pioneer with expanding horizons, for whom three continents were not enough. And if America had been discovered before his day, he would in all likelihood have made his way to these shores also, to bring the gospel of Christ. Besides this, although advanced in years, he was still in his prime. And he was needed everywhere. The churches which he had established here and there were young, inexperienced, and bristling with problems. Though zealous and eager to help, the Apostle was "in bonds" —in prison, in total frustration, in the presence of a need so great that it must have wrung his heart from day to day. Yet, we do not find him fretting, chewing his fingernails, tearing his hair, as some of us might have done. Instead, we find him serenely on top of his troubles and frustrations, having learned from the Lord Jesus Christ the difficult lesson of how to behave in prison. "I have learned, in whatsoever state I am, therein to be content" (Phil. 4:11).

We who have never experienced imprisonment can scarcely realize what the Apostle Paul endured. We have never known the experience of hearing the prison door clanging shut behind us and then spending hours, days, weeks, or months behind locked doors. But all of us have frustrations, and in many cases these frustrations are not less serious than prison bars. We might be surprised if we knew the frustrations of some of our acquaintances, like the man who had lost both legs, and who was known to his neighbors only as a cheerful, adequate, well-adjusted person. What was not generally known was the fact that he was walking on artificial legs. By the grace of God he had risen above his handicap; but when he died and his will was read, the opening line reflected something of the frustration which he had endured through the years: "Please bury me in a full length coffin."

A comparable frustration is that of the man in the grip of an incurable disease, who is unwilling to take the first doctor's diagnosis, and goes from one physician to another, always to have the same diagnosis confirmed. "There is nothing more that we can do; you may have only six months, and perhaps less, to wind up your affairs." I am thinking also of that person who is born with a hereditary handicap—a deformed, weak, inadequate body. Or that other person with an inadequate mind, with occasional flashes of inspiration and aspiration but always driven back and made to realize that he must move in a small circle and live a small, frustrated life. I was speaking to a woman who said her ulcers were about to get her down. "But you are too young to be talking about ulcers," I said. "What do you mean?" "Oh," she said, "that son of ours . . . injured in an accident, so that he almost died, now in an institution for the mentally afflicted! And here I am, utterly frustrated, unable to do a thing about it!" Her case is not unique. All around us people are breaking down, tens of thousands every year, because they have not the spiritual defenses and resources to endure the strains and pressures of every day living.

There is something which we sorely need to learn, and which we can learn from the Apostle Paul. He had achieved, at the time of his Epistle to the Philippians, several *successes* which point the way for us:

## I. PAUL SUCCEEDED IN FORGETTING ABOUT HIS IMPRISONMENT

1. *Listen to him.* "I do rejoice and will rejoice," he said. Four times he refers to his "bonds"; but sixteen times in that brief epistle we read the words "joy," "rejoice," "gladness"; and twice the Apostle speaks of "praise" and "thanksgiving." Look at him. There he sits. For the crime of preaching the gospel, he is in prison—hounded, persecuted, abused and threatened by those whom he had come to help, just as the Son of God had suffered at the hands of those whom He had come to help. Paul does not know whether he will ever see the outside of prison again, whether he will ever walk the street again as a free man; he does not know what day he might be led to the executioner's block. And yet, instead of smoldering in bitterness, he is radiant and serene. From the tone of his letter, one might imagine him a free man in a lovely setting, comfortable, relaxed, and surrounded with friends. "Blessed be the God and Father of our Lord Jesus Christ, who hath blessed us with all spiritual blessings in heavenly places in Christ . . . ." Thus he writes to the Ephesians out of the same imprisonment, and later in that Epistle he speaks of sitting with Christ in heavenly places (Eph. 1:3; 2:6). Where was he sitting? In prison! But that was not his real address. Where he really *lived* was, as he indicated, "in heavenly places with Christ Jesus."

The Apostle reminds us of an incident in *Pilgrim's Progress.* You remember how Christian was being guided around and was shown a place where a fire was brightly burning at the foot of a wall. A man was there throwing water on the fire, and the more water he threw on the fire the higher the blaze came up. Christian was utterly baffled until the Interpreter took him around behind the wall. There he saw another man with a vessel of oil steadily feeding the flame. The faster the water was thrown on the fire, the faster he fed the flame from behind the wall. The unquenchable radiance of the Apostle must have been baffling indeed to those uncomprehending pagan guardsmen who observed him from day to day.

2. *Listen to him again.* "For me to live is Christ and to die is gain." Can we say that without stuttering? We have not really attained to maturity in our faith until we *can*. We may need that kind of faith before we are through. We have been hearing over the radio that England has concluded that there is no adequate defense against atomic attack; the country is vulnerable and must rely upon deterrents rather than defenses. The only thing they can see to do is to plant enough installations of long-range missiles pointed toward the potential enemy, so that at the pulling of a trigger they can bring destruction upon half a continent. With these installations multiplied in all the countries, deliberately engineered, placed in strategic positions, aimed with all the factors of distance and direction taken into account, the pressing of a few buttons could bring desolation to much of the civilized world. If we think long enough and deeply enough upon the harrowing possibilities, it is something to make the blood run cold.

Some of us will remember reading in the history books, back in grammar school days, about that awe-inspiring spectacle in the heavens over New England during the past century when, we are told, it became dark at midday, with shooting stars flying in all directions. People were thrown into hysterics, believing that the end of the world had come. A maid in the home of a certain ripe old saint burst in upon this man in his study and shrieked, "The world is coming to an end!" He, in all calmness, turned to her and said, "The world coming to an end? Let it! We can get along without it." And that is exactly what every one of us will have to do one of these days—we shall have to get along without it (II Peter 3:10). In the faith of the Apostles, we look toward *"a new earth,* wherein dwelleth righteousness" (II Peter 3:13). Such was the faith which enabled the Apostle Paul to forget about his imprisonment, and even to be joyful in the experience.


## II.  PAUL SUCCEEDED IN DIGNIFYING HIS IMPRISONMENT

1. *Whose prisoner was he?* Paul gives the answer: " . . . my bonds in Christ." It seemed to draw him nearer to his Lord, thus to dignify his imprisonment. Was he a prisoner of Rome, or of Nero? No; he was "the prisoner of Jesus Christ," "the prisoner of the Lord" (Eph. 3:1; 4:1).

2. *Why was he here?* Was it because of the evil intrigue of his enemies who had hounded and persecuted him and sought to put him to death? No; but for "the furtherance of the gospel." Why else would his Lord have permitted him to be imprisoned? Paul was saying in all sincerity, "I'm here on business for my King."

3. *Whence came that unquenchable optimism* by which he was able to turn a dismal dungeon into a feasting chamber of rejoicing?
(1) He was convinced that "all things work together for good to them that love God, to them who are the called according to his purpose." This is what he had written to the Christians in Rome, some years earlier, while he was still in Corinth (Rom. 8:28). The promise is not to the unbelieving, who reject the grace of God, but to those "who love God." Noteworthy also is the stipulation, "all things work together." Taken separately, these things might have wrought his destruction; but taken together they were for his good. The medicines which make you well are often compounded of poisons which taken singly would kill you. But, compounded by a skilled physician in the right proportions they make for the healing

and restoration of the body. Grievous though some of the Apostle's experiences were, he knew that the divine sentries would not let a single experience get through to touch him except such as his Lord would coin into his everlasting profit. Thus he knew in advance the outcome of the things that were happening to him.

(2) He was in the happy position of the boy who was found awake late in the night, long after he should have been asleep; and the father wondered, as he saw light coming out beneath the door of the boy's room, what the boy would be doing to be up at this time of night. As he approached the door, he heard a voice inside. He paused, and he heard the boy chuckling out loud and saying something like this: "If you only knew what I know!" then he would chuckle again and repeat, "If you only knew what I know!" Here is the story that the father got from the boy afterward. The boy was reading a wild west thriller; and he had gotten toward the middle of the book where the plot was getting thicker and darker and unhappier all the time, and where the hero of the story was being outrageously wronged and persecuted and abused and disgraced. The villain of the story was winning at every point and was gloating in his triumph. When the boy could not stand it any longer, he did the obvious: He turned to the last page to see how the story was going to come out. There he saw the hero gloriously vindicated and the villain suitably punished. Now, returning to the middle of the story, instead of agonizing, he was rejoicing in the midst of the dark plot, because he knew that all would end well. So it was with the Apostle Paul. He was in a dark place in the plot, but he knew the outcome in advance, and knew that it would be good.

(3) He was "joyful in tribulation" (II Cor. 7:4) because he could see beyond. We may be sure that he did not enjoy tribulation any more than we enjoy it. But he suffered like the Lord Jesus, "who for the joy that was set before him endured the cross, despising the shame . . ." (Heb. 12:2). Surely, one of the darkest nights this world has ever known must have been the night that Jesus went to Gethsemane. Just before, in the "upper room," He had declared that He

must suffer and die; and that one of the disciples would betray Him; another would deny Him; and all the rest would flee. Then, in the deep gloom of that hour, what does He do? He rises up and leads them in the singing of a "hymn" (Matt. 26:30). A hymn is a song of praise, a "doxology." It is believed that the hymn which they are most likely to have sung was the 118th Psalm. This Psalm contains the middle verse of the Bible, "It is better to trust in the Lord than to put confidence in man" (v. 8). How perfectly this was suited to the unworthy behavior of the disciples in Gethsemane! But the Psalm reaches its climax in the verse, "This is the day which the Lord hath made; we will rejoice and be glad in it" (Ps. 118:24).

A devout Negro servant who seemed to be grieving excessively over a certain experience was asked by her mistress, "Why do you agonize so long and so deeply over your misfortune? Can't you get over it? After all, you are a Christian and you have the grace of God to help you over times like this." Here was her explanation: "Well, when the Lord sends me tribulation, *I tribulate!*" That is one way to deal with tribulation; "but be of good cheer," says the Lord Jesus. "I have overcome the world" (John 16:33).

A city editor of a daily newspaper, with whom I had business occasionally, seemed always to be under terrific pressure, working feverishly to meet some deadline. I wondered why any one would stay with a job like that. Surely, there were better ways to make a living. Some years later, a city editor of another newspaper was speaking to a group of us ministers. As he gave opportunity for questions, I asked him, "How can the flesh endure a job like yours?" I told him about the city editor whom I had observed in his work in another city. He said, "If you looked in just once in a while, you do not know half the story. You should see those irate politicians who descend upon us when it seems that something in our columns has been unjustly critical. And you should hear some of the tongue lashings which we have gotten from offended society women for having said too much or too little in our columns." This editor, after his years of service in a rather hectic setting, was still the calm, genial sort of person that he had always been. "It is not what happens to people that makes the difference between them," he said. "It is the way they take it." As another has expressed it, "It is not what happens *to us*, but what happens *in us*, that matters."

### III. PAUL SUCCEEDED IN CAPITALIZING HIS IMPRISONMENT

1. *In his imprisonment, Paul was determined that "Christ shall be magnified."* And Christ *was* "magnified." How perfectly human it would have been for the Apostle to become cynical and bitter! Humanly speaking, he had deserved so much better than he was getting. Instead of a loving response to his sacrificial ministry, he was suffering persecution. And even among professed believers there were "false brethren," whose behavior was calculated to "add affliction" to his bonds. But nowhere does his faith shine more brightly than in his imprisonment; nowhere does he bear a more convincing or effective testimony.

2. *Through his imprisonment, Paul secured a new congregation.* He was not preaching to a church; but he now had, as his congregation, one person at a time, the guardsmen that were set over him. Those of us who have ever done guard duty know something of the tedium of those long, dragging hours when you would give anything to talk to somebody—anybody—about anything, just to break the monotony. Here were these guardsmen, one after another, set over this strange and distinguished prisoner. And he was talking to them. What was he talking about? He was telling them about the Lord Jesus Christ. It seems that, in the aggregate, he must have had a fairly large audience there. And he had the most effective approach there is, as he dealt with them unhurriedly, one by one, man to man, telling them about the Savior.

Those Roman guardsmen with whom Paul was working, who were probably accustomed to witnessing cruelty and suffering cruelty and inflicting cruelty, were not the likeliest candidates for sainthood. But they were sinners for whom

Christ died; and some of the finest saints that ever walked were made out of that kind of raw material. They were not the aristocracy of their generation. But as they came through the experience of the new birth and were born into the household of God, into the family of Christ, they were lifted into the highest aristocracy on earth or in heaven—the sons of God! They are mentioned in the concluding verses of that letter to the Philippians: "All the saints salute you, chiefly they that are of Caesar's household." So, through his imprisonment, Paul was enabled to reach even into Caesar's household with the gospel.

3. *From his imprisonment, Paul extended his ministry to the ends of the earth.* Here he was prompted to write those "imprisonment Epistles" which have blessed millions who have never seen his face or heard his voice. There is not a person among us whose life has not been enriched by the fact that the Apostle was in prison in Rome and there wrote these Epistles, nearly two thousand years ago.

Charlotte Elliott was a bed-ridden invalid for thirty-seven years, a devout Christian, with a deep longing to do something for her Lord. From her bed of affliction she gave to the world one of the greatest songs ever written. I am sure that if the coming of the Lord should be postponed another thousand years there will never be an invitation song written that will be better, that will say more, and say it with greater force and effect, than this invitation hymn. Probably more people have walked down the aisles to confess Christ to the accompaniment of this invitation hymn than all the other invitation hymns put together:

> "Just as I am, without one plea
> But that Thy blood was shed for me,
> And that Thou bid'st me come to Thee
> O Lamb of God, I come, I come.
>
> "Just as I am, and waiting not
> To rid my soul of one dark blot,
> To Thee, whose blood can cleanse each spot,
> O Lamb of God, I come, I come."

This expresses the manner and spirit in which all must come who would enter the Kingdom of God—the rich and the poor, the high and the low, the slave and the king. Thank God for the bed-ridden, helpless, frustrating condition out of which Charlotte Elliott gave us this hymn! Among the redeemed in heaven there will doubtless be many who will gratefully testify, "The greatest hymn that ever was written, so far as I am concerned is the hymn that gave me the final prompting to yield my heart to Christ—*Just as I am*."

What spiritual defenses and what spiritual resources did the Apostle Paul have that we do not have? Exactly none. What Paul had, we too have or *can have:* "the helmet of salvation, the shield of faith, the breastplate of righteousness, the girdle of truth, the sword of the Spirit, which is the Word of God" (Eph.) 6:13-17). "They that wait upon the Lord shall renew their strength; they shall mount up with wings as eagles; they shall run and not be weary; they shall walk and not faint" (Isa. 40:31). Thus it is possible to live with our frustrations, to the glory of God and the blessing of others.

# 14
## Building for the Ages

John 4:5-14

1. It is good for us to be reminded from time to time that *the privileges and benefits which we enjoy are ours, in the main, not by achievement but by inheritance.* Like the children of Israel who came into the Promised Land and occupied houses which they had not built, and ate from orchards and vineyards which they had not planted, and drank from wells which they had not dug, we are enjoying privileges and benefits which we have not earned, but which are ours by the grace of God and the labors and sacrifices of those who have gone before us. Surely these our benefactors did not fail of their recompense, in time or in eternity; but did they ever realize in the course of their labors that they were building for the ages? Probably it was with them as with Jacob, that godly patriarch of antiquity, to whose obscure labors there attached a vast unrevealed significance.

2. In one of the most familiar Gospel incidents *Jesus and his disciples, journeying from Jerusalem to Galilee by way of Samaria, made a noonday pause by the wayside—and "Jacob's well was there"* (v. 6). This casual observation has far more than a casual significance. What is remarkable is that this well had been there for about seventeen hundred years, fulfilling its purpose: providing water for household needs and for the refreshment of weary and thirsty travelers.

*3. This wayside well,* which is still intact and which has so blessed the world for nearly four thousand years, *is a fitting symbol of the life of that godly patriarch,* from which we may wisely gather inspiration. In several *particulars* it is to this day a tribute to the life of the builder.

### I. HIS WORK HAS ENDURED

"Now Jacob's well was there" (v. 6).

1. *Here is a reflection of the character of the builder.* When we see a good piece of work—neat and sound—we know, without being told, that behind it there was a corresponding soundness of character. And when we see a slovenly piece of work, we know that behind it there was a corresponding slovenliness of character.

(1) Jacob probably built under real difficulty. Even today, with modern facilities, to dig a well ninety feet deep, eight feet in diameter, mostly through solid rock, is no small undertaking. What fortitude it must have taken to build such a well with the crude facilities of four thousand years ago!

(2) Jacob could have built more cheaply. He would not have needed to select his stones with such care, and shape them with such accuracy, and lay them with such precision. As a matter of fact, he might have managed to get along without building a well at all. The tribesmen who had preceded him did not dig wells. Like the Bedouins of today, they would settle down with their camels, donkeys, and goats wherever there was grass and water; and here they would remain until the grass was eaten down into the roots and the creeks and water holes were drunk dry. Then they would move on and pitch camp elsewhere and repeat the whole process. They made no improvements, and left no wells behind them, but lived as so many others of whom the poet declared: "They consume the fowl, the flesh, the fish; and leave behind—an empty dish!" How different was the legacy of Jacob!

2. *Here is a reflection of greater wisdom than the builder ever realized.* If only he could have known that some day his Lord would be traveling that road and making use of the well! And if every servant of Christ could know the ultimate significance of his labors, what dignity and joy would attend even the lowliest service!

(1) A troubled mother, agonizing over her sickly child, wondered if he would live to maturity. She prayed for him and dedicated him to the Lord before his birth. Then, through many anxious days and sleepless nights, she had watched over the cradle of the little one. Later, as one childhood disease followed upon another, there were more crises, more tears, and more prayers. When finally the health problem seemed to have been overcome, there was another problem. It seemed that every teen-age influence was in one mighty conspiracy to win him away from the path of godliness in which the mother had so long sought to establish him. Now there were more tears and more prayers. Thus the struggle continued, with the mother so close to her task that she never realized what a good job she was doing. It was not until the boy was approaching the prime of life that it dawned upon the mother, rather suddenly, that she had given to the world a great man! She had built more wisely than she knew. Let faithful mothers and fathers be assured, there is a God in heaven who sees every tear that falls, and hears the prayer of every troubled heart.

(2) At a Baptist convention in New Jersey, the chairman noted in the audience an old gentleman who had been for years the Sunday School teacher of Charles Evans Hughes, the boy who ultimately became the Chief Justice of the United States Supreme Court, and the first President of the Northern Baptist Convention. This former teacher, whom the chairman invited to the platform to be introduced, appeared to be well up in the eighties. He was frail, gray, and bent beneath the weight of the years. But as he emerged from his pew and started up the aisle, he straightened up, his step became firm and lively, and it seemed that half a century rolled off his back, as he realized afresh what a privilege had been his. He had for years participated in building into the life and character of Charles Evans

Hughes what now the Chief Justice was reflecting back to his country from the highest judicial bench in the land. This teacher also had been building more wisely than he knew.

(3) Last Sunday, in all likelihood, in somebody's Sunday School class, there sat a boy who is destined to be the Chief Justice of half a century hence, or a Governor or Congressman, or President of the United States. Of course, the teacher did not know. Let us hope that he was putting his dedicated best into the molding of that young life for God. Perhaps there was a woman teacher struggling with a room full of beginners. One little fellow was particularly troublesome; he has been a problem all along. Perhaps there have been moments when her natural inclinations would have been to bind him and gag him. But she continues patiently, prayerfully, and sweetly to try to bring out the good that is in him. She had better! That little fellow may be destined some day to be her son-in-law; and she may spend the last quarter century of her life under his roof. She too may be building more wisely than she realizes.

(4) A minister was telling, in the pulpit, about his lovely three-year-old daughter. "I fell to day-dreaming the other day," he said; "and I could see the day, not far distant, when she would be starting to public school. I could see her, with happy face, and with her hair done up in pigtails, trotting off to her first day in classes. It was a beautiful vision. Then I dreamed a bit further, and saw her graduating. There she stood, in cap and gown, tall and slender like her mother when first we met. That, too, was a charming vision. I dreamed a bit further, and saw her going off to college. Then I hit a snag. Her mother also had gone to college; there she met a young man; in the course of time there was a wedding, and a new home, and afterwards this little one in the home. What so greatly concerns me is the question, Where is that boy who is destined someday to be the life companion of our loved one? Where are his father and mother? I would go anywhere to find them, and I would implore them to bring him up in the nurture and admonition of the Lord and to surround him with every influence to insure his growing up clean and straight. Then we could look with assurance toward the day when the two would stand before the

marriage altar with the smile of God upon them." This minister was wisely concerned. Perhaps that boy was at that very moment in Junior Church receiving instruction in the things of the Lord, while his parents were in the sanctuary listening to the preacher. And perhaps the minister was even then building more wisely than he knew.

## II. HIS WORK HAS NEVER CEASED TO BE A BLESSING

"There cometh a woman of Samaria to draw water" (v. 7).

1. *The Samaritan woman reflected the gratitude of a hundred generations who have benefited from the well that Jacob built.* With veneration and affection she refers to "our father Jacob who gave us the well" (v. 12). Approximately seventeen centuries had elapsed, but Jacob was still being affectionately remembered. Such is the afterglow of a godly life. Truly, "their works do follow them" (Rev. 14:13). This is true in two senses: In the first place, they are followed into eternity by the consequences of their earthly labors. In the second place, as they pass through life there follows a trail of influences which will linger to bless and enrich the lives of those who come after them. Sometimes it is only when a life has been lived to its full length and is seen in perspective that it can be accurately appraised.

(1) A life well lived may be likened to the course of the sun as it passes overhead doing its day's work, without the benefit of applause, and with scant appreciation of its beauty. It is not until the day's work is done and the departing sun casts its multicolored glory upon the sky that its real beauty can be seen. Only then do we realize how beautiful and beneficial the sun has been all day long.

(2) A life well lived may be likened also to the painting of some gifted artist. Standing up close, we do not see its full beauty. We see brush marks which are anything but beautiful. But stepping back to a suitable distance, we see meaning and color and beauty, and we cannot but explain, "What a masterpiece!" Similarly, as we study closely the life of Jacob we come

upon passages that make us blink. In his weaknesses he was too much like ourselves. But as we view that life in full perspective we realize that it was a life of noble dimensions, lived to the glory of God and the blessing of posterity.

### 2. *Jacob himself was not without reward.*

(1) The satisfaction of a good work well done is its own reward. And when God is in the effort there is an added blessing and an element of eternity in every service. What we do may affect generations unborn and ages beyond the farthest horizons of our thinking. And what seems at the time like so much lost motion may prove to have been fruitful beyond all imagining.

A chapel speaker in a theological seminary was approached at the close of the service by a woman from the audience who told him, with deep emotion, "I owe my life to you!" He did not remember ever having seen her before. But she reminded him of a hospital call he had made many years before in a distant city, while he was a seminary student. Then she revealed that in her illness she had reached a point of total despair, when he, as a complete stranger, came to her bedside. "I was steadily sinking, and felt that the end had come; but something in your prayer gave me the lift of a new hope. It was at that moment, as I realized later, that the tide was turned and I started back on the road to recovery." Thus there will be many pleasant surprises for faithful servants of Christ when the books are opened for the final accounting.

(2) The reflex blessing of a good work for Christ's sake is often immediate. A warm-hearted philanthropist in New York City felt sorry for the boys who roamed the streets and alleys of a certain slum area. He conceived the idea of an all day picnic for them. On the appointed day several hundred of these boys were taken by boat to a beautiful picnic area far up the Hudson River. Abundant provision had been made for games, refreshments, and entertainment. When the frolic of those happy youngsters was at its height, someone said to the philanthropist, "Did you ever in your life see a bunch of boys having such a good time?" "No," said the philanthropist, thoughtfully, "but the boy that is getting the most out of this picnic today is not

one of the boys out there, but the boy here"—pointing to himself. We can not channel blessings to others without experiencing a blessing ourselves.

### III. HIS WORK BROUGHT COMFORT TO THE LORD JESUS

"Jesus . . . being wearied with his journey, sat thus on the well" (v. 6).

1. *Jesus not only visited the well that his servant Jacob had built, but made practical use of it.* He rested upon its curb, and he drank from its water. "Give me to drink," He said to the Samaritan woman, and presumably He was thus fully refreshed. Then followed that memorable discourse on the water of life (vs. 13-14), the spirituality of all true worship (v. 24), and His own Messianic identity (v. 26). And as He ministered to her and to those other Samaritans who came to him because of her testimony, that wayside well became in the truest sense a wayside pulpit, to the blessing and salvation of many.

2. *Jesus makes it clear that He derives comfort from every good work which is done to honor Him and to bless the lives of others.* No service is too humble, too obscure, or too trivial to be noted. "Whosoever shall give you a cup of water to drink in my name, because ye belong to Christ, verily I say unto you, he shall not lose his reward" (Mark 9:41). "Inasmuch as ye have done it unto one of the least of these my brethren, ye have done it unto me" (Matt. 25:40).

(1) How sobering, how comforting, how reassuring to know that all heaven is witnessing our humble services. In the Scriptures we are reminded of the great cloud of heavenly witnesses who look down upon us in our labors and struggles (Heb. 12:1), and again we are reminded of angel witnesses (I Tim. 5:21). How much more compelling is the reminder that our Lord Himself sees all, hears all, makes no mistakes, forgets nothing! "Therefore, my beloved brethren, be ye steadfast, unmoveable, always abounding in the work of the Lord, forasmuch as ye

know that your labor is not in vain in the Lord" (I Cor. 15:58).

(2) Beautiful in their simplicity, and perpetually relevant, are the lines of that little rhyme which the children so loved in Kindergarten:

> "Build it well, whate'er ye do;
> Build it straight and strong and true;
> Build it tall and build it broad,
> Build it for the eye of God."

Viewed in the light of the centuries, Jacob's well was a noble work which has stood the test of time. But as Jacob came to the closing moments of his earthly life, with his loved ones at his bedside, that was not what he remembered. Looking back over the long, tumultuous years of his life, he saw one thing that stood out like a brilliant star in the dark heavens. It was not the wells that he had dug, or the fortune that he had amassed, or the family that he had reared. It was that awesome night at Bethel, ninety-seven years before, when God came into his life (Gen. 28:11-22; 48:3). What gave eternal significance to the labors of Jacob is that he worked *with God*. "Without faith it is impossible to please Him" (Heb. 11:6).

Thus building with God, we build for the ages—something that will endure, something that will never cease to be a blessing, something that will bring comfort to the Lord Jesus.

> "May we be wise with His wisdom,
>   Our hearts aflame with His love;
> May we greatly build as we build with God,
>   For this world and the world above!"

# 15
## Always Ready for Life's Big Moments

Daniel 1:8-21

*Daniel purposed in his heart that he would not defile himself. . . .—Daniel 1:18*

1. *Daniel apparently was a boy of high school age when he was carried away in the Babylonian captivity and abruptly thrust into the demoralizing paganism of the Babylonian court.*

Here he demonstrated that it is possible with the help of God to live a pure, godly life in an impure, ungodly environment. His life was like the steady glow of a tiny candle which all the darkness in the world can not overcome.

Here by the grace of God he not only survived, but actually thrived, in the foulness of the Babylonian court, like the golden-hearted water lily lifting its clean, white face above the scum of its dismal environment.

Here he grew in spiritual stature, in reputation, and influence; and remained for three-quarters of a century as a living monument to the living God.

Here he demonstrated that it is not the soil in which a life is planted, but the set of the soul, which determines the outcome of its testings.

2. *Daniel set a pattern of character, conduct, and achievement*

*not only for the high school age, but for all ages up to ninety years and over.*

At varying age levels Daniel hazarded his life for God as he moved from obscurity to fame and immortality.

In successive crises God intervened on his behalf, manifesting equal concern for the teen-age youth, the man in middle life, and the aged saint.

In the background of every triumph stands the living God, speaking to Daniel and through Daniel to us: "You too are important," He is saying. "Whatever your age, your aptitudes, or your circumstances, you are unique; you are indispensable; you are irreplaceable. I have a place for you; and for this place you are the best qualified person on earth. I have my heart set on you; let me do my best in you and for you and through you. You too can be ready for life's big moments, like Daniel, whose extraordinary achievement rested upon his extraordinary devotion to his Lord, which met all the divine *imperatives*:"

### I. DANIEL'S DEVOTION TO HIS LORD WAS EARLY

1. *An early beginning is reflected in the inclusion of Daniel among the so-called "children" selected for service in the royal court.* Just how young he was when he came to terms with his Lord, we are not informed. But when that first great crisis came, Daniel was ready—with clean hands, a pure heart, clear vision, and a fixed purpose: "He would not defile himself with the portion of the King's meat, nor with the wine which he drank" (v. 8). Daniel's character was already formed. He did not need to run back to the laboratory to make up deficiencies or repair flaws in his character; nor would this have been possible.

Like Joseph, who had been sold into slavery in Egypt centuries before and who withstood such crucial testings in the courts of Pharaoh (Gen. 39), Daniel could be trusted anywhere. Did Daniel know about Joseph? Certainly he had the same lofty ideals, and was upheld by the same Lord and given the same extraordinary wisdom (Acts 7:10). Daniel was expected to conform; yet he purposed not to defile himself. But how was he to escape? He might so easily have excused himself as being bound by the customs and practices of the Babylonian court. And when his first request for exemption was refused, he might have felt doubly justified in dropping the matter. But with rare tact and perseverance he takes the further step that results in exemption and vindication for himself and his three young comrades for whom he had become the spokesman.

2. *An early beginning made possible a full career.*

(1) Occasionally a man who has wasted his early years will turn to the Lord in middle life, and through zealous devotion achieve mightily for God; but nothing can compensate for the years that have been lost. A late starter can not declare, when life draws to a close, "I have finished my course." At best he has finished only the latter part of his life's mission.

Those "pillars" of the church upon whom the life and health and fruitfulness of the church so largely depend are nearly always men and women who entered the service of Christ in childhood. Thus they have been nurtured through all the normal phases of growth, and have escaped those damaging practices, habits, and involvements which otherwise account for so many backslidings. At the same time they have developed those strengths and capacities which give stability and effectiveness to the church, and which require a full season to grow.

Trees that stand tall, straight, and symmetrical are not developed from undernourished, stunted, warped beginnings. Their ultimate beauty is the result of uninterrupted growth under favorable conditions throughout the growing season. The tree that has grown crooked, gnarled, and unsymmetrical through adverse conditions in its early life can not be redeemed later by any amount of extra care and labor.

Crops that are planted when the normal time of planting is past can not be brought to a full harvest. However fertile the soil, however favorable the weather, and however careful and diligent the cultivation, an essential part of the growing season has been irretrievably lost. Growth ceases with the first frost, and what might have been an abundant harvest has become a dismal failure.

(2) A pastor was asked if there had been any additions to his church over the previous week-end. "Yes," said the pastor, "there were two and a half additions." Pressed for an explanation, he added, "There were three persons who presented themselves for baptism on profession of faith—two children and one adult. That adds up to only two and one-half *lives* at most!"

3. *An early beginning makes possible a happy journey for the full length of life's one-way street.* "The days of our years are three score years and ten," and possibly "four-score years" (Ps. 90:10). The journeying might be pleasant and the scenery beautiful and inspiring; but the eyes of the "natural man" (I Cor. 2:14) are not open to this beauty, and his heart is not open to the "joy of the Lord." The longer he waits, and the more milestones he passes before coming to terms with his Lord, the less time he will have to enjoy the "abundant life" (John 10:10). The more he tastes of the ways of the world, the more there will be to regret in the years that are left. "Blessed is the man that walketh not in the counsel of the ungodly . . ." (Ps. 1:1). Hebrew scholars declare that a more accurate rendering of this verse might be: "Blessed is the man that *never did. . . .*"

A pastor was asked to visit a man ninety-one years old who was slowly dying of cancer in a "home for the aged." Asked how he was getting along, the old man declared that the time of his illness had been by far the happiest time of his life. "I have an inoperable cancer," he said. "When it took hold about two years ago, it was in one of those long, sleepless nights that I began seriously thinking about the hereafter. I remembered some Scripture verses that I had learned in childhood but which I had never heeded. Now they became intensely personal to me. Lying here alone in that dark night of suffering, I found the Lord! The days and nights ever since have been wonderful. My one great sorrow is that I could not bring back those wasted eighty-nine years that were past."

Daniel's remarkable career was off to a good start because his life of godliness had begun early.

## II. DANIEL'S DEVOTION TO HIS LORD WAS COMPLETE

1. *Completeness of devotion is reflected in the phrase, "in his heart"* (v. 8). There was nothing casual, superficial, or tentative about his purpose to keep himself undefiled. His heart was "fixed" (Ps. 57:7). When the heart is right, all else is right; and the graces of godliness appear spontaneously, revealing what is within. Out of the heart are the issues of life (Prov. 4:23). As a man "thinketh in his heart, so is he" (Prov. 23:7); and "the Lord looketh on the *heart*" (I Sam. 16:7).

Daniel seems never to have been overawed by the pomp and power of the royal palace; but again and again he reflects an awareness of the awesome presence of God, who "revealeth secrets" (2:28) and whom he must serve at all costs. Thus Daniel was never alone.

2. *Completeness of devotion is evidenced by the risks involved in "purposing" that which was at variance with Babylonian practice.* It was no small matter to turn down that royal wine cup and to sit at the table as a non-conformist. Daniel was risking his favored position as one of a small group selected to receive training and ultimately to stand before the king in the royal palace (v. 19), while his captive contemporaries labored as peasant slaves "by the rivers of Babylon" (Ps. 137:1). Not only was his position at stake; his very life was in jeopardy. Life was cheap, and the existence of alien captives was precarious at best. But Daniel, with rare wisdom and humility, took the risk, believing that the plebeian fare of slaves with the blessing of God upon it would be more wholesome for body, mind, and spirit than the sophisticated menu of the royal court.

(1) Actually, who was taking the greater risk—Daniel, who dared to be different, and who by the grace of God went on to renown as a godly and distinguished statesman, or those of his companions who in Babylon chose to do "as the Babylonians do," and who came to oblivion? Had Daniel faded into his environment, not even his name would be known to us. And had Daniel stood in his own strength alone, he would quickly have

gone down in defeat. Not in compromise did he make his way to the top, but in total commitment to his Lord.

(2) Which costs more—to be a Christian, or *not* to be a Christian? Perhaps too much has been said about the cost of being a Christian, and not nearly enough about the cost of *not* being a Christian. And perhaps there has been too little discrimination between total commitment and that so-called "Christianity" which is only nominal and which neither saves the soul nor brings the compensations of true godliness. Greatly to be pitied is that halfway "Christian" who has never presented himself *bodily* to his Lord and has never discovered "what is that good, and acceptable, and perfect will of God" (Rom. 12:1-2). Not only does he miss the best; he does not even know what he has missed.

### III. DANIEL'S DEVOTION TO HIS LORD WAS LIFE-LONG

*"Daniel continued even unto the first year of King Cyrus"* (v. 21).

1. *Daniel appears in one of his noblest portrayals when, at the age of approximately ninety years, he was cast into the den of lions* (6:16). Here again he had dared to be different. When the unalterable decree of King Darius required that for thirty days no petition be addressed to any God or man except to King Darius, Daniel continued praying to his Lord three times daily "as he had aforetime" (6:10). Thus to hazard his life required an enormous faith. It was not enough to have *begun* well; he was still dependent upon God as at the beginning. It was not enough to have *had* spiritual abundance; he needed it now more than ever. It was not enough to have *retained* the spiritual resources of his youth; he now needed the strength of greatly increased resources.

2. *Daniel worked for a solid lifetime laying up spiritual resources for crises which were unpredictable but sure to come.* Every crisis found him ready, and with every crisis he moved up to higher ground. There were at least five great moments of destiny:

(1) There was a time when *character* was enough—a pure heart, a life of faith, and a godly determination. Confronted with his first great crisis, Daniel "purposed in his heart that he would not defile himself," and God marvelously sustained him. It was here, as he turned down the royal wine cup, that he took his first long step to greatness.

(2) For the second crisis, character alone would not have sufficed. King Nebuchadnezzar was "furious" (2:12), and the lives of his counselors were in danger because they could not recall and interpret the strange dream which had so deeply disturbed him. By this time Daniel had been long enough in Babylon to have developed a disciplined mind, with knowledge and *understanding*; and had sufficiently established himself in the esteem of others to insure a hearing for him when he asked to go into the presence of the King. With rare grace and humility he met the King's problem, taking care to give God the glory (2:28).

(3) By the time of his third great crisis, Daniel had added a further dimension to his life. In addition to character and understanding, he now had the advantage of a *reputation* as well. King Belshazzar was in serious trouble. Terrified and trembling before the handwriting on the wall (5:5-9), he sought help from the "wise men," but they were helpless. The Queen had heard about Daniel (5:10-16), and so he was summoned before the King. Again, with the help of God, Daniel was equal to the situation.

(4) The fourth great crisis demanded even more than character, understanding, and reputation. King Darius had decreed that for thirty days no prayers should be made to God or any man except the King himself. Anyone failing to comply was to be cast into the den of lions. To defy such a decree required *fortitude* of a kind that does not come quickly, but through long years of experience in the intimate fellowship of God. Again Daniel was ready, and "the God of Daniel" was exalted in Babylon (6:26).

(5) The final great moment of destiny, and the crowning achievement of Daniel's life, seems to have fallen in the reign of King Cyrus (1:21; 10:1). Not much is revealed about Daniel's relationship with King Cyrus, but the Scriptures record a most

astonishing emancipation proclamation by King Cyrus permitting and encouraging the return of the captives to their homeland. "The Lord God of heaven . . . hath charged me to build him a house at Jerusalem, which is in Judah" (II Chron. 36:22, 23; Ezra 1:1-4).

What did this pagan monarch know about "the Lord God of heaven"? Somehow his heart had been opened to the supreme wisdom of the ages—to note which way God is moving and to fall in step with Him. The only explanation seems to be that Daniel, who had so long stood in his place of peril and privilege, had witnessed to Cyrus and had influenced him to bring the power of this world empire to the side of his Lord. By this time Daniel had come to full stature and maturity and had everything: character, understanding, reputation, fortitude, besides *influence*—without which he could not have succeeded.

Daniel survived the hardships and hazards of the Babylonian captivity, and the intrigue of the Babylonian court, because God was with him. He rose from the obscurity of a captive slave from a despised, alien people speaking a foreign tongue, because he was always ready for life's big moments when they came. He was always ready because of his extraordinary devotion to his Lord, which was *early, complete, and life-long.*

The God of Daniel still lives. The "rules of the road" which guided Daniel have not changed; the assurances which sustained him are forever the same; and every sincere believer is a potential Daniel.

**Charles W. Koller** (1896–1983) taught ministerial students at the Northern Baptist Theological Seminary for over twenty years, in addition to serving as its president. An influential preacher and a popular conference speaker, Koller earned his Th.D. degree from Southwestern Baptist Theological Seminary.